The Broadcast Voice

The Broadcast Voice

Jenni Mills

ELSEVIER

AMSTERDAM • BOSTON • HEIDELBERG • LONDON • NEW YORK • OXFORD
PARIS • SAN DIEGO • SAN FRANCISCO • SINGAPORE • SYDNEY • TOKYO
Focal Press is an imprint of Elsevier

Focal Press
An imprint of Elsevier
Linacre House, Jordan Hill, Oxford OX2 8DP
200 Wheeler Road, Burlington, MA 01803

First published 2004

Permissions may be sought directly from Elsevier's Science and
Technology Rights Department in Oxford, UK: phone: (+44) (0) 1865 843830;
fax: (+44) (0) 1865 853333; e-mail: permissions@elsevier.co.uk. You may
also complete your request on-line via the Elsevier homepage (http://www.elsevier.com),
by selecting 'Customer Support' and then 'Obtaining Permissions'

British Library Cataloguing in Publication Data
A catalogue record for this book is available from the British Library

Library of Congress Cataloguing in Publication Data
A catalogue record for this book is available from the Library of Congress

ISBN 0 2405 1939 6

For information on all Focal Press publications visit our website
at: www.focalpress.com

Typeset by Newgen Imaging Systems (P) Ltd., Chennai, India
Printed and bound in Great Britain

Contents

Contents

Preface

There is no such thing as a 'bad' broadcasting voice – only people who are using their voices badly.

I wanted to write this book because I firmly believe that everyone who works, or aspires to work, in broadcasting deserves to get help with their voice. The voice is every broadcaster's most basic tool. War correspondents and weather forecasters, DJs and documentary narrators, newsreaders and kids' show presenters – all of them rely on their voices to get the message across. Even in the visual medium of TV, a good voice enhances the programme; a poorly used voice distracts and weakens it.

Since I became a broadcaster, I have been fascinated by voices. I have been lucky to work alongside some of the most memorable broadcasting voices of their time. But as a documentary maker, I also recorded thousands of ordinary people's voices, which were often in their own way just as compelling, and I began to get an inkling about what it is in the human voice that can add so much to (or take away from) the story being told.

Teaching the broadcast voice is a curiously specialist field. It is not our job to change a voice, so much as to help you make the most of what is already there. As one of my female clients put it, it's more a facial than a face-lift – radical surgery usually doesn't come into it. It is not the same as teaching voice to actors. Actors require enormous vocal flexibility in order to become other people. Broadcasters only require the ability to be, and sound like, themselves. But exposing your true self and being 'natural' in front of an audience – even an invisible one – is not an easy job. Perhaps that is why actors for all their vocal virtuosity rarely make good broadcasters; it is hard to avoid the temptation to put on a mask and play a role. If you 'act' rather than 'be' in broadcasting, you can be sure the audience will know it, and respect you the less for it.

So you won't find in this book the kind of detailed voice routines that actors practise. Instead, you will find much more about how to use your voice to communicate successfully as a broadcaster. The exercises in the text are simple ones, designed with very specific goals in mind – better breathing, stronger voice support, and above all clearer understanding of what it means to broadcast. Although some are derived from classic voice work practised in the theatre, and owe much to the work of Cicely Berry, Michael McCallion, and J. Clifford Turner, I have been using and adapting these techniques over the years specifically with broadcasters in mind, recognizing that most broadcasters are allergic to vocal exercises and have to be persuaded of their effectiveness in relation to their craft.

The television presenter John Simpson wrote how he was told as a young reporter that there is no place for the word 'I' in the broadcaster's vocabulary. I am painfully aware that it keeps cropping up in this book. Although I write as a professional voice trainer to broadcasters and students, I still work in both radio and television, sometimes as a presenter using my own voice on air, sometimes as a producer and director striving to get the best from my contributors' voices. So I find it impossible to teach without sharing with students my own on-air experiences – not least because continuing to make programmes keeps me aware of all the technical difficulties broadcasters face when they are in front of a camera or a microphone. I understand how often the last thing on your mind, when writing to a deadline or grappling with sometimes unreliable equipment in the field, is the sound of your voice.

I also know just how vulnerable a broadcaster can feel about his or her voice. The voice is so personal, so much a part of whom we are, that criticism of the way we sound is as painful as criticism of the way we look. Finding an honest but sensitive way of helping people to hear what needs improving in their voice, without destroying their confidence, is a challenge that faces editors, producers, and directors, as well as voice trainers.

This book is aimed at both the student and the professional broadcaster, whether you have chosen to work in television or radio, news, factual, or entertainment. I write assuming that like many broadcasters today you will be moving between radio and television and back again. Only rarely is it necessary to make a distinction between the vocal techniques required. The accompanying CD-ROM is designed so you can hear examples of voice work. You should not look at it as a substitute for reading the book, but as an illustration of the problems and techniques addressed in the text.

There is always a debate in broadcasting about the purpose of credits. Who actually sits through them, apart from a few colleagues and your mum? To me, they are a way of thanking those who contributed to what is always a team effort, and this book is no exception. Many people have helped, directly or indirectly, in its birth. My thanks go first to those who gave practical support. They are: Bob Atkins and Colin Larcombe, at Cardiff University's Post-Graduate Diploma Course in Broadcast Journalism, who provided facilities for recording some of the material on the CD-ROM, as well as many helpful thoughts on content and approach; their students on the Diploma course, who bravely allowed their first faltering steps in voice-work to be used on the CD-ROM (they all sound much better now!); David Parker, Wendy Maclean, and their wonderful computer team led by Sam McFadden at Available Light Productions, who mastered the CD-ROM; Glenn Lewis, and Sue Bennett, also of Available Light, for computer help; Alex Parkinson, who filmed for me; Mark Richards, who drew the illustrations, and Helen Dunderdale and Chris Chapman who allowed me to photograph them. At Focal Press, I must thank Beth Howard and Georgia Kennedy for their patience as they answered my incessant questions about how to deliver the manuscript.

Numerous friends and colleagues provided both encouragement and useful suggestions: Janet Trewin, who gave me the initial spur to get my thoughts on paper; Carolyn Brown, Radio Four newsreader, who also appears on the CD-ROM; Gerald Hine-Haycock, of the BBC's SON&R training department in Bristol, and his assistant Tracy Hall; Andrew Edwards at the University of Central Lancashire for some extremely helpful comments on the finished manuscript; my former producer, Sarah Rowlands, now teaching at Staffordshire University; Iain Hunter, who advised on technical matters concerning microphones and recording equipment; and Frances Byrnes, Nigel Clark, Anne Malindine, Lesley Morgan, and Guy Smith, for dispensing coffee, wine, and sympathy during the process of writing.

There are also a number of people who have contributed to this book without ever realizing it. First, there were those who helped me when I was a young broadcaster: especially David Waine, who was my first station manager at Radio Bristol; and Douggie Chalmers, David Dunhill, and Roy Williamson, the BBC trainers who taught me so much when I was starting out. And then there are also the thousands of broadcasters who have been my clients, who kept me going with their enthusiasm. I hope they learned something from me, but just as importantly I learned so much from them.

Jenni Mills

1 Introduction

What is a 'good' broadcasting voice? If you ask any group of people – and I've been asking media students the question for a good dozen years or so – you'll get at least as many answers as there are people in the room.

Somebody will like John Humphrys because he sounds 'strong and doesn't take any crap'. Somebody else will loathe him because they think he is aggressive and hectoring. Someone will pick one of the Radio Four newsreaders (say, Peter Donaldson or Rory Morrison) or a TV voice like Dermot Murnaghan – 'rich, smooth, such authority' – and immediately there'll be a moan from the other side of the room that compared to the energy of voices on independent radio, his style is too formal, the pace too slow, the smoothness positively soporific.

Eventually someone will get around to remembering that women broadcast too, and we might then have a lively debate on Davina McCall ('sassy' or 'too sharp'), Sarah Montague ('cool and confident' versus 'public school head girl'), or Jenni Murray ('friendly' or 'too mumsy'?). Sara Cox on Radio One always divides people – some love her brashness and strong accent, others find it harsh and abrasive. We rarely reach a consensus as we compile our list, because voice is often inseparable from personality and the style of a network or programme. Indeed, the point is to demonstrate exactly how wide the range is of successful broadcasting voices. It would be a poor and colourless world where we all liked exactly the same things, and there will usually be a bit of a barney on whether Trevor Macdonald deserves the status of all-time great or all-time grate-on-you.

There'll be someone else who picks a voice specifically because it has an accent – and they will look defiantly at me as if they expect I'm going to shudder with horror like an old-fashioned elocution teacher. I remember deliberately trying to cause a stir at the first job interview I went for as a speech advisor with the BBC by telling them I thought Jonathan Ross had a brilliant voice (a man better known perhaps as Jonathan Woss), because despite his weak 'r', it struck me as being so energetic and full of character. On the other hand, being a product of my generation and background, I also have a lingering weakness for dignified voices like Michael Buerk or Martha Kearney. But a soft Scottish accent like Eddie Mair's glues me to the radio.

Inevitably the examples we come up with are those who have already made an impact in national network TV or radio, and those I have mentioned are for many people the voices that sum up the classic British broadcast voice of today. But we could never compile a definitive list. Broadcasting is of the moment, ephemeral, and by the time you read this book, these voices may already be broadcasting history. Already there will be an exciting new voice working its apprenticeship in local TV or entertaining listeners on hospital or student radio, which will one day muscle its way into our personal top tens. It may even be your voice.

SO WHAT IS A GOOD BROADCASTING VOICE?

Even though we can't always agree on our favourite voices, there are certain characteristics such voices generally share. A good voice is one that has an effect on us. It is something we can't ignore – we have to listen to it, it compels us in some way. We think of it as an expression of what we imagine to be the personality of the broad-caster and we respond to it. It doesn't matter whether I like John Peel and you like Kirsty Young – more interesting are the *qualities* we look for and find in the voices we individually like. It's like asking someone if Cindy Crawford is preferable to the late Princess Diana. Both will have their devotees and detractors, whether you consider them as beauties or as role models. But the real question is – what do we respond to that puts them, and others like them, in that exalted position for so many people?

So *whom* you think of as a good broadcast voice is not in a sense important. What we ought to look at instead are the common factors in the way people describe the voices they like.

For those of you who only feel you've learnt something if you do an EXERCISE – here's one to try right now.

Write a list of the broadcasting voices you like. I've left a big space so that if you've borrowed or stolen this book, you get to laugh at the ones picked by the person who did the exercise before you. Next to each voice, write why you like that voice. Try and think of the qualities it has for you. And try NOT to look onto the next page to see if you're coming up with the same things people usually come up with. It's supposed to be a surprise.

Broadcaster	Quality

When I do this exercise with students we always find the same qualities described over and over again, in very similar words. Here's a selection of the words that generally come up:

- warm

- friendly

- conversational

- clear

- strong

- authoritative

- trustworthy

- real

- natural

- relaxed

These qualities are what people seek in the broadcasters they come to like and trust, and they give us the direction we should be aiming in when we use our voices on air, in radio or television. Helping you achieve these qualities in your own voice is the purpose of this book.

Everything else is a question of style and personal preference – even perhaps of fashion. My mum thought Sylvia Peters – long, long ago an announcer on BBC Television – had a lovely voice. I suspect anyone hearing it today would think it strangulated, posh, and unnatural. But that was the 1950s. In those days, you had to have (with only a few token exceptions) a Home Counties accent to broadcast in Britain. People even spoke of a 'BBC accent', reflecting the stranglehold the Corporation had not only on broadcasting, but also on the nation's cultural life. Within my own lifespan in broadcasting, it is cheering to reflect how much things have changed in terms of the variety of voices on radio and television. Democracy has hit the airwaves, and that can only be a good thing.

On the other hand, the explosion in broadcasting outlets, and the medium's ever-insatiable hunger for new voices, has left us with one problem. The voices that used to appear in broadcasting were often *trained* voices. In the early days, announcers (sweet, old-fashioned term for it – and *announce* they did) were often recruited from the ranks of the acting profession. One thing they never had to worry about was making a pleasing sound, because most actors get plenty of training in how to use their vocal equipment. Standing up and declaiming, as they used to do in those days, was not a difficulty.

God forbid any of us should stand up and declaim these days, but nonetheless we usually have to sit down (unless you're doing a piece-to-camera or striding about a TV studio) and make ourselves intelligible to the audience. We have to deliver a script, because still a large proportion of broadcasting is scripted, and make it sound as if it were flowing naturally off the top of our heads. Reading aloud is something most people last did in primary school, and then probably not very well. We don't have the benefit of the actor's daily voice classes, or even those Saturday morning elocution lessons to which proud middle-class parents of past generations used to send their kids. Yet somehow we expect broadcasters to do it naturally. Natural? Warm? Relaxed? Friendly? Authoritative? Just *how* do they do it?

Is there such a thing as a 'bad' broadcasting voice?

Are some voices unsuitable for broadcasting? This is a question still hotly debated amongst trainers and editors. I prefer the positive approach: that there is no such thing as a 'bad' voice, only people using their voices badly.

With professional guidance, almost anyone can become a competent broadcaster. How much professional guidance a voice may need is another matter. One of my former clients was born with a cleft palate. She underwent a number of operations, had intensive speech therapy, and at the same time worked with me to improve her broadcasting techniques. She was an excellent journalist – which helped convince her employers she was worth the effort – and eventually got an on-air job in radio. You may have to put in a lot of work and go to some personal expense before you can convince broadcasting bosses to let you on air, but if you are really determined you can do it. Strong regional accents are no longer a bar. The only thing that will stop you from getting anywhere is either the unwillingness to learn, or your own lack of confidence in your voice.

Whether you are a novice broadcaster or an old hand, chances are you won't have had much in the way of professional voice training. Even at colleges and universities who offer courses in media skills, voice-coaching is often tacked on as a bit of an afterthought. There seems to be a notion that since we all use our voices everyday to communicate, we ought somehow to know instinctively how to use them in front of a microphone. Actually, that *is* true – but the trouble is something rather odd happens to people when they get into a studio or pick up a script, a kind of brain-freeze that destroys the normal ability to communicate instinctively.

If you listen to radio or watch television, you can pick up hundreds of examples of what I mean. Bizarre singsong rhythms. Breathless gabbling. Voices that ought to be strong, but sound tight and strangulated. This is not to decry the undoubted skills of reporters or presenters. I merely suggest that many could sound much better, more authoritative and more natural, with a little help.

I have trained well over a thousand broadcasters and the one thing they have almost all had in common is a surprising insecurity about the sound of their own voices. Some have been hardened war correspondents who without turning a hair have been to places and seen things that are the stuff of my worst nightmares. Yet in the broadcasting studio, they are as touchingly nervous about their voices as is the greenest media student. They are often conscious they don't have the control over their voice that they would like. Some days they feel better about it than others, but are not quite sure why. They know that voice can be a big factor in determining whether or not you get the job you want, whether you are a young journalist looking for your first break in a local newsroom, a DJ pleading to be given a chance to prove yourself on the graveyard shift, or a seasoned broadcaster aiming to make the move into presentation on a national network show.

So whatever your level of experience there should be something in this book that will help you, particularly if you have not yet found a way to get any specialist voice-training. Of course, I also hope it might convince you that training from a specialist is valuable too. Working alone with a book can take you so far, but there is no substitute for one-to-one advice, tailored for your own voice!

What you immediately discover when you enter the great wide world of broadcasting are whole newsrooms and production offices full of the 'hard-knocks' school of voice coaches. By which I mean helpful colleagues only too anxious to pass on the benefits of their own experience. This is both a blessing and a curse. Most of us have learnt a great deal from colleagues, and you should always be prepared to listen to their tips. Many of my own trainees made a quantum leap in the quality of their broadcasting the minute they set foot in a real radio or TV station, and it is certainly helpful to watch and listen to people who are doing it for real, day in and day out.

On the other hand, a large part of the work of any professional voice coach consists of trying to unstitch the extraordinary vocal patterns some people pick up unwittingly as the result of well-meaning advice from colleagues. Often, it is not necessarily the advice itself that is wrong but the way it gets put into practice.

A good example of this is the person who is told they need to get a little bit more 'oomph' into their delivery. 'You need to punch it out more', they will often be told. Generally the helpful colleague is right – the broadcaster in question sounds like the vocal equivalent of a limp lettuce. The trouble is that trying to 'punch it out' can mean different things to different people. There's a danger you could end up sounding like a limp lettuce with laryngitis if you push your voice too hard in the wrong way. Besides, what's so great about sounding 'punchy'? To my ear, a broadcaster whose only vocal technique is to place more stress on words is the aural equivalent of someone whose only body language is to thump the table. Call me old-fashioned, but I prefer something a BIT more subtle than being constantly HIT on the HEAD WITH words which MAY or may not BE the right ONES to stress. (For more on this, see Chapters 7 and 8.)

A small aside here – just about everything you will read in this book is born of bitter experience. You think I didn't make that mistake at some point in my broadcasting career? I still catch myself sometimes failing to take my own good advice. We all know broadcasters whom we imagine sounded totally wonderful from the word go, whose first flawless 'Mummy' or 'Dada' was captured by proud parents on the family cassette recorder and who have never quailed in front of a microphone since. All I can say is that if this rare breed truly exists, I was not one of them. And almost certainly neither are you. Getting your voice in top shape takes work, and it never really stops throughout your career.

So the aim of this book is to try and demystify some of the advice you may be given as you set out in broadcasting, or embark on a new direction in your career, and to give you some suggestions about how to get a sound that is 'warm, natural, relaxed, authoritative …' etc. You might find it's easier than you think. After all, most of us manage to sound warm, natural, relaxed, and authoritative when we're chatting to our friends. All you have to do is translate that to the microphone.

HOW TO USE THE EXERCISES

A word about the exercises contained in this book. I am the world's worst exerciser. Successive tutors – from my piano teacher onwards – have despaired at my inability to go home and practise what they have shown me.

As a result of this, I cannot play the piano. On the other hand, I *can* drive a car, swim, and operate rather complicated computer editing equipment.

The difference is that with the car, the swimming pool, and the computer, I both enjoyed and could see the point of practising what I was doing. The latter especially was essential to my chosen career. In all cases, I learnt by doing. What I read about the processes – if anything – might have been useful, but it wasn't until I put the advice into practice that I really began to learn.

If you want to learn how to use your voice for broadcasting, there is no substitute for doing, and that is why I have included a number of moments where hopefully you will break off from grappling with interesting theoretical notions in the text and have a go at it yourself.

The cringe factor

The exercises are important for two reasons. First, they are all designed to help you realize that you are capable of controlling the sound of your voice – and we all often do that, totally unconsciously, in various situations.

The second reason is that they are also designed to help you develop an 'ear' for the sound of your own voice, and a way of judging it dispassionately. I have yet to meet the person who truly loves the sound of their own voice. I certainly don't love mine, and generally have to be tied to the sofa to watch a programme on which I have done the voice-over, cringing all the while as I imagine the forty different ways in which I might have done it better. Indeed, the more people I train, the more I am convinced that this person who loves his or her own voice is a mythical beast. Without exception the usual reaction I get to 'Now let's listen back to the recording we just made of your voice' is a terrible groan, accompanied by 'Do we have to?'

The answer is unfortunately, yes. Unless you get over the cringe factor to some extent, it will be hard to make progress, and if not learn to love your voice, at least be able to assess it dispassionately and positively. So whenever possible, I would suggest you use a sound recorder of some sort to help you with the exercises.

As I shall explain later, one of the reasons we all tend to 'hate' our voice is that we are not used to hearing ourselves as others hear us. The more you get used to what you really sound like, as opposed to the voice resonating in your skull, the more you will get over the cringe factor. You may never perhaps be entirely satisfied with your voice, and that perfectionist attitude should keep you on your toes as a broadcaster. But it is important to develop a level of confidence in how you sound, because confidence itself strengthens the sound of your voice.

I have noticed over time that the people who make most progress with their voices have also developed the ability to listen – not just to themselves but to other people. A good ear is just as essential to a good voice as a good mouth or a good pair of lungs. All these organs are not necessarily something you're born with, they can be developed. Actually most of us *are* born with good ears, mouths, and lungs – we just forget how to use them properly.

Feeling self-conscious

Many of the exercises are what I think of as 'privacy of your own bathroom' ones. They are best practised at home, and not on the audience. The time to do exercises is *not* when you are actually on the air. Also you may feel silly doing some of them, and there is nothing worse than getting caught mid-exercise by one of your more hard-bitten colleagues who has just happened to wander into the studio and wants to know why you are on all fours panting like a dog. (Don't worry; I decided not to include that one.)

One of my first jobs as a voice-coach involved taking over a course of students who had been subjected to a different coach in their first term. She had come from an exclusively theatrical background and was not, I suspect, used to the scepticism of most broadcasters. She had made them all lie on the floor in a big group doing breathing exercises, and naturally they had felt deeply self-conscious. 'You're not going to make us do that, are you?' they said to me. I explained that I was interested in a different approach – for a start, they would all be taught one-to-one, and as broadcasting was rarely carried out from a supine position I thought it unlikely anyone would spend much time on the floor unless it was me, chewing the carpet in frustration. Nevertheless, by the end of the course, they all knew a great deal more about how to control their breathing, and I think we achieved it without anyone feeling too daft.

On the subject of breathing exercises, there is one golden rule. If you start to feel dizzy, stop. It's easy to overdo things with breathing if you are trying too hard to get it right. Before you know it you are hyperventilating and someone has to pick you up off the floor. Just let your breathing return to normal – remember, breathing is a reflex and if we stop thinking about it, it gets easier.

There are a few exercises that require a long-suffering partner. Broadcasting is about communication, and you need to remind yourself that there is a real person at the end of the process. Pick someone you feel comfortable with, and can have a good laugh with if you get to the point where you feel really silly.

You will feel less ridiculous if you can understand the point of an exercise. Better to feel silly now than to wonder why it always goes wrong when you get into a 'real' situation.

Revisiting the exercises

Remember these are no more than exercises – ideas for you to try to see if they work for you. I have learned as a voice coach that no single definitive route works for every individual person. The metaphor that presses the right button for one person may be meaningless to the next. There are certain basic principles which hold true – but the paths by which you arrive at that truth can be as varied as the people who choose to go into broadcasting.

So I would suggest that sometimes you might want to go back to read a particular chapter again and return to its exercises after you have looked at what follows. It might have seemed not to work for you at the time, but in the light of other things you discover later, it may suddenly start to make sense after all.

At first, it may seem overwhelming. So much to get right, so many ways to go wrong: pitch, intonation, pace, posture, and breathing. But when you sit hunched over your recording machine in despair (except after reading Chapter 2 you won't do the hunching bit) just remember what it was like when you learned to drive. That horrific moment when it struck you that you had to have one foot hovering over the clutch, another pressing the accelerator but ready to shift any second to the brake, both hands clutching the steering wheel so firmly it would have taken a crowbar to unclench your fingers – oh, but don't forget to keep an ear out for the engine starting to labour so you're ready to change gear, an eye on the rear view mirror – and on top of all that, you've got to look where you're going … I can still remember freezing in utter terror at the complexity of the mental and physical processes involved in driving a car when my Dad – never the most sympathetic of instructors – said 'Oh for goodness sake, you just *do* it.'

Yeah, yeah, Dad. It's OK for you, you've been doing it for years. But damn it, he was right, though it took me a good while to realize that. And you will too.

2 Are you sitting comfortably?

*Why it's important how you sit (or stand, or swing from the chandelier) while broadcasting. The state of your body has a big effect on your ability to make a convincing and pleasing sound. Your position determines your capacity to breathe properly and control the flow of breath. It also affects your body's potential to act as a resonator for your voice. A shift of literally a few centimetres can make all the difference to the tone of your voice. Also, what's happening in your body has a reciprocal effect on your state of mind – and as later chapters will show, mind-set is often the key to better broadcasting. A physically confident position produces an audibly confident voice. Refer to the tutorial on **posture** on the CD-ROM.*

Before we go any further, I would like you to try something. Sitting just as you are (I assume you're sitting down to read this), I want you to take the deepest breath you can manage. Hold it for a count of three, and then let it out slowly and easily.

Now change the way you're sitting – not to put too fine a point on it, try sitting *up*. Put your feet flat on the ground so they act as stabilizers for your body. Shift your weight firmly onto what I always think of as the 'sitting bones' (yes, there are bones there under all that padding, and once your weight is settled on them you'll become much more aware of them). Now let your spine lengthen upwards – you won't need the chair back to support it any longer if your weight is balanced on the sitting bones – and let your head lift too. Your ribcage should lift in the lengthening process. In this taller, straighter position, let your shoulders and neck relax (which doesn't mean that they slump) and now take the deepest possible breath you can manage, just as before.

Notice a difference?

What you should have felt if you really sat up properly is how much easier it is to breathe deeply in, and to control the flow of breath out, when you are in a more upright position.

It is breath that supports the sound we make with our voice – a fact that is so obvious it hardly needs stating. But if we know this, why don't we make more effort to give our bodies every chance they possibly can to breathe easily and to make a comfortable sound?

FREEING YOURSELF UP TO BREATHE

Before we can make a good sound, most of us need to spend some time undoing a lifetime's bad posture habits. Cicely Berry, the Royal Shakespeare Company's voice coach for many years, came up with a startling illustration of this. She points out how effortlessly a baby fills its lungs and bawls – sometimes for hours on end, as any parent knows. Despite producing such a sustained volume for long periods, the baby doesn't suffer any vocal damage. Yet leave an adult male at a rugby match for a couple of hours and he will shout himself hoarse. (Indeed I've often wondered whether the huskiness of some Welsh voices has anything to do with the national passion for rugby!)

Cicely Berry's point is that all of us are capable of making a strong sound without any huge effort that would harm the voice. But somewhere along the line we forget what we instinctively know, and develop all sorts of physical habits that prevent us from using our voices properly. As a result, as soon as we make any unusual demand on the voice, we run the risk of damaging it.

The answer, of course, is to try and unlearn some of these awkward physical habits and return to first principles.

Which is why I ask – are you sitting comfortably?

WHY POSTURE MATTERS

Most (but not all) voice work in broadcasting is undertaken from a sitting position. In spite of what some people will tell you, this doesn't necessarily put broadcasters at a physical disadvantage when using their voices. It all depends on how you sit – and it is also true that even if you are standing, you may still be using your body disadvantageously.

The exercise at the beginning of the chapter has probably shown you how little thought we give to body posture normally. Even a relatively small change in position can help improve breath control, by freeing up the midriff area of the body so your diaphragm and lungs get a chance to work more easily.

But it is a little more complicated than that. It is not only your lungs that have to work freely. There is a whole system of interlinked muscular processes that combine to produce the sound of the voice, any of which can be interfered with depending on your posture.

Let's run through a quick anatomy lesson. Your lungs are inside your ribcage, and they always move to follow the shape of the cavity.

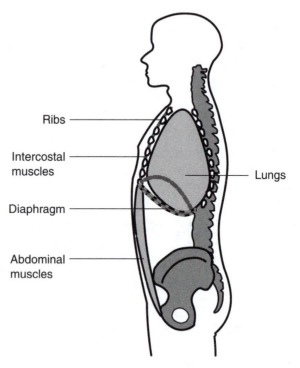

Figure 2.1
In an upright posture, the muscles are free to move to control the airflow

When you need to breathe in, your nervous system activates your diaphragm – a dome-shaped slab of muscle attached to your breast bone at the front, your spine at the back, and following the line of your lower ribs. It flattens out, working together with the abdominal muscles, which lengthen as you breathe in. Meanwhile, intercostal muscles between the ribs lift your ribcage, increasing the size of your chest cavity so your lungs expand to pull air in like a bellows. If any of these processes are constricted by poor posture, your lungs won't fill properly. (So it's a good idea to forget vanity and not worry about holding your tummy in. Tight waistbands, sprayed-on jeans, and 'look-five-pounds-slimmer' underwear are not helpful either!)

As you breathe out, those abdominal muscles contract, pushing your guts upwards so they help the diaphragm to form a dome again. Meanwhile, another set of intercostal muscles pulls the ribs closed, so the air is pushed out of your lungs, passing en route through the vocal cords in the larynx. These open and close as you speak, turning the airflow into a series of puffs that are essentially the basis of your voice. The strength and power of your voice is directly affected by how well these processes work.

While your lungs are the powerhouses that provide the breath sup-porting the voice, the precise sounds we make are moderated by other parts of the body. Air passing through the vocal cords is only the first stage. Sounds are shaped by our mouth parts – tongue, teeth, and lips, not to mention less familiar structures like the hard and soft

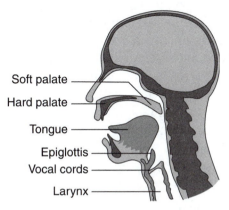

Soft palate

Hard palate

Tongue

Epiglottis

Vocal cords

Larynx

Figure 2.2
Sound shapers in the head

palate, acting together in various ways to make vowels or consonants. We use other cavities in the head and body to give the voice resonance and richness. The chest provides some of this, in a similar way to the sounding box of a stringed instrument. But there are other resonators, like the mouth. Similarly, how much of the airflow passes through the nose – producing the effect called nasal resonance, often a rather harsh and metallic sound – alters the sound of the voice.

It is not the purpose of this book to provide a comprehensive elocution tutorial – many other helpful textbooks on this subject already exist. But it is important to understand that the state of the body has a strong influence on the sound you make, and at the most basic level, it is a question of *relaxation* so the muscles can work properly.

RELAXED POSTURE

If you ask someone to sit in a 'relaxed' way, it is interesting to watch what happens. Bizarrely the position most people will assume is anything but relaxed. The shoulders slump, the spine curves, the head sinks forward – all actions that put tension into the muscles of the neck, shoulders, and back, and take a surprising amount of physical effort to maintain. You're probably not conscious of this effort. You're used to it, because you've let your body develop lazy habits – you probably rely on the back of the chair to hold you upright. That might seem to be 'relaxed' to you, but nonetheless your body isn't free. Just breathing normally is taking more effort, though you don't realize it, because your lungs are squashed up in that big abdominal slump. So instead of breathing deeply and freely, you're taking little shallow breaths that are sufficient to keep your body functioning, but not equal to the demands you are going to place on it if you want to have a strong confident voice.

Men, I've noticed, have a particular take on this. Sorry to sound sexist, but it's rare to come across a man who gives much thought to how he sits. When I ask them to relax, I can see them mentally flinging themselves on the sofa in front of the telly and opening a can of lager. Nice try, guys, but broadcasting requires just a tad more authority in your posture than that.

On the other hand, simply asking someone to 'sit up' may do just as much potential damage. Up comes the chin, pulling on neck

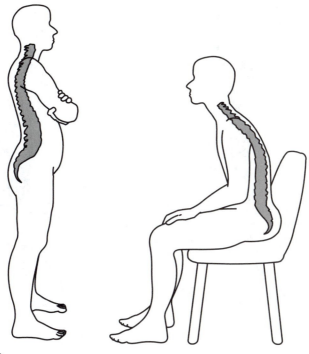

Figure 2.3
The slumper. Sounds as tired as she looks

Figure 2.4
The sprawler. Lazy posture, lazy voice

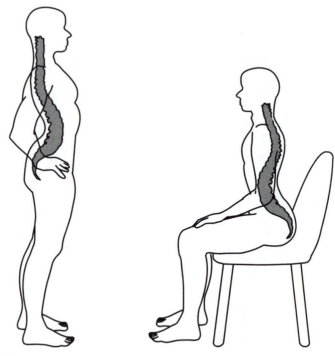

Figure 2.5
Uptight. Holding yourself too rigid, the voice is as tight as the body looks

muscles and squashing the vertebrae of the neck. Back go the shoulders, out puffs the chest, and the spine arches to match.

None of these positions is ideal, because they all involve shortening in the spine and tension in the muscles. The 'slump' position makes breathing more difficult, but although the 'uptight' position has improved the freedom of the abdomen and diaphragm, the muscles are still not free enough. This posture takes a lot of effort to maintain and has introduced extra tension in the neck, back, and jaw.

So it's time to change the bad habits of a lifetime.

Picture yourself taller

I am still often surprised by the extraordinary effect that words and mental images can have on the state of the body. They need to be

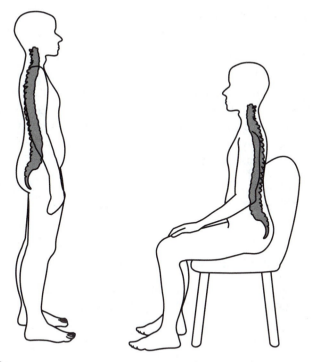

Figure 2.6
At ease, free and upright – good posture, improved voice

used with care, for a word or image that means one thing to one person can have a radically different affect on another.

The way that teachers of the Alexander Technique (a body movement system that was originally designed to help the voice) usually describe the effect we are looking for is 'back long and wide, head and neck free'. This may be a useful image to bear in mind as you move towards the ideal position to free up your voice. I like to think of it as a position of perfect balance that takes no effort to maintain. The weight of the body and the head – for the head is one of the heaviest parts of your body – are supported by your spine and skeletal frame, resting on those 'sitting bones' I mentioned earlier. The feet are firmly on the floor, acting as stabilizers for your body. (Actors often refer to this as 'grounding' themselves, and it does conjure up good images of both using the floor to give you support, and a flow of energy between you and the earth.) Because the spine is lengthened, the rib cage is lifted and the mid-section of your body is free to let your lungs work. The head rests on the top of the spine, chin and nose are not tilted up, and the jaw and neck are easy.

In this position, everything is free to work as it should in the production of your voice. Also, it takes physically less effort to maintain. Notice, however, that I have avoided using the phrase 'hold' the position. If you feel you are 'fixing' or 'holding' a particular posture, you are already beginning to introduce tension into the process. Essentially, you should be able to feel you are free to move in any direction you choose.

If you find it difficult to grasp what I mean by 'a long back', there is a simple exercise you can try to help yourself.

Exercise 2.1: Lengthening the back

Stand easy with your back against a wall. Your back should be touching the wall at your shoulders and at your buttocks. Your heels will be against the skirting board, but the whole of your feet should be on the floor, supporting your weight. (Shift the weight forward onto the balls of your feet, then back onto your heels, so you can find the balance point to distribute the weight between the two.) The back of your head will not quite be touching the wall, and your chin is level.

You are using the wall not to support yourself, but to give a guide to your spine. It should feel 'long and free'.

Now bend slightly at the knees, and as they flex let your back – still long and straight – slide down the wall. From this position, let the top of your head lead you upwards as you return to a normal but tall standing position.

Now return to a chair and sit down on it, trying to maintain that length and freedom in the spine. Let your knees bend, your tailbone come out and down to lead you back into the seat of the chair, while your head remains easy and balanced on the top of your spine. Let your weight rest on your sitting bones, as your spine moves back – still long and free – to the upright position.

It is sometimes helpful to do these exercises where you can see your whole body in a mirror, but the best test for checking

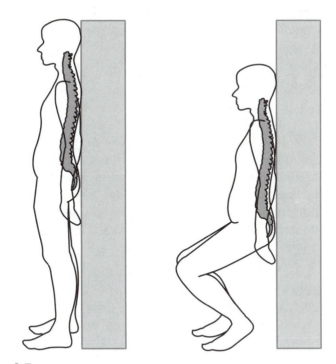

Figure 2.7
An exercise to lengthen the back

if you have found the right position is how it feels to you. If you feel comfortably balanced on your sitting bones and your feet are acting as 'stabilizers' flat on the ground, you won't need to use the back of the chair to support you. Your diaphragm should be free, the ribcage slightly lifted, there will be no feeling of 'squashing' your stomach, and breathing should seem effortless. If you want to see how it should look, refer to the drawings or the tutorial on **posture** on the CD-ROM.

This position should always be your starting point. Just remember, though, that rigidity is your enemy. You don't have to freeze yourself into this position as if turned to stone by the basilisk stare of the TV camera or microphone – there must always be the *possibility* of movement, and as we will discover in a later chapter some movement can help you remind yourself that you are talking to someone. I would point out, however, that on television this does *not* mean constantly shuffling about or waggling your shoulders, which can be immensely irritating for the viewer. It is also wise before you start to move around during a radio performance to check that you are not sitting on a squeaky chair, or moving so dramatically that you appear to be 'coming and going' on the microphone by moving out of its sensitive field.

Exercise 2.2: Hearing how good posture helps the voice

Sit in front of a microphone and find that perfect sitting position again. Resisting the temptation to lean into the mic (move it towards you instead), read a few lines of script, recording your performance. Notice as you do how it feels. Is your breathing easier? Do you feel more relaxed? Is the whole performance somehow more effortless?

You should be feeling generally freer in the way you are using your voice. If not, it may be that you have allowed yourself to lean slightly forward, or have tipped back to rest on the back of the chair. It is also possible that, terrified you are going to lose this unfamiliar position, you have made your muscles rigid in order to maintain it, and you are sitting poker straight, afraid to shift by even a millimetre. 'Fixing' like this is just as unhelpful as slumping, so try again. Once you are in the right position there is no need to tense your muscles to hold it, because your body is perfectly balanced, supporting the weight of your head on your spine.

Now listen back to your recording. If you have an earlier recorded version of your voice compare the two. Does this sound more relaxed? Does your voice have a subtly richer, fuller sound? If you think it does, that will be because you have increased the resonance of your voice by making it easier to fill your lungs in this position.

Why this position helps

In essence, you are allowing your body to work as it was intended to. The ease in your relaxed muscles makes it possible to fill your lungs – and when you do that your breath can support your voice. Because you have created space in your body, your voice will sound subtly richer, stronger, and more resonant – you'll see why this is important when you read Chapters 4 and 5. But above all everything becomes easier, and, therefore, more enjoyable. You feel more confident – and confidence is one of the key factors in sounding good.

Some common mistakes

Some people – and it's very often men who do this – imagine they are sitting up straight when, in fact, they are slightly leaning back onto the base of their spine – the coccyx. They are probably relying on the chair back as a support. In this position, the abdomen is still being squashed, the rib cage is not lifted, and the diaphragm is not free – they won't be able to fill their lungs as easily.

If you were to continue in that position for several hours, your body would soon tell you how uncomfortable it was. Your coccyx, which is not designed to carry your weight, would become sore – you'd develop what my nephew calls 'a numb bum'. If that is your characteristic sitting position, you probably have suffered this already, if you've been to the cinema and sat through a long film. You thought you were sitting comfortably, sinking back into that plush seat, but after an hour or so you began to shift around trying to ease the soreness. I expect you blamed the cinema seat. I always did. Then one day I tried sitting differently, weight on sitting bones instead of the coccyx – and got through the whole of *The Lord of the Rings* without the slightest trace of discomfort.

The opposite of this – and equally unhelpful – is a slight tilt forward. Again you will be squashing your abdomen, with your weight settled on your thighs. It takes some determination to avoid this. There is something about a microphone or a camera that draws you towards it. I have watched many a client carefully adopt a perfect posture, then as they begin to broadcast unconsciously lean forward. Even an inch or two can make a noticeable difference in the voice. The tension in your muscles is enough to restrict the resonating spaces of your body, and your voice will sound less warm and strong.

If you suspect you are falling into either of these traps, shift your weight around from buttock to buttock until you locate those sitting bones. And sit up! It may feel odd at first – but it certainly won't be uncomfortable.

Your feet

It is worth re-emphasizing how important your feet are in establishing an ideal, relaxed position for your body. Good posture starts at ground level.

It seems absurd, doesn't it, that these two much-neglected appendages, far away from what seems like the business end of

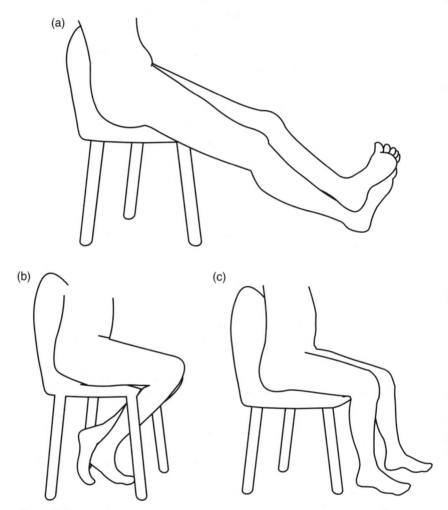

Figure 2.8
(a) Feet doing little to support the body. (b) Single point of gravity, no stability. (c) Feet acting as stabilizers for your body

your body (your head and mouth) could have much to do with improving how you sound? But because they help to balance you as you sit in front of the microphone, or stand in front of the camera, they are very important indeed.

I tell people to get their feet right – firmly planted flat on the ground, and *not* tucked under you on tiptoe – as soon as they sit down to broadcast. That way, they become a reminder to you of all the other processes involved in assuming a good posture. So *start with the feet*. And watch out they don't creep back, as if they had a mind of their own, while you are making yourself comfortable.

They are your body's stabilizers. If they are tucked under you and crossed at the ankle, you are operating on the equivalent of three wheels instead of four. This may be fine for some varieties of motor vehicle, but it doesn't suit the broadcasting body. It would be rather like doing a piece-to-camera (PTC) standing on one leg.

Standing to broadcast

How important are your feet when you are standing to do a PTC? I would always advise you to plant your weight firmly on both feet, slightly apart, which will give you a sense of balance and

Figure 2.9
Natural poses for PTCs

confidence. Your weight should be on your heels rather than your toes. You might want to put one foot slightly in front of the other, if it feels more natural, in which case the weight will naturally shift to the foot that is further back. Try to keep *both* knees relaxed, rather than rigidly straightening the back leg.

As a TV director, I sometimes ask my presenter to take up a position where he or she is leaning on something; it can make you look and feel more relaxed and natural. But I will always make sure whatever the position, they can still support their voice by being able to breathe easily and naturally. And good voice support starts with the feet.

If posture's so important, why don't we always broadcast standing up?

In the very early days of broadcasting, people did just that. Announcers stood at the microphone. But fairly soon it became apparent that if there was a long news bulletin to read, for instance, and script papers to manage, life would be much easier for all concerned if the broadcaster sat down.

In more recent years, there has been a trend for some DJs in commercial radio to revert to standing at the mic. This is understandable if they come from a club background where the DJ almost always stands. Unfortunately, any advantage that might be gained from standing is lost as soon as the DJ or presenter has to bend over the turntables or broadcasting desk to operate the equipment. They immediately start to hunch and the voice is no longer strong and free – indeed if they are trying to produce it at volume, they run a very real risk of causing voice strain.

Nowadays, most local broadcasting equipment is self-operated, and even the national networks are moving that way. One or two stations have experimented with 'stand-up' desks, but the main problem is that not all broadcasters come at a standardized height, and short ones find themselves on tiptoe, while taller beings have to bend down. At least with sit-down desks the chair height is adjustable. So – until someone invents a broadcasting desk that rises up and down like an old-fashioned cinema organ – you are really far better off sitting if you have equipment to operate or scripts to manage.

Adjusting chair height

Any chair in a broadcast studio should be height-adjustable. It is not so important to alter the angle of the back (unless it is at an awkward angle) because in the ideal posture for making the best of your voice, you do not need to rely on the chair back for support. But the height is important. You need to be able to get your feet flat on the floor to balance you, at the same time being high enough to operate the equipment comfortably.

If you can't adjust the chair to this ideal position, don't panic. By moving your backside *forward* on the seat (now you really won't be able to rely on the chair back for support!) you can ensure that your feet reach the floor comfortably.

Getting the chair height right is not just important for your posture. The height of the chair you sit on can give you a psychological boost. Think of how you might feel if you went to a job interview and you were made to sit on a lower chair than the interviewing panel, or on such a high stool that your feet dangled like a child's. Find a position that not only makes you comfortable but also gives you confidence.

Think TV, even when you are on radio

Some years ago, I began training young broadcasters on one of the first bi-media journalism courses in the BBC. Although I had, for some time, been working with both TV and radio journalists on voice production, this was the first time I had tackled a group of journalists who were being trained to work interchangeably in both media. The course fell into two parts – in part one they learnt about radio, and in part two they tackled television. In the first part of the course, I was scheduled to give them a couple of sessions of voice training, with further follow-up during the second part.

As the course progressed, I noticed something interesting. As soon as the journalists began the television part of the course, the quality of their voices (which had been so far slowly and steadily improving) suddenly underwent a quantum leap. They became much better almost overnight.

This fascinated me – why such a sudden, marked improvement? At first I thought it was because this generation of broadcasters might be much better attuned to television than to radio – although mine was a TV generation, as children we were also surrounded by radio voices (no daytime TV then, so our mums brought us up on a solid diet of *Woman's Hour* and the Home Service). I still think there may be some element of truth in this, but nonetheless simply being confident in a more familiar medium did not seem sufficient explanation for the dramatic change.

Eventually, I realized it was something much more simple. Facing a camera, the journalists had discovered the truth of what I had been telling them all along – they needed to sit up straight. Up until this point they had not really absorbed what I had been saying – and it was only when they began to read from autocue, and saw how they looked on camera if they slumped, that their posture truly improved – with noticeable effects on the voice.

The lesson I drew from this is that it can be very useful for someone working in radio to think of him or herself as speaking to a TV camera. It brings the head up into balance, which in itself can give you a big boost of confidence. Nobody – as I am constantly reminding radio broadcasters – ever conducts a successful conversation with their head sunk between their shoulders and their eyes cast downwards. Besides, with your head down, you end up directing your voice onto the tabletop rather than directly into the microphone. Some tables in broadcasting studios are covered in felt, which absorbs the sound – other harder surfaces may reflect it back – but whichever is the case, the sound is poorer for being distorted in this way.

Looking the listener/viewer in the eye

It is not just a matter of body balance reducing the tension in your speaking parts. How you sit has an effect on your **mind-set** too. Sitting up straight, relaxed and balanced gives a sense of well-being, calm, and confidence. And it makes you feel – with your head up facing the camera, real or imagined, instead of being buried in a script that's flat on the desk in front of you – that you are *talking to someone*. Most of us never talk with our head hanging

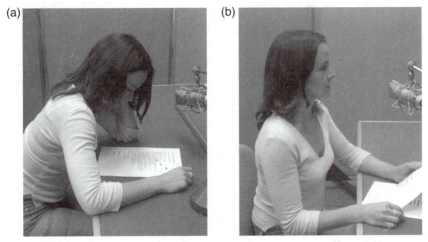

Figure 2.10
(a) Since when did you talk to anyone like this? (b) Looking your listener in the eye

down, failing to look anyone in the eye, unless we are either severely depressed or ashamed.

We are used to thinking of mind-set and body-state as being two quite separate things. But they are interlinked. While we are prepared to accept that the body often reflects the state of mind – that if you are nervous your body will tense, if you are calm it will relax, etc. – it is not always so easy to grasp that your mind is reciprocally affected by your body. Physical ease produces mental ease, and putting your body in the right position for talking will also help you feel that you are indeed communicating. As a result, your delivery will almost magically improve.

What do I do with the script?

The usual objection at this point from radio broadcasters is 'But what do I do with the script?' To which the obvious rejoinder is 'Try holding it up'. You don't need to clutch it obsessively with both hands – I suggest you pick up one page at a time with one hand (leaving the other one free to wave in whatever expansive gestures you might choose) and lay it aside as you read the bottom line, ready to pick up the next from the desk in front of you.

Figure 2.11
Holding the script firmly, one page at a time

You should see the horror on some people's faces when I suggest this. You'd think I had asked them to do something extremely difficult. 'But it will rustle!' they squawk. 'We've been told to be really careful and never let the script rustle!'

Good advice, sure – after all, broadcasting is built on trying to create the extraordinary illusion that you are talking, not reading, so it would be sacrilege to let the audience realize there's a piece of paper there with the words on it. But if you hold *one page at a time*, the script won't rustle unless you are obsessively rubbing it as you talk. If you grip it firmly and confidently there is no danger at all it will make a sound. Of course if you want to *make* it rustle, you could wave it around like a mad conductor – but you're not going to do that, are you?

The only time the page could make a sound is when you lay it aside and pick up the next sheet from the table. You have to change sheets whether you're holding the script up or leaving it flat, so there's just as much chance of rustle if you *don't* hold the script up. If your microphone is set up in a sensible position, any rustle should be well away from the microphone's most sensitive field (see Chapter 12 for positioning microphones). So I am not going to let you use that as an objection against holding the script up, unless you happen to be suffering from some violent shaking disease, which seems fairly unlikely.

Exercise 2.3: Reading with your head up

Test out what I have suggested by trying it for yourself, recording your performance. Once again, ask yourself as you read how it feels. Does the process seem easier? It should because with your head up, your neck muscles are freer, and you are no longer squashing your vocal apparatus. And you should feel more as if you are actually talking to someone. You may even feel bold enough to lift your eyes off the script occasionally, as if you were making eye contact with a listener.

Now check back the recording to see how you sound. A little less strangulated, perhaps? More natural?

Script rests and computer screens

Someone many years ago invented a cunning device called the script rest – a sloping surface so that the script doesn't lie flat on the desk. Unfortunately, these are somewhat limited in their usefulness, as on a standard self-operated desk they would be in the way. They also don't lift the script to a level with the eyes, so unless the broadcaster is aware of the need to keep their head up, they may still end up speaking into the script rest. Personally, I feel they are only really useful in TV dubbing suites, where the need to watch the pictures on the monitor should keep the head up anyway, and those are the only circumstances in which I ever use one.

The days of paper scripts may be numbered. Many broadcasting organizations now read the news from a computer screen, which does have the advantage of keeping the newsreader's head up. But some care needs to be taken with the positioning of the screen so that it is adjustable to eye-level. If it is fixed too high, shorter broadcasters may end up with their chins in the air and tension in the neck. One engineer, who had clearly never broadcast, suggested saving space by sinking the screens flat into the desktop – fortunately, this particularly idiotic notion was never adopted.

I like the idea of reading off a screen, which like autocue in television does help to keep your head level, and remind you that are speaking outwards to somebody. But anyone who has less than perfect vision may find they need to remember their glasses.

Leaning forward and peering at the screen will undo much of the good. Perhaps broadcasting organizations moving towards this technology should make sure that the position of the monitor and the size of the typeface are adjustable for the short- or long-sighted!

Checking your position in the studio

A short while ago, I was booked to do a voice-over for a TV documentary. It wasn't the best day to be doing it from my point of view – I was going on holiday the next day, I had a programme edit of my own to complete before I went, and my head was full of how I was going to get through everything before going away. It was a real effort to concentrate on the script and, of course, I was feeling tense.

We began the recording. I was immediately aware of something wrong with my voice. It wasn't bad – it just wasn't quite as relaxed as it normally is, and sounded a bit thin. I also found it harder than usual to control it so I could hit the right stresses and make the intonation sound natural. In between takes, I paused to assess what was going wrong. And the first thing I noticed was that I was poised on the edge

Figure 2.12
Leaning slightly forwards – the body is out of balance and the resulting tension will subtly affect the voice

of my chair like an athlete in the starting blocks. My feet were tucked under me and crossed at the ankle. Certainly my spine was long and straight, but I was leaning slightly forward, all keyed up to go for the start of what I seemed to be thinking of as a race.

I knew immediately why my voice sounded wrong. In that position, I had to tense my muscles simply to keep upright, or the weight of my head would have dragged me forward and down. Instead of acting as a balance, my feet crossed beneath me had destabilized my body and shifted my centre of gravity – only muscular tension in my back was keeping me upright. And that physical tension – the reflection of my own inner mental tension – was just enough to have an effect on the sound of my voice, robbing it of some of its usual resonance.

Nothing was going to take away the mental tension, I told myself – you can't alter the fact you've got a lot to do and time is ticking by. But you can do something about physical tension. It felt the very opposite of what I wanted to do, but I made myself move my feet forward, flat on the floor, shifted my weight back off my thighs and squarely onto my bum, so that I stopped leaning in to the mic. My head had probably moved back no more than a few centimetres but I instantly felt taller and more relaxed. We didn't even have to adjust the position of the mic. But I could hear the difference in my voice – fuller and more resonant. That in its turn gave me confidence, and by the time we finished the session, I was feeling great. The mental tension had gone too, because apart from anything else it had taken remarkably little time to record a set of perfect takes. I hadn't stumbled; I got the intonation spot-on every time, and the director was gratifyingly effusive about my performance.

The point is that even seasoned old hacks like me can screw it up. I ought to know how to sit – indeed I *do* know how to sit to get the best out of my voice. The trouble is on a pressured day your body slips back into its old bad habits, and that 'athlete in the starting blocks' posture sneaks in without you even noticing it has happened.

You can just about get by in that position, if your voice is already strong. The effect on the sound is subtle. You might be the only person who ever notices, if you know how your voice should sound at its best. But the muscular tension in your back creeps insidiously through the whole of your body and increases the chance of stumbling over words. It makes it more difficult to hit the right pitch on the upward and downward inflexions of your voice, the subtle signposts we use in everyday speech to highlight meaning. It makes the difference between a great performance and a merely adequate one. You are the cake, without icing. And worse, it can add time to a recording session because you somehow can't get anything right first time – you trip over words, you gabble sentences, you garble the meaning.

So *check your position before you start*. Check it in the middle of recording too, between takes. *Ease back, and get your feet working for you*.

It's one of the miracle cure-all tricks I use with the people I coach. If someone is sent to me because they keep stumbling over their words, or because they need to strengthen their voice in some way, their position will be one of the first things I look at. Dead simple, but usually dead effective.

Never move your body to the mic, move the mic to you

There are all sorts of psychological factors that can affect how you sit, and interfere with the process of finding the right position to get the best from your voice. One of them is where someone else has left the microphone.

Just because someone before you has set the microphone into the position that suits them, that's no reason to assume it is right for you. We'll talk more about microphones and their sensitive fields later, but for now I just want to remind you that microphones are *adjustable*. You can move them nearer to you, instead of leaning in to them. If necessary you can move them further away. You can angle them so they feel right to you – but please, please, *do not adjust yourself to them*.

It's simple. So blindingly obvious I feel patronizing saying it, but you would be surprised at how many people I have to remind of this when we're working together. You should sit down and get yourself comfortable at the desk so you can reach anything you need to reach, adopting the best position for your voice which by now I hope is becoming second nature. Feet on the floor, spine long and free, weight on sitting bones. Then you pull the mic towards you until it is about six to ten inches from your mouth, and it doesn't feel as if you have to lean in to it. In a professional dubbing studio, where there is an engineer to set it up for you, make sure he adjusts it when you are sitting in your optimum position.

If for any reason the microphone is not adjustable, have words with your boss or the station engineer. Not everyone is the same size or height – for a microphone to be suitable for broadcasting it must be possible to adjust its position.

If you are out on location and have to hand-hold a mic, don't hunch over it – even in the teeth of a howling gale. Find a sheltered spot instead and turn your back to the wind – you are going to need all the breath you can muster to compete with the noise of the storm. Keep your shoulders free as you hold the mic up towards your mouth. Don't clutch it – remember tension anywhere in your body has the habit of spreading, like ink on blotting paper.

We'll talk about lip mics in a later chapter – I hate them, and I'll tell you why, but some broadcasting organizations insist on using them, so you may have to find a way of adapting to get the best out of them.

But the mantra to remember is – move the mic to you, not you to the mic.

The Alexander Technique

I (and many others who use their voice professionally) have been helped immensely by practitioners of the Alexander Technique – a way of working with the body that was originally developed early in the last century by an actor interested in voice production, but which has since been found to help people in many other ways. Practitioners claim it frees up movement, releases more energy in the body, and can alleviate a range of physical problems including back pain and joint difficulties. I first became interested in it when I realized that almost every book I had picked up on voice enthused about it, but it was not until I began to suffer from a frozen shoulder and neck pain that I tried it myself. Since that first session (in which the neck pain magically disappeared never to return again), I have become a devotee.

Broadcasters who work in television may find it useful for another reason – it can give movements a wonderful grace, as well as being a good antidote to the stress of working to deadlines.

You will find an address for the Society of Teachers of the Alexander Technique at the back of the book. However, it should not be regarded as a 'quick fix' for posture problems – to get the full benefit you need to make a commitment to lessons on a regular basis, and for that reason it may be beyond the budget of some student broadcasters. How much you get from it will also depend on the relationship you build up with your individual teacher, and not everyone finds it easy to fit the lessons into a busy lifestyle. I would recommend one-to-one sessions rather than large classes, if your budget will stretch.

SUMMARY

- Voice is a physical process, and how you use your body affects your voice.
- Your muscles need to be relaxed to make a good sound. To get that relaxation throughout your body, your posture is important.
- Sit up, weight on sitting bones – not leaning back on your coccyx or forward onto the thighs – and balance your body by putting your feet firmly flat on the floor.
- Don't 'fix' – you must always feel free to move, but be able to return to the base position.
- Now your ribcage is lifted, your diaphragm is free, and your lungs can really take in air easily.
- There are also psychological benefits – you feel more relaxed and that boosts your confidence and helps you feel more authoritative.
- Avoid the temptation to lean in, however slightly, to the mic. Bring it to you.

3 Who are you talking to?

> *Every broadcaster learns quickly that you are only supposed to be talking to one person. But which person? Does it matter? And are you really, honestly, talking to one person – or 'broadcasting to the nation'?*

The most important process in broadcasting is what is happening in your head while you are in front of the microphone or the camera. In fact your mind-set *is* the broadcasting process – it is what makes the difference between 'reading' and 'telling', 'acting' and 'being'.

Everyone will tell you that a broadcaster sounds best when he or she is being 'natural'. But achieving that is – apparently – the hardest trick of all when everything about your situation screams out that broadcasting is NOT a natural act. What after all could be natural about sitting in a small, perhaps windowless room, with carpet or its equivalent all over the walls, on your own yet miraculously talking to thousands or millions of people?

Of course, I am going to attempt to show you that this can *become* natural. Once again, remember how it felt the first time you sat behind the steering wheel of your car. That probably did not feel exactly 'natural'. But for most people, driving – or any other process that involves the tricky combination of physical and mental processes, aided by technology – becomes sooner or later something you do almost as 'naturally' as breathing.

And just like driving, some people take to broadcasting more quickly than others. Some will always feel awkward and self-conscious while doing it – we've all heard of people who took seven goes to pass the driving test, and if you don't do it every day, of course you can get a bit rusty. But with practice, you can become more natural.

I like the driving analogy because it is something that most of us do, and do reasonably competently, in spite of the accident statistics. It seems to me that this is the way we should look at broadcasting – not as a mysterious talent but an everyday skill. You don't have to aspire to Formula One to be good at it.

THE INVISIBLE PASSENGER

Unlike driving, however, in broadcasting you *always* have a passenger with you. There will always be someone somewhere listening to you when you are on the air. If this notion fills you with terror, I am going to try to help you at least get familiar with the idea, and hopefully you might even learn to welcome their presence. I want you to understand that the listener/viewer is one of your most important aids in becoming a good broadcaster.

In some broadcasting circles it has become fashionable to be cynical about the listener/viewer. It is tempting to go along with that, especially if you have been on the receiving end of those extraordinary letters from 'the green ink brigade', criticizing your programmes and often you personally. 'I saw you at an outside broadcast' began one I received once from a listener. 'Do you really think it was suitable to wear shoes that high with that skirt?' This particular lady took my fashion sense so much to heart that she once turned up at the studio with a carrier bag. 'I bought this for you at a market stall', she confided, unwrapping a hideous turquoise-blue crimplene dress at least two sizes too big for me, which was not exactly flattering. But she meant well, as most do.

If you allow yourself at heart to despise the listeners or viewers it will show in your on-air performance. What you have to remember is that for every madwoman lurking outside the studios with a carrier bag, there are hundreds of sane, intelligent people who are listening or watching because they want to be informed by you. You owe it to them to treat your audience with respect. If you do that they in turn will respect you.

To carry on the driving analogy a little further, you should perhaps think of the listener or viewer not simply as a passenger, but as a *destination*. Without their unseen presence your words are going nowhere.

Performance

Before we go any further though, we should look at the notion that the broadcaster is – as well as being 'natural' – someone who *performs*. Someone who is in some senses a little larger than life.

This is a tricky area because the concept of performance can seem to contradict the idea of being natural. A 'performer' is in most people's definition someone who is not being their real self. They are adopting a mask, a *persona*. But what do we mean by 'our real self'?

Most of us have a number of equally 'real' selves that we use in different situations. At work or at home, having a drink with friends or walking alone in the countryside, there are several different faces we show to the world. These are all 'real' aspects of our personality. We are still the same person, whether we are dealing with someone's grief, or having a laugh with our mates. It should not be a question of 'acting' sad when we are happy and someone else is not, or 'pretending' to be decisive when we haven't a clue what to do – as the situation demands we can *become* those things. All it takes is awareness of what the person we are interacting with needs from us. So in one sense we all 'perform' in different situations.

Performance, in the broadcasting sense, is this. It is not getting up on a stage and *pretending* to be something as part of a piece of fiction. It is finding that part of you that can *be* the person the situation demands.

The simplest example of this is the person you become when you are comfortable with a small group of people. Perhaps, for example, the 'you' who goes out after work on a Friday evening with a group of friends for a meal or a drink. (Alcohol, of course, is not necessary to this process – but relaxation is!) The working week is over and you feel pretty pleased about what you have achieved. Even if you've had a hell of a day you can put that behind you now. Someone might start talking about something you feel you know about – you can put them right, whether it's the performance of your favourite football team, the pros and cons of genetically modified foods, or the motivations of characters in your favourite soap. You begin holding forth. You're confident; you have the facts (and your own personal interpretation of them) at your fingertips. You have authority. People begin to listen – they're interested in what you are saying. Your voice grows stronger, knowing that people are actually taking note. (They might argue later, but for the moment you hold the floor and they're paying attention.)

Isn't that what broadcasting is?

So who are you talking to?

What I hope you will have noticed, through all the examples I have given above, is how they all make reference to the person you are talking to. Our multiple 'real selves' do not exist in a vacuum. They are called forth depending on the relationship we have with the person we are with.

At the heart of real broadcasting is the notion that we are *with* someone. We have a relationship with the listener/viewer. We're talking *to* them, not *at* them. You can hear the difference on the CD-ROM, in the section on **Who are you talking to?**

It may not be a close relationship. There may be no emotional ties between you and the person listening or watching. But it is not a formal or distant one either. Your listener/viewer knows you, because they have probably heard you before, and hopefully they will hear you again. We reflect that in the kind of language we use in broadcasting – colloquial, spoken English, rather than formal written language. There's a particular reason why I chose to call this chapter 'Who are you talking to?' The grammar check on my computer urges me to use the old-fashioned grammatically correct case 'Whom?' But when did you last hear that used in spoken English?

We'll look in more detail at broadcast writing and language in Chapter 9. For now, the important point to grasp is that you are not alone when you are at the microphone or in front of the camera, and that the person you are talking to must be real and connected to you.

ONE OR MANY?

Broadcasting is in fact rather a misleading term. It implies a vast audience – scattering our message over a sea of people. The temptation is to think of yourself on a stage, staring down at an auditorium full of faces.

For most of us this is a rather difficult experience to imagine, and can be somewhat paralysing (especially if you try to put a number on those faces – your local football stadium for instance would not hold the number of people who are in the audience even for an off-peak regional TV programme). Possibly, the last time you faced even a moderately sized audience was the day you were hauled up at school assembly to read something out – and although there are people who thrive on that kind of thing, standing up in front of a large audience is intimidating. You are immensely conscious of being watched, and judged, by a whole variety of opinion. Not only that, you are terrified you will not be heard – or perhaps even terrified you will be heard! Some people sink into themselves and start to mumble. Others puff out their chests, forcing their voices into something between a shout and a strangled screech in an attempt to reach the very back of the hall. Even those who find it less scary very often put on an act to get through it – they become mannered or put on a 'posh' voice.

So the idea of an 'audience' is not really a helpful one. It leads at worst to paralysis, at best to the idea of 'broadcasting to the nation', rather like the Queen delivering her Christmas Day message.

When you broadcast, you are only ever talking to one person. It is perhaps the oldest and most familiar cliché in the slender manual of advice given to new broadcasters. But like most clichés, it is based on a fundamental truth.

Unfortunately it is one that, even when we think we understand, is remarkably hard to put into practice. So I am not the least bit apologetic about trotting it out again. But what I want to do is examine what we really mean by it.

Who's talking to me?

Just for a moment, let's turn the whole thing on its head, and look at the experience of the person who is listening to a broadcast.

As far as the listener is concerned, hearing a broadcast is rarely a communal activity. Once upon a time, it is true that whole families gathered before the crystal wireless set, but these days most radio listening is a solitary experience, usually undertaken while the listener is occupied with some other activity – driving, washing up, working, or maybe (this is me) lying in bed trying to persuade oneself it's time to get up. (There are exceptions: as one of my clients at BBC World Service pointed out to me, there are still communities in the developing world where the whole village may gather to hear 'London calling', as they used to say.)

But there is also something about listening attentively that is solitary in itself, no matter whether you are with people or not. Even when a whole family is gathered in front of the TV set, the experience of each member is an individual one. If you look at your own experience of watching or listening to a good broadcast, you will find that the over-riding sense is of being addressed directly, one-to-one.

Push it a little further and you will see why it is that little old ladies say goodnight to the weatherman or continuity announcer before switching the set off. The good broadcaster becomes someone with whom we feel we have a relationship, even if sense tells us they wouldn't know us from Adam. We feel they are talking to us. We feel at liberty to write to them and tell them we hate their taste in ties, or ask them for a signed photograph; we're sorry or titillated to read in the tabloids about their divorce. We think of them in some senses as a friend, someone who has been in our living room or living space, and we are terribly shocked if they are ill or feel betrayed if they turn out to have committed a crime.

So for the person at the receiving end of the broadcast, we can say that *he or she likes to feel they are being talked to as one person –* one-to-one.

The implication of this is obvious. You don't *broad*cast – you *narrow*cast. You focus in on that single listener/viewer.

THE FOCUS POINT

So far, so obvious. But how do you, as a broadcaster, pull off this trick when everything around you tells you that these are very unlikely circumstances in which to be talking to one person? In a radio studio, or a TV voice-over booth, you're likely to be on your own. In a TV studio, there are masses of people bustling around, and on location, filming a piece-to-camera, you may find yourself in the presence of several people who make up the crew. But none of them ever look to be the slightest bit interested in what you're actually saying, because they are far too busy concentrating on getting the exposure or the sound levels right. In all these situations, there is one over-riding point of focus that lures your attention like a hideous siren – the piece of technology that gets your voice or your face to the masses: the microphone or the camera itself.

You need to recognize that microphone and camera are only *channels* that take you to a listener/viewer, like an open doorway. If you were sitting in the living room talking to someone in the kitchen through an open door you would hardly focus on the doorway itself, would you? Yet if you ask most new broadcasters who they are talking to – and wade through a lot of guff about 'the audience/my grandma/the person next door etc.', which you know perfectly well is only so much lip service to what they think they ought to say, because they haven't really thought about it before – you will eventually come to the answer 'the mic' or 'the camera'.

Wrong.

You should not be talking to the mic or the camera, you should be talking to the *person* who is *beyond* them.

When you talk on the telephone – another technological portal of communication, but one we are all much more familiar with – do you in any sense 'talk to the phone'? I think not – on it, maybe, but not to it. Although he or she is not physically present in the same room, you have a real sense of there being a person at the end of the process – and most of us have no difficulty whatsoever in visualizing them and talking to them *just as if they were in the room with us*. (Answering machines are rather a different matter – like listeners, they don't talk back to you, though you may hear from them later!)

Let's take a step back and look at the process of communication in a real situation we can all identify with.

You are talking to someone you know. You are entirely comfortable with them. He or she may not be a close friend, but nonetheless you are easy in their presence and once again you are talking about something you know.

What are your eyes and your voice doing?

Most of the time they are focused on the person you are talking to. Effectively, you have *eye contact* (we all know about that, and how shifty someone looks if they don't have it) and you also have what you might think of as *voice contact* with them. Your voice – without you having consciously to think about it – is pitched to the precise distance between you.

Exercise 3.1: Talking to a person

Try an experiment. Sit with someone you know – your long-suffering partner perhaps – at a comfortable distance of let's say six feet apart – and begin talking to them. Now ask them to move further away, into the corner of the room, and continue talking to them. Notice what happens to the sound of your voice.

Then ask them to move very close – say a couple of feet away – and continue to talk to them. You should notice that your voice drops – and not just in volume. The pitch of your voice also becomes lower and more intimate.

Now that you have made yourself conscious of the difference, ask them to return to their original position six feet or so away. Now talk to them using the voice you used to reach the furthest corner of the room. And then drop your voice to use the pitch you used to reach them when they were only a couple of feet away. It will probably help if you focus your eyes on those distances rather than on where they actually are. Ask them how they feel about those different voices you are using.

It's worth repeating the experiment with yourself as the listener to see how much difference it makes in your judgement of the voice.

Like many of the exercises in this book, it's designed not only to show you how much unconscious control you have in real situations over your voice, but also to encourage you to listen and develop an 'ear' for what your voice is doing. Unless you can learn to assess your own voice dispassionately – without the usual cringing – it's hard to move on.

Focus and pitch

A quick scientific aside here: sound waves travel across distance through air more or less successfully not just according to their amplitude (volume), but also according to their wavelength. The higher the pitch of the sound, the greater the frequency and the shorter the wavelength. A higher pitched sound travels further than a lower-pitched sound, which is one of the reasons car alarms streets away may wake you up at night. Somehow – without having studied GCSE level physics – our bodies *know* this. Without having to think about it, our voices will adjust to the distance we are from the point of focus.

So if in normal conversational speech, we have a point of focus that determines the pitch of our voice – and which makes it sound 'right' to the listener – it follows that we need to pick a point of focus in the studio if we want broadcast speech also to sound easy and conversational.

Focus and distance

The average studio microphone sits something like six to ten inches (15–25 cm) away from your mouth. The average person you talk to

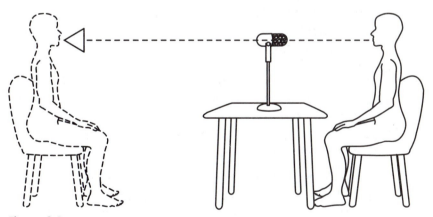

Figure 3.1
Direct and focus your voice beyond the microphone (or camera) to an imaginary listener in the same room

in conversation (if there can be said to be any such thing) sits about three to eight feet (90–250 cm) away.

Clearly, I am not talking here about the kind of intimate conversations we might have with our nearest and dearest under very special circumstances. I am thinking of the sort of situation you will find yourself in if you are having a normal conversation with someone you may know (but not necessarily well) – the kind of comfortable position we all pick for conveying information.

There is generally nothing accidental about this distance, though it is one we choose instinctively and often unconsciously. It places the listener close enough to hear your voice without you having to make any great effort to project it (or them to strain to hear) yet at the same time it preserves a polite, culturally determined space between you. We're all familiar with the notion of 'personal space' and we all resent any intrusion into it, except under very particular circumstances. A normal conversation preserves both the speaker and the listener's personal space – though there may be moments where you use your voice to draw someone metaphorically nearer to you, by dropping the pitch. (More on this in Chapter 7.)

You might like to spend some time noticing exactly what that distance is – and how you may vary it depending on the tone of the conversation, and your relationship with the person concerned.

One of the things I notice particularly is that there is a distinct one-to-one 'teaching' distance. Very often it is not necessarily chosen by me – when the client comes into the room, they will pick the chair that happens to be at that distance. (Though sometimes which chair they pick tells me a great deal about how nervous or defensive they feel about the experience that is to come!) It tends to be perhaps slightly further away than your best friend might choose to sit – the important thing is that it feels for both of us a comfortable distance to start from when one of us has the task of conveying information to the other.

There are many other situations where you will pick a similar distance to convey information (always supposing someone else hasn't got there first and arranged the chairs in a pattern you feel too nervous to disturb). Just imagine where you would most like to sit at a job interview, to impress them with your confidence and tell them everything they need to know about you to give you the job. It certainly isn't on their lap (unless you have a very dubious method of getting employment) but equally it is not at a huge distance – think of those intimidating interview settings where you are placed at the end of a boardroom table with the panel glaring at you from afar.

Distance is crucial in the relationship you wish to establish with the person you are talking to. And so it is in the broadcasting setting. You need to establish for yourself what that ideal distance is between you and the listener. Forget about where they actually are (which could be on the other side of the world, or in the next room). The critical thing is where they would want to be if they were in the room with you.

This may vary according to the type of broadcast. Radio DJs for instance – especially late at night – often pick a relatively close focus point, as if they have an intimate relationship with their listener. But DJs who play dance music clearly visualize themselves at a greater distance, to create the illusion of being in a club atmosphere. A current affairs presenter seeks a more formal relationship and so puts the listener a good five to six feet away (150–180 cm). Newsreaders are more formal still and reach out yet further with their voices. You need to experiment to find the distance that is right for you and your subject matter and style.

Finding the right focus point is one of the reasons that your colleagues will urge you to remember you are only ever talking to one person (it's not the only reason, but we'll come to that). It is the easiest way of directing your voice to somewhere specific, and setting the right pitch so that it sounds 'natural' to a person listening in their own setting.

You are going to be in the room with the listener or viewer when your voice reaches them – so put them in the room with you.

Tips and tricks

There is a trick that some broadcasters use, but which you may need to be wary of. To remind themselves that they are talking to a person, they draw a smiley face and stick it on the desk in front of them. This is not a bad idea at all, and I've known it work really well for some people, but you must remember that your voice needs to reach *beyond* that smiley face to someone sitting the other side of the desk from you.

It is also worth emphasizing that your imaginary listener is not simply at a certain distance from you – they are at a *precise spot*. Sometimes you will hear a voice, which although it is pitched right, still feels as if it is not quite focused on you – the equivalent of someone who is looking at a spot just to the side of your face, as if talking to a monkey perched on your shoulder. Voice contact needs to be as precise and personal as eye contact – and so you may find it useful to use your eyes to lead your voice when trying to focus on that exact point. I encourage people occasionally to glance up from the script while they are broadcasting, to remind them they are not alone.

I can already hear the protests. You are thinking that if you lift your eyes from the script you will instantly lose your place and stumble. If this is so, use your eyes to locate the spot before you start reading the script, and remember it. So long as you know where it is, even if you don't look at it you can talk to it – or rather the person who is in your imagination there.

THE IMAGINARY LISTENER/VIEWER

But the technique of 'imagining' a listener or viewer can be taken further still, by personalizing your broadcast as if you were talking to a real person with a specific identity. Even though this is the hoariest of old broadcasting tricks – and perhaps the most tried and tested – it seems to be one which many people have immense difficulty with. After years of hearing squawks of protest about how impossible it is to imagine anyone there, I came to the conclusion that if it is to be at all useful it needs to be examined and properly understood.

I have already explained that its main purpose is to give you a point of focus that will make your voice sound natural and unforced to the real listener. There is a physical explanation for why it works – based, quite literally, on the laws of physics. And quite frankly I don't care if you talk to a person you see in your mind's eye or to a spot on the wall – so long as you can focus your voice. But some people find that their voice improves if they take the idea of visualizing a listener/viewer a step further.

Once I worked alongside a journalist who read the news really well. He told me the secret of his success was to imagine his auntie sitting just across the table from him. Throughout the broadcast, she was nodding and smiling and expressing great interest in what he was talking about.

Now I had some trouble with this. I have always had difficulty with those exercises, so beloved of alternative therapists, where you visualize yourself walking through a lovely path in the woods down to a golden beach. My imagination is the sort that goes off at unhelpful tangents – I would start thinking about how very dark it was under the trees, and when I got to the beach I'd remember how I loathe getting sand into every crevice of the body. So if I visualized my auntie sitting across the table from me, all I could think about was how she wasn't that interested in the news anyway – or she would start making comments about the different stories. 'I really don't trust the Prime Minister, you know. He smiles too much...' It was most off-putting. My colleague clearly had a much better relationship with his aunt than I did.

After some thought, I came to realize two things. One is that if you are going to make this trick work, *whom* you imagine yourself talking to is a critical decision. My colleague's aunt worked for him because they had a good relationship – she was an intelligent woman, interested in news, and imagining her listening attentively to the story acted as a positive reinforcement for his confidence. My aunt made me feel awkward. I was to discover a similar trap later, when I picked someone different – but we'll come to that.

The second thing was that imagining a listener – be it your auntie or anyone else – is not an end in itself. It is simply a method of getting you to sound right. You don't want it to become a distraction. If it helps, wonderful. If not, find a way of adapting the principles behind it in a way that *is* helpful to you. The imaginary listener is a technique worth trying, but it is one that you may need to come back to at a later stage in your experience of broadcasting, if you find it doesn't work immediately.

But first you must think about who it will be.

Exercise 3.2: The imaginary listener

If you have access to a studio setting – preferably at a time when no one else is desperate to use it to make a programme! – this exercise should be carried out there. Alternatively try it at home using a sound recorder. Try and make the setting as much like a studio as you can – sit at a table, with the microphone in front of you on a stand if possible. It is best to use a real broadcasting script if you can, as it is always easier to read aloud something written for the ear rather than the eye. (More advice on this in Chapter 9.) However, the point of this exercise is to get your mind-set right – and with the right mind-set you could read the telephone directory and make it communicate something. Choose a well-written story or novel with simple syntax (this is an occasion where Jeffrey Archer might be better than Henry James) if you don't have a broadcast script to hand.

Before you begin, make a list of people you think you would feel comfortable talking to, and whom you could imagine might be interested in the subject matter of your broadcast.

Now imagine them sitting opposite you at the kind of distance we have already discussed, one by one, and tell the script to each of them in turn.

Afterwards, compare the results you have recorded. Do the results sound better with some than others?

Also try to remember what you felt at the time. Were you really able to visualize them? Were some, in your mind's eye, more helpful than others? Did you feel differently about the script you were reading – did it seem to you that you were explaining, telling, rather than reading or performing?

This may be an exercise you should return to later. It is also, like most of the exercises in the book, one that is far easier to try out initially as an exercise rather than in a real broadcasting situation. The time to apply it to the airwaves is only when you feel more comfortable with the technique.

I can't tell you who will work for you. I can however make some suggestions about the kinds of people who may not be ideal as imaginary listeners, and why.

- **Mothers**, I generally find, are not helpful. Maybe this is just a reflection of my own relationship with my mother (love her dearly as I do), but there is something deeply off-putting about the idea of my mum beaming proudly across the table at me. I want to wriggle with embarrassment. I immediately return to uncomfortable, unconfident, little-girl mode, and all hope of sounding authoritative flies out of the window.

- **Spouses and other close partners** may be tricky. The same question of embarrassment at doing your job in front of them – they have an uncomfortable knack of cutting you down to size, even when they think they are being supportive. And it would be very bad news if you had had a row with them over breakfast. Whether they become your ideal listener or not depends on your relationship with them.

- **Best friends** can either be wonderfully helpful – if you can imagine them truly being interested in what you say – or a real hindrance. For news broadcasters, who often have friends who are also news junkies, they may be the perfect listener. If though you keep thinking 'But I wouldn't talk to my best mate using these words', or you can only imagine them laughing their socks off at you, they are best avoided.

Sometimes it is better to imagine someone you know slightly less well – though it is important that you should not feel they are judging you critically and finding you wanting. A former college lecturer can therefore be good or bad – similarly colleagues. You need to find someone encouraging.

But at all costs, avoid the greatest pitfall – *someone you do not know at all.*

Doris from Dorking – a woman to be avoided

There is a school of thought that suggests that your ideal imaginary listener should be typical of the kind of people who listen to your particular station or network – as if this will somehow remind you not to swear on air or offend their delicate sensibilities. While it's a good idea to be mindful of your target audience's tastes and background, it is but a short step from this to 'dumbing down' your delivery to the point where you begin to insult the intelligence of your audience. Lately, I have come across a number of younger broadcasters who spend their time talking to a fictional 'Doris from Dorking' (or Dunstable, or Doncaster), with generally dire results, and this is definitely not a technique to be recommended.

The point is that none of us really knows anyone like Doris from Dorking. She is a fiction, a construct based on stereotypes and prejudices about audiences we don't know as individuals. She, and her nephew Kevin the Sales Rep, who listens to music radio while he's driving, were born out of misconceptions about the kind of people who phone or write in to local stations. Most of us have never written to or phoned a broadcasting organization in our lives, and indeed most of your audience won't either. If you base your 'personal' listener on these fallaciously 'typical' listeners, you run the risk of patronizing the vast majority of your real audience.

I learned this the hard way. I began my on-air broadcasting career in local radio. I was twenty-three. The average age of my listeners was probably closer to fifty-three. I knew this; I was just about astute enough not to play the Sex Pistols on air with any great regularity, though I did sneak them on once or twice for the hell of it. But the idea of how you talked to fifty-three-year olds was much more problematic for me.

For a while I had in my head an imaginary listener who was as close to the stereotype of an old-age pensioner as it is possible to get. She lived alone in a council flat in one of the less-affluent suburbs of Bristol, and spoke with a broad local accent. She kept a budgerigar, her basement flat smelt slightly, and she was very careful with money because she only had her pension to live on. She kept her teeth in a glass by the bedside at night and sometimes forgot to put them in during the day.

This woman did not exist – or if she did, I certainly did not know her. I had no notion of how to talk to older people, except to treat them as if they were slightly hard-of-hearing (which I thought she probably was) and on the verge of senility. As a result, I talked down to her and the rest of the listeners.

It embarrasses me to recall just how dreadful I must have sounded, and I might have gone on sounding like that if it hadn't been for a friend of mine – Rosi, the wife of a colleague, and therefore a genuine listener to the station – who pointed out how patronizing I sounded on air. She didn't know it was because of my imaginary Doris from Downend, but neither did I – until I went on the air, upset and furious, thinking, 'Right, Rosi, I'm going to show you I'm not patronizing...' And all of a sudden, I heard myself talking to Rosi instead. She was a woman of my own age whose intelligence I respected, and by that simple trick of accidentally imagining her listening, I became instantly warmer and friendlier. I felt I was talking to somebody like myself: an equal, genuinely interested in the things that interested me, who would share my take on the world around me.

The side-benefit of this for all the *real* old ladies listening to Radio Bristol was that they must have felt suddenly that I wasn't talking down to them any more. Here was someone talking to them as if to a friend – an equal.

It taught me a lot about how to talk to people generally and genuinely. My then voice coach used to hammer on about broadcasters needing 'the common touch' and it took me a while to recognize what he meant. It isn't about trying to moderate yourself to fit in with an ill-conceived stereotype of what you imagine your listeners are like. It's not 'coming down to their level' or 'putting yourself into their shoes'. On the contrary – you put them in your own or similar shoes to yourself. You allow them to be on a level with you. You talk to them as you would to anyone you genuinely know and respect.

This, of course, is the other reason why the imaginary listener – not so imaginary, after all – can be a useful concept: if and only if you can make them real.

WHEN IMAGINATION FAILS

I mentioned that there was another way of adapting the 'imaginary' listener technique to your needs. If you find it just impossible to visualize a listener, whoever it might be, stop wasting effort and attention trying to do so. Concentrate instead on *behaving as if* there was someone there with you. You don't need to imagine a person to do this. Just analyse what you do when there is a person there – and reproduce it even when there isn't.

I am not talking about acting – 'acting' for a broadcaster never works. I'm talking about 'being', or rather 'becoming' (paradoxically, at the heart of great acting too). If you adopt the gestures, body language, mannerisms of someone talking to another person, you will actually start to talk to another person.

First though, you will need to break down what it is that you actually do in conversation.

Exercise 3.3: Using body language

Next time you have a real conversation with someone, allow a little of your attention to dwell on what you are doing as you talk. Remember we are looking at a process in which you are supposed to be communicating information with confidence and authority, so choose a situation in which you feel you are able to do that – not, for instance, the sort of humiliating conversation in which you try to justify yourself to the boss who's picking holes in your latest piece of work.

Notice: do you use your hands? Where do you look? How do you sit as you communicate information? Is your head up or down? Do you allow your body to move as you speak? If you are still, are you also rigid, or do you feel there is a possibility of movement? What expression is on your face? Are you smiling or frowning?

There's quite a lot to notice and remember here and if you try to reproduce it all at once you may get into difficulty. So pick just one or two of the things that struck you particularly about the way you behave physically when you are talking, and retire at your convenience to either a studio, or your makeshift studio set-up at home. Again using a broadcast script if you can, record yourself delivering it while making an effort to use your body 'conversationally' (though not sacrificing any of the advantage you have gained from improving your posture).

Personally being a great hand-waver in conversation, I find that it is the easiest way of tricking myself into behaving conversationally. You don't need to make great sweeping gestures – most of us use our hands to some extent in conversation, even if it is no more than the occasional flick of emphasis with the fingers or palm.

Figure 3.2
Behave as if you are talking to someone

Now listen back and see what effect it has had on the way you read the script.

Smiling

Many broadcasters find that a smile helps them sound more natural. Not necessarily a huge grin, so much as allowing the corners of your mouth to lift in the kind of real, unfaked smile you use when you meet up with someone you like. Smiling relaxes the muscles of the face and makes it easier to talk.

We'll return later in the book to this subject of 'talking a script' and being conversational. But mind and body are beautifully co-ordinated in the good broadcasting voice, so in the next chapters we'll consider how to continue the physical process of improving the sound you make, by studying breathing, resonance, and pitch.

SUMMARY

- At the heart of the broadcasting process are two people – you and the listener/viewer. You can't broadcast in a vacuum to no one – there must always be a listener and you must have a real sense of relationship with that listener.

- Whatever trick or technique you use to remind yourself of that, it is the starting and finishing point of all broadcasting, and the most fundamental influence of all on the sound of your voice.
- A final thought – broadcasting is no more than a sophisticated version of a telephone conversation. The only difference is that the person at the other end cannot immediately answer back. But they are there – and they are hearing what you say.

4 Breathing easy

No one can make a good sound unless their voice is supported by their breath. In this chapter, we discover how to improve your breathing to increase the power and resonance of your voice. We will also look at when to breathe; what to do to avoid noisy, gasping breaths; why opening your mouth wider helps; and how to make sure your diaphragm is working properly.

If there is one secret worry that is shared by almost all broadcasters, it is how to breathe.

Anyone, even hoary old pros, can experience a sense of panic about breathing. You find yourself in front of the mic, facing a long unpunctuated sentence that appears to go on for an entire paragraph (not, hopefully, one you wrote yourself!) with not the faintest clue how you are going to get through it without turning puce or possibly exploding.

The irony is that breathing ought to be the most basic and natural action our bodies perform. It is a reflex. If something knocks you unconscious, you generally carry on breathing.

But perhaps because breath is so essential to life, we have a tendency to panic about it. And that panic has exactly the opposite effect we want to achieve. It inhibits our ability to breathe naturally. The breath doesn't stop; it just becomes awkward and tense. The tighter and shallower it becomes, the tighter and more strangulated the voice.

Voice *is* air. When you speak, the air from your lungs passes out through the larynx, opening and closing through the action of the vocal cords to cut the air stream into a series of little puffs. It is those rapid, ever-changing puffs that create the basic note, which is then altered by the shape of the mouth and the movement of the lips, tongue, and teeth to make vowel sounds and consonants. The more air you have available to you, the stronger the sound.

But you also need to be able to control the flow of air so that your voice can be flexible: loud or soft, high or low. So getting the breath right means that you will have much more control over the sound. That's why people like me talk about 'supporting' the voice with the breath.

Breathing properly can do wonders for the pitch of your voice. In the next chapter, we'll look in more detail at how to achieve a natural pitch, but simply following the techniques described in this chapter should help you to a deeper, fuller sound. By opening up your body to breathe properly, you will increase the resonance of your voice – in musical terms, you'll be adding lower harmonics to the note your vocal cords are producing in the larynx.

But breathing in the right way will do more than that. It will relax you, make you more alert mentally, help your listener to understand more easily what you are saying, improve the clarity of your voice, give you confidence, cure stumbling problems... I could go on and on. Kindly do not skip this chapter. Breathing is as necessary to your voice as it is to life.

BREATHING AND THE RESONANCE OF YOUR VOICE

The first thing to look at is how you are sitting in front of the microphone. (See Chapter 2.) Remember you need:

- to sit upright
- weight on your sitting bones
- feet flat on the ground to balance you
- neither slumped back nor leaning forward
- with a long spine and a wide back
- your head up but level so that your neck feels long and free
- without tilting your chin up or down or forward.

Don't fix; be free. The more relaxed your muscles – and remember they *are* more relaxed in this position because they are not having to support the head's weight, as the skeleton is providing the framework for that – the more resonant you will sound, as you have effectively opened up your body. In this position, as we have already seen, it becomes dramatically easier to breathe.

But posture is only a starting point. The next thing to look at is *how much air you are taking in*, and *how easily*. A good lungful of air within a relaxed chest cavity will improve your resonance no end.

It sounds absurd that you should need to learn to breathe properly, but if you watch inexperienced broadcasters you will probably be able to see for yourself how many *wrong* ways there are of filling your lungs.

For a start, there is the shallow breather who rarely uses more than the top third of their lung capacity. Not only does this make it difficult to get to the end of a sentence without having to pause for breath (not a cardinal sin, but dire if you happen to run out in the middle of a connected phrase). It also makes the voice sound thin and weak. I have noticed that people who run for relaxation and fitness can sometimes seem guilty of this, because they have become used to rapid, shallow breathing to keep fresh oxygen flowing. On the other hand, swimmers tend to be much better at filling their lungs, to give them extra buoyancy, as well as the ability to keep the head down for longer.

Then there is the person who hauls in a good big lungful of air, but lets it all out on the first words of the sentence. By the time he or she gets to a suitable breathing point, they are practically strangling the last couple of words.

And there is also the gasper – incapable, it seems, of taking in air without huge physical effort and maximum noise. More on gaspers later – they deserve their own special set of exercises.

HOW TO BREATHE

You used to know this. When you were a baby, you did it quite naturally. Unfortunately you may have unlearned it along the long road of life. So now is the time to relearn.

Although it often seems easier doing breathing exercises standing up, most broadcasting is carried out sitting down. You can try these exercises in either position, but as you are eventually going to have to put them into practice sitting down, be sure you do at least some from a chair, as if you were in the studio. Look at the CD-ROM to see how these exercises are carried out.

One other suggestion. Most of us were taught that it is polite to breathe through the nose, and keep your mouth closed. 'You'll get a fly zooming in there, if you keep your mouth open,' mothers used to say. Please forget your mother's advice while you are doing these exercises. (You can close your mouth again afterwards in case there is a plague of flies.) Because your mouth opens when you speak, you generally breathe through the mouth while speaking, and these are after all exercises to help your voice. I would also like you to get into the habit of opening your mouth more widely, to get the tension out of your jaw. A relaxed mouth enunciates more clearly – it's easier to get your tongue and lips round the sounds. And an open relaxed mouth is another of those spaces where your voice can resonate, so make the most of it.

Exercise 4.1: The big breathe in and out

Sit comfortably and straight in a chair (see Chapter 2). Your weight should be on your sitting bones, your feet on the floor, your back long and wide, and your diaphragm free. Rest your hands comfortably in your lap, and begin by taking a deep breath through your open mouth for a count of three, allowing your lungs to fill completely without straining. Then let the air out again over a count of three. Do this several times.

Now raise your arms and put your fingertips on the tips of your ears. (This lifts and opens the ribcage.) Again breathe in deeply over a count of three, and out again for three, several times.

Now rest your hands in your lap again, and return to the first exercise. Is there a difference? Has the experience of opening up the ribcage increased the depth of your breathing in the more 'normal' position?

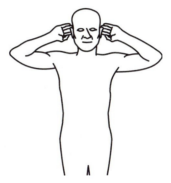

Figure 4.1
Fingertips on the tips of your ears to open up the ribcage

Let's see if that has had any effect on the sound of your voice by reading out a simple sentence or two. You don't have to use my text – pick one of your own, something you can enjoy the sound of. I've written a simple news story but it's up to you to choose whatever you feel is appropriate.

It is helpful to do this part of the exercise with an audio recorder, if you have one to hand, so you can record yourself and listen back. If you are doing that, make sure you have the mic set up in front of you so you don't feel tempted to lean in to it. As we've already discussed, your position is important, and you can undo all the good of the exercise by reverting to bad posture. If you are going to hand-hold the mic, don't clutch it and introduce more tension that way. Keep sitting up, don't hunch over the mic.

If you don't have a recording machine, try and listen to the sound of your voice in your own ears. Do those deeper breaths help?

> Police are today hunting the owner of a five-foot python found in a garden shed. Paul Smith, of Rochdale, was tidying his tools when he realized he was being watched by a large snake. 'I thought it was sizing me up for dinner', said Mr Smith. An animal handler from the local zoo was called in to catch the python.

Three deep breaths

You can use your experience with this exercise to help you relax before you use your voice on air. Before the red light goes on and the microphone becomes live, take three deep breaths. Each time allow your lungs to fill to capacity, and then let the air out slowly. It reminds your body that it's time to open up, so you make a good strong sound supported by a big lungful of air. It might also remind you about the importance of opening your mouth!

It will make you both relaxed and alert as all that oxygen hits the brain. I still use this exercise, especially when things are fraught and pressured. It seems to create a space and separate me from the pressure, so that I can just focus on what I need to do next – use my voice to communicate.

CONTROLLING THE AIRFLOW

But all that air isn't going into your body just to increase the reso- nance and strength of your voice. It's also there to help you form sounds – and you need to be able to control the flow of it so that you have exactly enough to get you to the next point where you can refill your lungs. I say exactly enough, no more, because holding onto breath can be as bad a habit as letting it all go too quickly. If you are still reserving much air in your lungs, it is difficult to take a deep full breath, and you'll be back to your old shallow breathing habits again.

Exercise 4.2: Letting breath out

Sit comfortably again on a firm chair, weight on sitting bones, spine long, head balanced and neck free. This time, I want you to put your hands on your rib cage. As you breathe gently in and out, notice what is happening to your ribs. They will be moving in and out, because here are the **intercostal** muscles we use to control the flow of breath. As you breathe in, the diaphragm, which is a big dome-shaped slab of muscle attached to the breast bone at the front, and to the lower ribs at the back, flattens out, creating a space above it so that the lungs can expand and pull the air in. Between the ribs, one set of intercostal muscles relaxes and lengthens, expanding and lifting the ribcage. But as you are breathing out, the intercostal muscles are tightening so that the ribcage narrows down again, pushing the air out of the lungs.

Breathing is a reflex, which means you do not have to think about it. In fact thinking about it tends to mess up the natural process. The more you worry about your breathing, the harder it becomes to breathe naturally. So what I would like you to do – a fine distinction – is rather than think about your breathing, simply allow yourself to notice it.

Let's demonstrate that. Take your hands off your ribs, and place them relaxed on your thighs. You might find it helpful to do this with a friend who can talk you through the instructions, because you need to keep your eyes closed throughout, so that you concentrate fully on the experience of letting yourself breathe easily and naturally.

In this exercise, you are only going to concentrate on your breath OUT. Pay no attention whatsoever to the breath in. Breathe easily and normally for a few breaths, putting all your focus on the breath out. At first I want you to notice the sensations in your mouth and ears as you breathe out: the feel of the air as it passes over your tongue and lips, the sound of it quietly whispering in your ears. Then let your attention move lower in your body. As you do this, start to lengthen each breath out. Feel the sensation of your stomach apparently rising to push out the air, and those ribs narrowing. Make each breath very slightly longer, so you begin to have to make more effort from your abdominal muscles to push out the air. Feel as if you are really beginning to squeeze the very last few cubic centimetres out of your lungs. We all tend to leave a little reserve in the bottom of our lungs, but let's clear that stale air out.

And now, quick as a flash, right after your strongest stomach push, switch your attention from the breath out to what has happened to the breath in. Don't do anything to alter it; just notice what has changed by itself while you have been concentrating on breathing out.

Then gradually, easily, let your breathing return to normal.

Close your eyes and have a go.

What you should have noticed

As you concentrate on lengthening the breath out, your body naturally adjusts the breath in, so that your breathing will over the course of the exercise have become very deep but also totally relaxed. This should teach you that you don't have to make an effort to breathe deeply. The real effort involved is in expelling the air, not in taking it in. If you concentrate on the out-breath, the in-breath will look after itself.

I suggest you now record yourself reading a few lines, to see if this has helped to make your breathing more relaxed and whether anything has happened to the sound of your voice. Notice particularly whether there seems to be a stronger, more supported sound to your voice.

Deeper breathing, deeper voice

If you found that your breathing after the exercise seemed much easier, you would also have noticed probably that your voice sounded stronger and subtly richer. As you open your body cavities to take in more air, you create a relaxed resonating space for your voice. Chest resonance, as this is called, adds extra richness in the form of deeper frequencies to your voice. You have effectively turned yourself into a cello or a double bass, instead of a violin.

But remember, you will only be able to breathe this freely and easily if you put your body into a state of relaxation. As we saw in Chapter 2 that means a relaxed but upright posture, perfectly balanced, without any slumping back or leaning forward.

WHEN TO BREATHE

In ordinary conversation, no one ever thinks about when to breathe. It happens as if by chance whenever you run out of breath. But wait a minute – is it in fact quite so random as you imagine? As you talk to other people, notice when in fact you do pause for breath. Usually it is when you have finished a thought. Language tends to package thoughts into easily understandable chunks – clauses and sentences. When you have finished a sentence, you take a breath before moving onto the next thought. And while you are filling your lungs, you have the opportunity to marshal your next thought, and the person listening has an extra moment to absorb the sense of what you have just said.

Breathing is a kind of punctuation for spoken language. Indeed, that is where written punctuation originated – as an attempt to break up thoughts into understandable chunks. It is the equivalent of the breath pauses in speech. So use written punctuation in the script to be your guide for where to breathe. That's why getting the punctuation right is so important; a point I will be stressing again when we come to look in Chapter 9 at how the writing can help or hinder your voice.

Full stops are an indication of an opportunity for a BIG BREATH. If there are commas in the sentence (and we hope there will be), marking off separate ideas, those are also an opportunity to breathe. In this way you can move from punctuation point to punctuation point, without having to think consciously about where to breathe.

But what if some inconsiderate person has failed to punctuate within the sentence? Do you have to make it from one full stop to the next? Of course not. Look at how the separate thoughts occur within the sentence. (When you have read Chapter 7, *Signposting the sense*, you will become very practiced at this.)

> The Chancellor of the Exchequer Gareth Moneybags today announced a new tax on breathing which is due to come into force next November.

This can be separated into thoughts:

> The Chancellor of the Exchequer/Gareth Moneybags/ today announced a new tax on breathing/which is due to come into force next November.

The thoughts being:

> WHO (his position)/HIS NAME/WHAT he's done/
> WHEN it's going to happen.

A good punctuator would have written:

> The Chancellor of the Exchequer, Gareth Money-
> bags, today announced a new tax on breathing,
> which is due to come into force next November.

If necessary, you could breathe at any of those points without spoiling the flow of the sentence. In reality, you probably would not have to breathe at more than one of them. But remember that the more you keep your lungs filled, the greater the resonance, so you may want to 'top up' at another of the commas.

You can breathe between thoughts – but woe betide if you breathe in the middle of a thought. Imagine hearing someone read (and I have heard the equivalent of this many a time):

> The Chancellor/of the Exchequer Gareth Money-
> bags today/announced a new/tax on breathing
> which/is due to come into force next/November.

It makes it much harder for your listener to follow the sense, and it sounds irritatingly breathy.

But as I told you not to think too hard about breathing, how do you achieve this control that enables you to hop effortlessly from comma to comma?

Here's an exercise that will remind your body it can do it, without you having to think very hard about it.

Exercise 4.3: More out-breath control

We are going to make those intercostal muscles – the ones between the ribs – work again, so having assumed your comfortable sitting position, balanced and upright, put your hands on

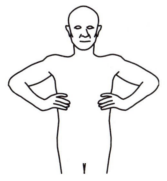

Figure 4.2
Feel the movement of your ribs

your ribcage. This is so you can feel what is happening in your body during the exercise.

It is helpful if you use a studio clock with a second hand to time you through this exercise. Alternatively you can persuade a friend to count you through it. If you do your own counting you may be tempted to cheat!

Take a big deep easy breath over a count of three, taking care not to hunch your shoulders. Then let the air out over a count of TEN (or ten seconds on your clock). You should time it so that at TEN your lungs are empty. Pace the breath out steadily, so that you don't run out of air early – but neither should you have any air left when you reach TEN.

At first you may find it is tricky getting right the pacing of the out-breath. You may well find you have either run out too early, or you still have some air left at the end. Try it again until you get it right. Then try it a couple more times, this time altering the length of count for the breath out. You could try SEVEN for instance, or FIVE, or TWELVE. Anyone with a normal pair of lungs should certainly have no difficulty in making it as far as FIFTEEN.

What this exercise does is help you discover that controlling the flow of breath out is not at all difficult. You simply need to re-educate your body to make it second nature. This is in effect what we should do instinctively when we begin speaking a sentence.

A deep breath to begin, then control the airflow out to get to the next breathing point, the comma or full stop.

By practising the exercise using different counts, you are helping your body become familiar with the way you control the airflow. The more you practise this now, the less you will have to worry about it when you are on the air because it should become an automatic process.

When you feel confident in your ability to do the exercise without needing to cheat, try vocalizing the count, saying the numbers aloud as you let the air out.

NOISY BREATHING

The exercises I have shown you should help iron out most of the problems you are likely to have with your breathing. They should also have helped increase the strength and resonance of your voice, so it will sound richer, fuller, and deeper.

But there is another common problem that many broadcasters suffer – *noisy* breathing. In fact, that is usually the excuse they offer when I ask them why they don't take in deeper breaths in the first place. 'Oh, I couldn't possibly do that!' they say. 'It sounds so loud on the microphone.'

It is true that the microphone picks up the sound of your breathing, and if it is noisy it will make you, and the audience, very aware of it. Listeners get irritated and sometimes are even moved to write in to complain.

But that is no reason to stop breathing in deeply. The solution is to find a way of taking a breath that doesn't sound noisy; and that isn't as difficult as it sounds.

Don't edit breaths

Some broadcasters who edit their own material have discovered that with computer editing it is remarkably easy to cut your own breaths out of the finished recording. Unfortunately this is *not* a solution to the problem of noisy breathing. Without breaths, the recording will sound false and unnatural. Sentences may be butted so close to each other that the natural pauses have disappeared. The listener finds this disturbing because you appear to be some sort of superhuman being who does not require breath – we expect to hear some sort of intake of air, even if we don't enjoy noisy gasps – and it undermines your credibility.

I would be lying if I tried to persuade you that I had never edited a breath out of a recording. But if you must cut a breath, don't remove it altogether but trim only the noisy front end. Better still, replace it with a softer breath from elsewhere in your material. You need to be a skilled editor to do this so that it sounds natural. But do not do it as a matter of course. Instead, learn to breathe properly. It will save you editing time.

Quieter breathing

The cause of noisy breathing is tightness and obstruction in the airway. If you narrow a channel, and suck air down it, it stands to reason you will hear the sound of the air rushing through. The wider and more unobstructed the channel, the more soundless the flow of air.

People tend to narrow the breathing channel at three points: the mouth, the throat, and the upper chest.

These are the places where tightness in your muscles can obstruct the passage of breath. Each adds a slightly different sound to the breathing. Tightness in the *mouth* makes you a **gasper** (and sometimes a clicker or a lip smacker as well, if the tongue and lips are not relaxed). Tightness in the *throat* makes you a **rasper**; and tightness in the *chest* can make you a **wheezer**. I sometimes amuse myself by deliberately tightening the muscles in each of these areas in turn to show clients what wonderful but appalling noises you can make as you breathe.

If you can relax your body (and you have already made a start on that) you will be able to pull in the air unimpeded, and therefore silently.

Gaspers

Gaspers have tight jaws and they start to breathe before they have opened their mouth properly. Their tongue and lips are possibly also tense. They may incidentally have difficulty enunciating words because they don't open their mouth enough, and could find stumbling and slurring a problem.

If you were to video a gasper talking, with a big close up on the lower part of the face, you would probably notice an unusual immobility in the jaw. You would see the mouth opening in a letterbox shape. The lips part, but the words escape between two horizontal lines. The sound of the voice may be slightly hissy, because the speaker isn't making full use of the mouth as a resonating space. And most noticeably of all, the breaths are drawn in with a loud hiss. As the mouth opens, you can hear the air being obstructed by tongue and teeth, and there may even be a wet, smacking sound to the intake of breath as it encounters little pockets of saliva.

The answer is simple. Relax your jaw muscles and allow the mouth to open fully downwards (more of a round cave than a letterbox) *before* you start the breath in. Some gaspers may protest that they do open their mouths into a more rounded shape, but I would bet that they are beginning the breath intake before it is fully open, so the airway is still obstructed.

The big question is how far to open your mouth. We can demonstrate this easily, and you may be surprised by it. Stand in front of

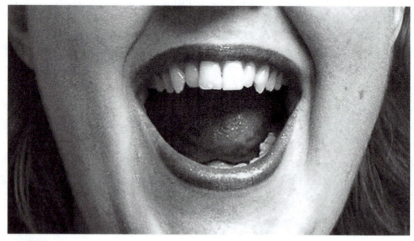

Figure 4.3
A big mouth!

a mirror, and open your mouth as if to start talking. Say the words 'A big mouth', and stop with your mouth open just as you are in the middle of the word 'big', before you get to the 'g', or on the 'ou' of 'mouth'. Now see if you can insert the knuckle of your thumb between your teeth. No? I would suggest that you are not opening your mouth wide enough.

There are many wonderful exercises to help you get used to using your mouth properly; too many to include in this book. Meanwhile, I will suggest just one for you to practice in the privacy of your own bathroom, which will help increase the mobility of your jaw. Please do it gently; you are not aiming for a mouth that could swallow a hamburger whole, but simply a relaxed, more rounded opening.

Exercise 4.4: Opening your mouth

Again stand in front of a mirror so you can see what is happening. Stand straight, and let your head be balanced so that your neck feels long and free. Don't tilt the nose and chin up; this shortens the neck and scrunches the vertebrae.

Let your lips and tongue feel relaxed and free. It's important to let the tongue rest low in the mouth, not forcing it down but letting it lie easy and relaxed. Now allow the jaw to open by letting it drop easily downwards, wide enough to insert a couple of fingers between your teeth. Make sure you are not tilting your head back as you open the jaw.

You will not need to open your mouth quite this wide when you speak. But the point of the exercise is to train you to get used to being free enough in the jaw to encompass any movement you are likely to need to make when you talk.

Now, keeping the neck easy, and again not tilting your head back, let the opening develop into a soundless yawn as you draw breath easily in. You should feel the back of your mouth arching, and your throat opening. Let your tongue relax on the floor of your mouth with its tip touching the lower front teeth.

If by this stage you are hearing a series of appalling clicks, it suggests that your jaw really is unused to working properly.

Never over-do the yawn, but it is worth continuing to practise this exercise until you are used to a feeling of freedom in your jaw.

Adding mouth resonance

Relaxing the jaw and opening it wider has a delightful side benefit. It puts more resonance into your voice, created in the space you have opened up in mouth and throat. Resonance adds richness to the tone.

Opening up in this way helps to lift the soft palate, and so prevents you from over-using nasal resonance, which gives the voice an unpleasant quack or twang. You'll hear more about this in the next chapter.

Raspers and wheezers

Once again, the problem here is usually that muscles are tightening and fixing, probably at the end of your breath out, so you are not letting go enough to allow free passage to the next breath in. Ask yourself if your throat feels congested and tight when you are speaking. Watch yourself in front of a mirror, to see whether as you come to the end of a breath, particularly when speaking, your body seems to be pulling down. (Pulling down is not helpful because it locks the breath in.)

There are physical exercises that can help this sort of problem. I firmly believe that all but the most simple of these are best done under the supervision of an experienced voice teacher, who can see better than you where things are going wrong in your body. But I have found that sometimes a simpler approach can work just as well by asking you to visualize your body in the right state.

If you are having a problem breathing easily and silently, try imagining your air passage as a wide, open channel. First, of course, you must make it possible for it to be a wide-open channel by making sure you are sitting correctly, as outlined in Chapter 2. Try not to throw your body forward as you begin to breathe or speak, or tilt your head back, but find an image that helps you see yourself as a relaxed open conduit for air. Some people find it helpful to picture a wide funnel or chimney through which the air can stream unimpeded, with no effort involved. You don't haul it in or push it out; you let it flow.

Once you feel your body is open and easy, your abdominal muscles can work properly to allow the air in. You should notice that your stomach actually moves when you are breathing correctly – it will go out as you breathe in. If you let your stomach move and open the channel, you will notice you can get in a big breath without any noticeable sound at all.

Test this in front of a microphone by turning the volume in your headphones up, and practising deep silent breaths. It will soon become a habit if you make a point of practising.

Tight waistbands are not helpful in breathing correctly. Personally, I have always blessed the person who invented lycra and discovered how to incorporate it in jeans! Fortunately, most men these days seem to wear their trousers on the loose side. In my youth, there was a notorious broadcaster who would ostentatiously undo his trousers in the studio before starting a broadcast, 'to improve my breathing'. Well, that's what he claimed ...

Raspers and wheezers are also not doing themselves any favours if they smoke. Over time, smoking clogs the airways with mucus and you can often hear it bubbling away in the voice.

THE DIAPHRAGM

There is one final part of your body to consider when you are breathing. It is a part which most people feel rather nervous of, because they can't see it, and most of us take its operation so much for granted that we don't actually feel it working either. It is the diaphragm: a big dome-shaped slab of muscle attached to the breastbone at the front and the spine at the back, following the line of the lower ribs at the sides and back (see Figure 2.1). When you breathe in, it flattens out, creating a space above it so that the lungs can expand and pull the air in. You can think of it rather like the membrane of a pair of bellows.

Because of its position, it is often very difficult to tell if the diaphragm is actually moving – take it from me that it is, because otherwise you would not be breathing. What you can feel though is a big sheet of abdominal muscle, which releases during the breath in, and contracts during the breath out, shoving your digestive organs upwards to help the diaphragm resume its dome-shape. As you breathe, you can place a hand on your middle and feel those abdominal muscles move *out* as you breathe in, *in* as you breathe out, reflecting what is happening to your diaphragm.

But the diaphragm plays another part when you start to speak. Although it moves upwards into the dome-shape as you breathe out, as you vocalize, it can also begin to flatten, the way it does on the in-breath, in order to keep the air-pressure just right while passing through the glottis where the vocal cords are working.

That is why as you speak, if you keep your hand on your abdomen you should feel a whole set of more complex movements out and in. You won't be able to feel the diaphragm itself (unless you have a particularly svelte midriff) but you will feel the knock-on effect of it moving as the abdominal muscles release outwards.

Of course, it may be that if you are still tense in your muscles, you will be interfering with the diaphragm's ability to regulate the air pressure. The sound of your voice will be less rich: either breathy, or tight sounding. You can test that out by trying this exercise.

Exercise 4.5: Say hello to your diaphragm

For once I am going to suggest that you try this exercise standing up. Stand easy and tall, applying the same principles of planting your weight firmly on both feet, back long and wide, head balanced on a long free neck. Put one hand on your midriff on the fleshy triangle just underneath the breastbone, keeping the fingers flat. Try not to dig them in as you do this exercise; it will hurt, for a start, if you do, and you are more likely to feel the movement if a wide area of your hand is in contact with your middle.

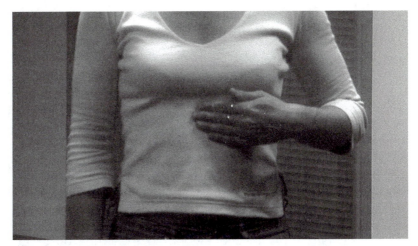

Figure 4.4
Feeling the movement of your diaphragm

Now take a medium-sized breath, and instead of letting it out slowly, use your stomach to push it out quickly in a little huff. You should feel a kick from your midriff against your fingers, because you have started to use the diaphragm as a pressure-regulator. You will feel tempted to keep on doing this to be sure you can feel the kick, but don't go on too long or you may start to feel a little dizzy. (If you do, sit down and let your breathing return to normal.)

Now the big test. Will your diaphragm respond in the same way if you vocalize? This time turn the huff of air into a 'hoo' sound. Can you still feel your diaphragm kick against your fingers?

If you can't, you will probably also be feeling the sound right up in your throat, as if all the push is coming from there. The sound will be thin and tight. You may be inadvertently tightening the upper body and locking the air into your chest, so the diaphragm cannot work properly.

See if you can relax your throat and your upper chest so that the push feels as if it is coming from where your fingers are. You want to feel that you are allowing the sound out of your body, as an impulse that rises from your middle, rather than forcing it out. Now you should feel the kick from your diaphragm, and the sound should be different too – more relaxed and full.

When you've mastered the 'hoo' sound, turn it into a more conventional 'ooo'. Then try the same exercise with 'aaah' and 'eeee'. Eventually you could try whole sentences, trying to keep your diaphragm in play as much as possible as you speak them.

This is one of the more tricky exercises in the book, but don't worry if you can't get the hang of it at first. Go back to some of the earlier breathing exercises and come back to this one later. Or save it for another day and run the whole set through again.

Once you get it right, you will know immediately what people mean when they say you should 'talk from your diaphragm'.

One further trick that may help. When I was studying the Alexander Technique, my teacher and I did a session on breathing. Under scrutiny, I started to get tense, and was locking the air into my chest. My teacher suggested a curious idea to help loosen me, by starting the relaxation process at the other end of my body. 'You should feel like you're peeing air', she said. Once I'd recovered from a set of embarrassed giggles, I realized this strange notion did actually work. Sometimes it helps to shift the attention away from the muscles you're trying to unlock, and unclench some others. In fact, the big sheet of abdominal muscle stretches right down from the lower ribs to the pubis, and by asking yourself to imagine you are 'peeing air' you are asking that long stretch of muscle to relax.

Walk, don't run

None of this useful advice will work if you have been so foolish as to belt down the corridor into the studio at the last minute. Running – especially upstairs – is not a good idea before you broadcast. Allow plenty of time so you can walk, and keep your breathing steady.

Being aware of breathing

Breathing 'properly' isn't just something to do when you're in front of a microphone or a camera. For it to feel natural, you will have to make it a lifetime habit. You shouldn't become overly self-conscious about it, but it is worth letting yourself be aware of your breathing occasionally, wherever you are, whatever you are doing. You will begin to see how those deeper more relaxed breaths can help you whatever the circumstances.

Once you get into the habit of using the breath to support your voice, you are well on the way to sounding stronger and more confident. But you may still have some niggling worries about the overall sound, especially related to the pitch of your voice. Read on – that's what we'll look at in the next chapter!

SUMMARY

- Voice is air, so getting the breathing right is important.
- More air and easy breathing means better resonance, and your voice will sound deeper and richer.
- Make sure you fill your lungs properly – don't just take shallow breaths.
- Make sure you empty your lungs properly too – don't lock breath in, or you won't be able to take a proper breath the next time.
- Breathe at the punctuation marks, not in the middle of a connected phrase.
- Open your body – chest, throat, mouth – to avoid noisy breathing.
- Relax and enjoy it – breathing is natural!

5 Pitching it right

Why do we still think of a deeper voice as being more effective than a lighter one? Is this a chauvinist hangover from the days when most newsrooms were staffed and run by men (deep male voice equals serious, high-pitched female voice equals frothy) or is there something else going on that we ought to heed? This chapter helps broadcasters explore the full range of their voices. It re-emphasizes the importance of what is happening in your body as you speak, and how your mind-set can also influence the sound you produce.

The one question I am asked as a voice coach more frequently than any other is 'Can you do something about the pitch of my voice?' It's not only women who ask. Men too are often troubled that their voice doesn't sound as deep and strong as they think it should.

Broadcasters are particularly vulnerable in this area because there is a perceived wisdom that deeper voices carry more authority. Notice I say 'perceived'. I think it's a myth worth questioning.

Most of the people who ask the question have perfectly normal voices, well within the usual range for their age and gender. But the Deep Voice has become one of those obsessions in broadcasting. Just as we'd all like longer legs or bigger chests, we'd all like to have a deeper voice.

Perhaps one of the reasons this becomes an obsession is that almost everyone is horrified by the sound of their own voice when they first hear it recorded and played back to them. Normally, we only ever hear our own voices as we are speaking, and because our ears are set against the head we hear a disproportionate amount of the skull's resonance. We get used to the sound of the voice that way and it's a shock to hear it the way everyone else hears you speaking, at a distance. The contrast makes us think we have a higher voice than we had imagined, and so we may get caught in the loop of believing we need to do something about the pitch of our voice. It is rather like the person who only ever looks at themselves in their favourite mirror. Seeing themselves on video ('Gosh, who's the fat bird?') is a startling revelation. It may reveal genuine flaws they could change; but it may also spark a neurotic obsession with some facet of their appearance that everyone else accepts as perfectly normal.

If you work in broadcasting, you have to get used to the sound of your own voice as it really is. You can't avoid hearing recordings of it played back to you, and though painful at first, it is one of the best ways of learning how you can improve your voice. Whatever you might think the pitch is often *not* the first thing that needs attention.

But there are times when you do need to consider the pitch – and ask yourself whether there is something you are doing when you broadcast that is forcing the pitch of your voice up above what would be your normal speaking range.

WHAT DO WE MEAN BY 'A NATURAL PITCH'?

A natural pitch is often hard to pinpoint for yourself – yet we all recognize in other people's voices what sounds like a natural pitch. Our voices never produce a truly pure note; we are not human tuning forks. What we hear in a voice is, just as in any musical instrument, a note that carries **resonance** to a greater or lesser degree – resonance created by the different spaces and substances of which our bodies are made. Your chest cavity, the amount of air in your lungs, the relaxation of your muscles, how much you open your mouth, and (as anyone with a cold knows) the state of your nasal tissues all have an effect on the amount of resonance in the voice. Resonance is also produced by your surroundings; the room space can add to the resonance of your voice.

Very often when we are talking about pitch, we should really be talking about resonance. A voice sounds deeper the more it resonates, using the body as a kind of sounding box. If it loses that resonance, it sounds thinner and squeakier. The breathing techniques

in the last chapter will set you on the way to increasing the resonance of your voice, but it may help to understand a little more
about why posture and breathing are so important to the broadcaster.

Dead acoustics

Broadcasting is full of traps that can steal the natural resonance
from our voices. For a start, it is often carried out in situations where
we can't get any help from our surroundings to increase the resonance. You may have noticed that you sound great when you sing
in the bath or even in the car. What surround you in both those situations are hard, sound-reflecting surfaces that bounce your voice
back, and add to its natural resonance. You notice you sound good,
you relax, and so you sound even better. Similarly theatres may be
acoustically designed to increase the resonance of actors' voices.
Speak in a church with good acoustics and you can sound glorious
with very little extra effort.

Studios are the reverse, designed to be a relatively dead acoustic.
They have carpets, and absorbent material on the walls. Even the
table at which you sit is probably covered with felt. This is because
the sound doesn't need to carry in a studio – the microphone does
that for you. And sound reflecting surfaces wouldn't just pick up the
sound of your voice – they would also magnify and bounce around
all those extraneous and distracting noises (for instance if you were
surreptitiously scratching your leg), which would otherwise be outside the microphone's range (see Chapter 12 for more about a
microphone's active field).

Sometimes just being in a dead acoustic can cause you to try and
force your voice. The 'deadest' acoustic in which we ever normally
find ourselves is the great outdoors. Vast open spaces have no way
of feeding back sound reflections to you. If you want your voice to
carry over a long distance, what you do instinctively is *raise the
pitch* of your voice. Higher frequency notes – let's not get too technical here – with their shorter wavelengths carry further through air.
So your natural response to being in a dead acoustic is to pitch up.

Resist this impulse. The microphone is there to take your voice the
distance it needs to travel – you rarely need to boost your frequencies.

Headphones

In a dead acoustic, wearing headphones can be helpful, once you get used to the sound. They send your voice back as it really is on mic, and by setting the volume at a comfortable level you can use them as the bathtub singer uses the hard surface of the tiles, to give you a feedback of reflected sound. That is why I always prefer to work with headphones. Hearing my voice coming back to me stops me from pushing against the dead acoustic and over-pitching my voice upwards.

But not everyone feels comfortable with headphones, and I have met people who feel so self-conscious with them on that they actually sound better if they work without them. Keep an open mind, and see which way works best for you. In radio, however, you will almost certainly have to get used to wearing headphones. They are an indispensable studio tool when you are prefading recorded inserts or music to set sound levels. You will also be wearing them outside the studio if you have to do a live insert or two-way, so it is best to get used to them. You can always wear them one ear on, one ear off.

Tension

A dead acoustic is not the only trap. This is after all broadcasting and there is a vast unseen audience out there – you may be nervous, especially if you're not completely used to it. You get tense, you lean into the mic – every muscle tightens, you can't breathe fully and deeply, and your body stops acting so effectively as a resonator.

And then there is that overwhelming need to get a bit of power into your delivery. Perhaps someone has planted the idea in your mind that you aren't really getting through to your listeners. You want to emphasize your message. So instead of relaxing and allowing your body to give you the power you need, you start using the pitch of your voice to *over*-emphasize the words you think are important. Every single WORD you want to make CLEAR to your listeners goes UP – and UP and UP. You remember how I have already described over-emphasis as sometimes being the vocal equivalent of the fist thumping the tabletop? This particular variation is what I think of as the sharp finger poking your listener in the chest. Not a

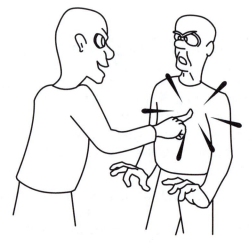

Figure 5.1
How your listener feels when you over-emphasize

comfortable experience for him or her – and whoops, up goes the overall pitch of your voice.

So as you can see, it may not be a question at all of lowering the normal pitch of your voice. It's much more a question of *not raising it in the first place*.

WOMEN'S VOICES

This is not sexism. Women's voices are different from men's. It's a fact of life. And they deserve a special section to themselves, not because being a woman I happen to be particularly interested in women's voices, but because bizarrely they are still an issue in some areas of broadcasting.

I sincerely hope you are shaking your head and muttering *surely not*. But because this is a chapter about the pitch of the voice, it would not be complete without looking at the Great Depth Debate as it relates to women.

Any keen student of broadcasting history who has spent time watching old TV programmes (and especially those wonderful, stagey ads *c.* 1962) will have noticed that something very odd seems to have happened to women's voices in broadcasting. They've got deeper over the years. Of course, you could always try blaming the frequency response of old recording tape – both sexes do sound a bit thin compared to what we hear now – but nonetheless there is a marked difference between the kind of range women used in the earlier days of broadcasting and the range we expect them to use now.

It is partly to do with social class. Our background determines the voices most of us use – we learn to adopt similar tones to the people who surround us. Back in the 1950s and 1960s, most of the people who worked in radio and television came from a very narrow middle-class background. Arguably that's still to some extent true, but in those days your voice identified your class to a far greater extent than it does today. Educated people, it was felt, should aspire to a sort of national standard of speech. What that meant for women was that they should all sound rather like the Queen does today – clear, slightly clipped, using the upper part of the range.

There were of course exceptions, but most women then in broadcasting used a similar light, feminine, Home Counties voice. You have to remember also that in those days women were not considered to be serious-minded enough to read the news or report on it. The appointment of the first female newsreader on BBC Television in the 1970s, Angela Rippon, caused an immense sensation.

But once women began to penetrate news and current affairs broadcasting, they found themselves working in newsrooms still largely staffed and run by men. Old attitudes died hard, and although I would hesitate to accuse the broadcasters of that day of deliberate sexism, I suspect there lingered a feeling that there was something about women that made it hard for them to be taken seriously in news. Men could be authoritative when delivering the news because they had deep, serious voices. So women began to develop deep, serious voices too. It wasn't terribly difficult, because most of us have a reasonably wide vocal range. We just started using a different bit of it – more of the chest voice, less of the head.

It wasn't the only way in which women adopted protective colouration to enable themselves to be taken seriously in newsrooms. Where else did the convention of the neat, short female reporter's haircut come from, or the only slightly feminized jacket that is still practically a uniform for most news women on camera? 'Simple is best' is the usual justification for this, and there is certainly some truth in that. 'You don't want to distract the viewer.' Nonetheless it's the men who get away with some of the most outrageously garish ties on camera, and it's thought to be an endearingly eccentric quirk. No woman in her right mind would dare wear a flowery blouse or a colourful scarf in the news studio, even though those are acceptable parts of the female wardrobe in almost any other walk of life.

Feminist rant over – well, almost. The legacy of all this is that we still associate deep with serious. What this means for voice coaches like myself is that we are confronted with a stream of young women who are worried that their voices aren't deep enough for broadcasting, and we are frequently asked by news editors (women as well as men) to do something about so-and-so's 'girly' voice.

But could there also be something intrinsically more effective about a deeper tone? If we are agreed that we look for 'authority' in the voices we want to hear on air, does any of that authority come from the depth of the voice?

AUTHORITY AND DEPTH

True authority comes from *knowing what you are talking about* (see Chapter 6 for more about authority). But we also need to remember that every voice is carrying a subtext – the subtext that tells your listener what is going on in your head, irrespective of the words. The pitch of the voice can be read as an indicator of your state of mind – and we already know what happens when you get tense and nervous. The body literally tenses; the tightness of the muscles makes breathing more difficult, and the effective space in your body that acts as a resonator for your voice is reduced. Result: you squeak.

So anyone listening to a voice that sounds thin and high-pitched is going to make a series of judgements about that voice. This person is nervous, they will conclude – he or she is uncertain of what they are saying. Goodbye authority: it's trapped somewhere inside and can't get out.

So there is some truth in the idea that a deeper voice is taken more seriously. But the human ear is also quite capable of discriminating between the rise in pitch that is produced by tension (because the resonance of the voice has disappeared) and a voice that is naturally higher-pitched even when it is in a relaxed state.

There have been many successful women broadcasters who do not have low-pitched voices. Indeed, they may even be at a slight advantage to the men – a higher voice is often easier to hear, and clearer, especially if it is competing with crackle and mush on a badly tuned receiver. This advantage will be to some extent eroded as digital sound reproduction takes over, but for listeners who are slightly harder of hearing, a higher-pitched voice is often the one they prefer because of its clarity.

The Thatcher factor

When Margaret Thatcher took over the leadership of the Conservative Party, she consulted image-makers to see if there were ways in which she could increase the authority of her personal presentation. The consensus seems to have been that as well as adopting a more masculinized wardrobe (with some carefully chosen concessions to femininity; Mrs Thatcher was never one to deny her gender, and used it to great effect on many an occasion) she should also do something about her voice. It was very much a product of her class, age, education, and upbringing, and similar to those I have described as being so prevalent amongst women broadcasters in the 1950s and 1960s. So the Iron Lady set about ironing out the shriller notes, and with the aid of voice specialists who no doubt acquainted her with the hitherto unfamiliar use of the diaphragm, she succeeded in pitching her voice far lower. I am not sure if it was entirely successful. There was always for me something rather forced and fake about the breathiness of her delivery, which suggested that if anything the diaphragm was being over-used.

This is a well-known story, and anybody who heard Mrs Thatcher pre- and post- the voice lessons cannot have failed to notice the difference. It's probably the best-known anecdotal example of what voice lessons can do for a woman. (The second most familiar tale being that of the young Sue Lawley locking herself in her room at university and not emerging until she had rid herself of her Dudley accent, though I have my doubts about the veracity of that one.)

What Mrs Thatcher did, sadly, was to reinforce the notion that only the deep-voiced woman is to be taken seriously. As a voice coach, I long to get to work on the less than dulcet tones of another female politician, Ann Widdecombe. But there's also a part of me that wants to cheer every time her voice hits those absurdly shrill notes. She certainly does not have a melodious voice and I may sometimes want to strangle her, though she sounds like she's doing that effectively enough to herself. But at least she's making no concessions, and doing her best to prove a woman can be taken seriously no matter what the pitch of her voice is.

'Girly' voices

Most of the women I see who complain (or whose news editors complain) that their voices are 'girly' and high-pitched are having problems relaxing their body when they speak. It isn't that there is something fundamentally different about their range – it is just that they are preventing themselves from using the body's own resonance and denying themselves some of the richness that is literally only a deep breath away. So the first thing to check out is how well you are using the breath to support the voice, by returning to the exercises in the last chapter.

The other factor that may affect the depth of women's voices appears to be age. There is a body of opinion suggesting women's voices mature rather later than men's, in the mid-twenties. There may be some physical or even hormonal factor affecting this, but personally I have always leaned towards the opinion that it is as much experience of life that deepens girlish voices as they grow older. As you become more relaxed in yourself with maturity, more certain who you are, so your voice relaxes and deepens. We should leave aside other factors such as the accumulated effect of twenty fags a day or a regular tot of whisky. These may appear to have a roughening, deepening effect on the voice, but are *not* to be recommended. Indeed, for the voice, the damage they ultimately do far outweighs any dubious short-term benefit.

Exceptionally girly voices

There are, however, some women – only a few, mind – who whether they realize it or not have made a deliberate choice to use only the higher part of their range. This is going to sound brutal, and I can hear the voice in my head that accompanies me when I write sounding rougher and deeper by the minute, trying to deny that I might ever have made use of such a shameless device myself. But let's face it, girls, we all know how very effective that little-girl voice can be when you want to appeal to a big tough man. They just melt.

Some women get stuck in that voice. Can you blame them? It's worked very well for them throughout their earlier lives – first daddy, then a whole succession of other males turned out to be suckers for its wheedling tones. Unfortunately, it rarely works that way in broadcasting, unless you happen to work in children's TV. It just goes to prove what my mum used to say about making silly faces – the wind will change and you'll get lumbered with that expression – or that voice.

But cheer up. You can do something to tune the pitch of your speaking voice.

TUNING YOUR VOICE

Nature assigned both male and female voices a range of pitch, and although you can do some vocal exercises to extend the comfortable range of notes a little at either end, you can't really alter the basic equipment that determines your potential range – how your body is constructed.

Voice specialists divide the potential range of the human voice into two basic 'registers' – the **first register**, the 'chest' voice, and the **second register**, the 'head' voice.

Most of the male range lies within the first register, the deeper chest voice. When men move into the 'head' register it produces the effect known as 'falsetto'. Women share part of the same range and they too tend to make use of the deeper chest register for the normal speaking voice, but most of their range lies within the second register, the higher head voice. They tend to move automatically up into that when they get excited or tense, and they will also use it in their normal speaking voice for *inflexion* – pointing up a word by altering the pitch. They will more often do this than men since the majority of their range is in the head voice.

Although people imagine that men's voices are deeper because they have bigger frames – bigger chests – this is not the main factor in determining the pitch range of the voice. It is the action of the vocal cords, not really cords at all but folds of muscle in your throat that open and close the larynx. In adolescence, the male hormone testosterone causes the Adam's apple to enlarge in boys, affecting the development and tension of the cords so that a boy's childish treble voice will 'break' and eventually become deep and gruff. An adult male's vocal cords are longer than a woman's.

Female-to-male transsexuals take testosterone supplements and their voices do indeed deepen. (Meanwhile male-to-female transsexuals have operations to reduce and re-align the Adam's apple, putting a tension on the cords to lighten their voices.) But most of us are quite happy with the gender fate assigned us and however tempting it might be to take a pill to get a deeper voice, would women really want the hairy chin and the male-pattern baldness that also go with an extra dollop of testosterone?

The way to develop the depth of your voice most effectively, for both men and women, is to look at how you are using it. Are you, for instance, only using the upper part of your range? And could you increase its apparent depth by making it richer with resonance, to increase the lower harmonics?

As we saw in Chapter 4, unless you are using your breath properly to support your voice, you will not be able to make much headway with altering the pitch successfully.

But it is also possible to make other small adjustments to help you pitch lower if you think you are only using the top end of your range. You might want to seek the help of an experienced voice teacher. For once, I would urge you to look outside the field of broadcast specialists, and find a good drama voice coach. Sometimes when people try to do this kind of work on their own, they end up forcing the pitch of the voice too far down and can cause damage to the cords. But, proceeding cautiously, we can explore the lower end of your range and find ways of making more use of it. You may discover you have far more range in your speaking voice than you thought.

Pitch control

Let's start by trying a simple exercise to see how much control you have over the pitch. Many people claim they have trouble adjusting the pitch of their voice. For some strange reason, although we are all prepared to have a go (with varying degrees of success) at hitting different notes when we sing, there seems to be some curious inhibition about using the same mechanism to alter the pitch of the speaking voice, where you need nothing like the same degree of pinpoint accuracy in following a set of notes!

It is simply that you are not used to thinking of yourself as being able to do it, because pitch in the speaking voice is generally under *subconscious* control. But you can, as this exercise will demonstrate.

Exercise 5.1: Spoken scales

Singers practise scales to improve their pitch control. Speakers can do something similar, though I am not going to ask you to repeat this exercise to the point of tedium. It is adapted from a classic exercise used by actors as part of their daily routine. Just run through it a couple of times to prove to yourself you can consciously alter the pitch of your speaking voice.

Before you do so make sure you are sitting (or standing) comfortably and easily, weight balanced on sitting bones, back and neck long and free, head level.

The note you choose to start on should be comfortably in the middle of your range. (If you are not sure where that is, this exercise is going to help you find out!) First we are going to go upwards. You are not going to try to hit perfect notes, simply to make each word a little higher than the one before.

```
                                                        up
                                                goes
                                        voice
                                when
                        choose
                can
        I
```

Now try it in the opposite direction – downwards.

```
        I
                can
                        let
                                my
                                        voice
                                                ease
                                                down
```

One thing you should notice is the word '*ease*' on the downward scale. This is because I want you to realize it is not a question of forcing your voice down; you should be thinking of allowing it to move effortlessly deeper.

Many of us – women especially! – are rather too good at moving the voice upward. We are used to using upward inflexions to point up words we want to emphasize, because pitch is associated with loudness and the carrying power of your voice. Remember though it is just as useful to inflect downwards.

When you have practised this exercise a few times, try extending the range covered by adding '**and up**' to the upward scale, '**and down**' to the downward scale. Keep your head level, your neck relaxed, your chest and throat open – don't push, just let the notes rise (or fall) naturally.

Which end of the range are you using?

I hope this exercise has shown you it is not very difficult to exercise control over the spoken pitch. But it may have also revealed some other interesting things about the way you are using your voice.

I find that the note people unconsciously choose as a starting point for their scale can reveal how natural a pitch they are using as a matter of habit. If for instance you found that when you did the upward scale, you were running out of top notes towards the end, you are probably over-using the upper end of your range. You automatically picked a note to start which was already well into the upper end of your range. The downward scale probably surprised you by being not nearly so difficult as you thought it might be.

If, on the other hand, it was more difficult to move down, you probably have a tendency to use the lower end of your range in your speaking voice, and you started on a 'chest' note that was already towards the bottom of your range. Keep the throat relaxed and open, and be careful that you are not pushing your voice further down than you need to. Many women in broadcasting do this, and in the long run it can cause voice strain.

Such women are afraid to let their voice move up from the first to the second register and they are keeping it all in the chest. The telltale signs are a constrained sound to the voice. It sounds tight, and even sometimes muffled or breathy. It is often uncomfortable for the listener – his or her fine-tuned antennae for the nuances of falsity in a voice are going to pick up that something is not quite right. It is this that gave Mrs Thatcher's voice that strange, sighing quality, because she rarely allowed her voice to rise into the head register. We knew her voice wasn't 'natural' because of that.

This problem is most often encountered in women, but men are not immune to it either. If you have convinced yourself your light and probably very pleasant tenor voice really ought to be a deep baritone or bass, you too may be pushing your voice down further than it can comfortably go.

So beware! An unnaturally deep voice is as uncomfortable for the listener as an unnaturally high one. If your voice is tight and constrained at either end of the range, it lacks resonance and even authority, because it sounds false. In the end it will damage your voice, and you may actually lose its range and flexibility altogether.

Exercise 5.2: Easing down – and up

To reinforce the effortless nature of your ability to control your pitch, you can practise gliding down (and up) on a sound. Try this on an 'ooo' sound first, then move onto 'aaah', and then 'eeee'.

Start in the 'head' register (which will be falsetto for men) and – keeping a constant medium volume – let your voice glide slowly down until you reach what feels to be a comfortable low note in the chest register, one that you can sustain easily. You should keep your mouth and throat open and relaxed.

When you've practised a few easy downward glides on all three sounds, try some upward soars, moving from the chest voice up into the head voice, and again finishing on a note that is high but comfortable.

If you have been over-pushing the lower end of your range, the upward soar will prove much more difficult. You will find that your voice tends to break up and crack as you try to make the transition into the head voice. Continuing to practise this exercise should help, but remember always not to force your voice. Let it emerge effortlessly from an open throat and mouth.

Opening the mouth and throat

If you are having trouble with a smooth easy move between the registers, your muscles in and around the larynx may be tightening without you realizing. The overall effect of habitual tightening is to make you always sound as if producing the voice is a bit of a struggle; it will be forced and rather harsh. What is probably happening is that you are normally staying in one register only. When you try to make the change to the other it becomes an uneasy transition instead of a gentle merge.

Another sign of this is a metallic, twangy quality to some of the vowel sounds. This happens because you are not opening your mouth and throat fully to exploit their natural resonance. The soft palate is not lifting enough in the back of the mouth, so more of the airstream is being forced through the nose. Your tongue may be pushing too far back, and your larynx is too high in the throat because the throat itself is tense.

'Oh, great', I can imagine you saying. 'Nice analysis of the problem – but what on earth am I supposed to do about it? I can't actually feel these organs, you know. I haven't a clue where my larynx or soft palate are, let alone where they're supposed to be.'

In fact, you don't need to know precisely where they are to cure the problem. (If you want to look at their relative positions, refer back to Fig. 2.2.) The best solution is to use a simple visualization technique. Imagine the roof of your mouth opening like an arch at the back. Feel how that opens up your throat too, especially if you stop tightening your tongue at the back of the mouth and let it rest easily on the floor of your mouth. Don't force it flat; just allow the mouth and throat to gradually open and the palate to arch. Now you can let your voice rise up the back wall of your throat and across the roof of the mouth, like a bird skimming the roof of a high cave. You will find it much easier, and a fuller and richer sound will emerge.

Make sure too that you are not tilting your head on your neck. The neck should be long and free, and your nose and face should stay level, not lift up, so that as you arch the back of your mouth your spine and neck lengthen and your whole body feels as if it is growing upward in the same direction.

Try the gliding exercise again to test out how this feels.

We can take the same exercise a little further by using words instead of vowel sounds. This is a good introduction, by the way, to improving the variety of intonation in your voice.

Exercise 5.3: Flexing the voice

You are going to try flexing your voice both up and down, this time using words. Let's start with a name:

You start the first syllable low, and then glide up to the second syllable, as if you were calling for Henry – 'Where are you?'

Now try the opposite: the first syllable high, gliding down to the second syllable to reach a low note. (This time your subtext is shock and rebuke – Henry's been a naughty boy.)

HEN
-RY!

You can have even more fun flexing up and down on insults. (How rude you want to get is up to you.) For instance:

GET \(high)
(to low)\ STUFFED!

And then, in a tone of outraged surprise:

STUFFED? (high)
GET (low)

And then try starting high, gliding down, then up again:

AND   TOO!
YOUR FRIEND

We can imagine the retaliation:

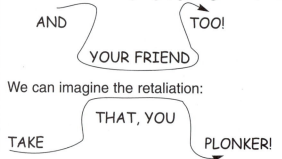

THAT, YOU
TAKE   PLONKER!

Making more use of your lower range

Provided you don't force the voice, you should find that there is room to explore in the lower end of your range. Now that you know you have conscious control over your voice, you can start to get into the habit of *choosing* the note on which you will start a sentence. (This is going to prove very useful when we look at how to avoid rhythms and patterns in a later chapter.)

Starting on a lower note will often bring down the overall pitch of your voice. At first, you will be making a conscious attempt to do this, but the more you practise, the easier it will become, until it is eventually automatic to start lower.

I am not asking you to start on your *lowest* note, because that would only give you the opportunity of moving in one direction – up – for the rest of the sentence. Give yourself flexibility and room to manoeuvre, so that whatever note you start on you can move up or down from it.

A word of warning though – it is important that it is not always the same note! People who start every sentence on exactly the same note fall into patterns that make the voice sound monotonous and boring. And please remember what I told you earlier – you must not push your voice down beyond its natural range. If you feel tightness in your throat or chest, you are pushing too hard. Relax, and your body will help you find your lower notes naturally.

Exercise 5.4: Starting lower

No time like the present to try that out immediately and record the result. Here's a paragraph to practise on. Don't worry too much about the sense of the story for the moment. Just try and go for those lower notes as you start, and move effortlessly up and down within the piece. Don't force it, relax and let it happen. Even if you don't manage to sustain it the whole way through, listen back to what effect it has had on your voice.

Fish in the River Soar are about to get a sweet treat. But they may find there's a catch in it. Local anglers are trying out a new kind of bait – jelly babies. A Leicestershire scientist claims that fish are attracted to sweets. He says anglers can increase their catch by using jelly babies instead of the more traditional worm or maggot. And different species respond to different colours. Cod choose black ones, eels go for orange, and catfish apparently prefer pink.

ADDING RESONANCE

You will find that working carefully in this way should get you into the habit of making far more use of the lower end of your range.

You can also improve the apparent depth of your voice by making fuller use of the resonant spaces in your body. Instead of altering the base note that your larynx produces, you will be adding layers of lower harmonics so that your voice sounds richer and fuller. By using the breathing techniques described in the previous chapter, you'll be opening up the resonating area in the **chest**.

But the chest is by no means the only resonating space for your voice. The **mouth** too is an important resonator. Simply opening the mouth a little wider can add another layer of richness to your voice, without sounding too plummy.

Nasal resonance – good or bad?

A third area of resonance also deserves a mention, if only because the resonance it produces is so frequently abused in broadcasting. Your **nose** acts as a resonator, and the sound it adds to your voice varies according to how much of the airflow you direct through the nasal cavity. In the back of your mouth is an area of muscle called the *soft palate*, and depending on how much you lower or raise it, more or less of the airstream goes through your nose. When I asked you earlier to arch the back of your mouth, you were in fact raising the soft palate to direct more air through the mouth instead of the nose. Believe it or not, the soft palate is under our conscious control, though some are better than others in being able to move it precisely to where we want it. Impressionists like Rory Bremner have superb control of their soft palate, and are able to use it to mimic voices with pinpoint precision.

Many people who lower the soft palate to produce nasal resonance as they broadcast are not aware they are doing so. It produces a sound that is strong but rather unpleasant, a bit like the quack of a duck. You could also describe it as a metallic honk, rather thin and twangy, having a lot of brightness to the sound but very little real depth. Once you understand what it is, it is instantly recognizable, and there is an example on the CD-ROM for you to hear. Voice specialists will describe it as 'nasality', which is somewhat confusing as most ordinary people think of a 'nasal' voice as being quite the opposite. They associate 'nasal' with the bunged-up sound of someone who has a heavy head cold. In fact, when you have a cold there is little or no nasal resonance at all, because the air can't get down the blocked nasal passages, and consonants like 'n' and 'm', which require nasal resonance to sound right, come out as 'd' and 'b'.

Over-use of nasal resonance may be a habit you have had since childhood. Some accents make use of it – the Essex twang, for instance, or the slightly whiney sound of an Australian voice.

But the most common reason for broadcasters to 'talk down their nose' is because someone somewhere told them at an early stage of their career their voice wasn't powerful enough. Without any expert guidance, they discovered they could make a stronger, more penetrating sound by over-using nasal resonance – and it does have considerable carrying power. Unfortunately it also sounds false and horrible, as you discover as soon as the person concerned turns away from the microphone, and asks brightly in the perfectly normal pleasant voice they use for everyday conversation what you think of their performance. It is an example of a 'put-on' voice that doesn't really work for broadcasting, and you should avoid it at all costs.

It is a voice that I all too often hear on the less well-resourced local stations, where newsrooms are using young inexperienced staff and not giving them proper voice guidance. Women particularly are prone to adopt it, because the main part of our range is the head voice, and nasal resonance is particularly effective in boosting a voice that is only using the upper part of the range. Men with lighter voices will sometimes try and use it too, with the same unfortunate result.

It is a habit that needs to be carefully unpicked, and sometimes I have a hard job convincing someone who is using it that I really can give him or her a strong voice they will like much better using different techniques. I really would recommend that you don't start using nasal resonance in the first place. If the boss is complaining you need to 'beef up' your voice and add some 'power and punch', resist the temptation to talk down your nose, and get some professional voice training instead. In the long run it will produce a far better result, one that is exportable to any style of broadcasting.

In the meantime, look back in this chapter to the section on tuning your voice, where I discussed how to **open the mouth and throat** when you move between different registers. I asked you to imagine yourself arching the back of the mouth and relaxing the tongue. This helpful little visualization is often enough to give people some conscious control of their soft palate, so they stop honking and instead increase the mouth and throat resonance, which sounds much more pleasant. And remember especially to relax and deepen your breathing, because that is how you can add extra power to your voice *without* quacking like a duck.

***

Broadcasters need to do more than just get their voice physically into shape. Now that your voice is stronger we need to explore some of the ways you can use it to connect better with your listener/viewer. The next chapters are going to focus you back on the sense of what you're saying, by looking at what we mean by 'conversational' speech, and intonation – that mysterious process of 'signposting' the meaning.

SUMMARY

- Broadcasting is full of traps that can force your voice higher than usual – nerves, tension in the studio, or the tendency to over-use upward inflexions to emphasize individual words.
- Make sure you are sitting in a relaxed, comfortable way, weight balanced, back and neck long and free.
- Use the comfortable lower end of your range, and train yourself to choose lower (though not your lowest) notes to start on.
- Everyone has a 'natural' range, and you should not attempt to force the voice beyond it.

- Adding resonance will boost a thin voice and give you a richer, deeper sound, but avoid 'talking down your nose'.
- Before worrying unnecessarily about the pitch of your voice, make sure it really is a problem, and not just a hang-up! Deep does not necessarily equal authoritative.

6 Being conversational (or trust me, I'm a broadcaster)

What do we really mean when we say broadcasting is conversational speech? Taking account of your listener's reaction; and being a real person without having to emote all over the script. Voice – the Great Betrayer – and why it's easier to lie when someone can see your face. (Honestly.)

By now you will have realized that I approach the question of voice from two directions – what's happening in your body and what's happening in your head. The two are often interlinked and I find it helpful to switch back and forth between them. So, after all that not-so-hard work improving your physical approach, it's time to think again about this business of mind-set.

If you watch or listen to the best broadcasters, the overwhelming feeling is that they are communicating with you, even if you know perfectly well that at least some of the words they use are coming off an autocue or a piece of paper.

But why do others – and maybe this includes you – sound wooden, flat, bored even, delivering the words with all the impact of a piece of wet cardboard? The answer often lies in what is happening in their heads; are they *reading*, or *telling*?

Some otherwise talented broadcasters have huge difficulty with this. You occasionally hear them on local radio magazine format shows. They may have a lovely warm personality that comes across wonderfully on air so long as they are chatting 'ad lib' to the listener, introducing records, nattering about last night's TV. But sooner or later, they have to pick up a piece of paper and read out a weather report or the lead-in to the next interview. And my goodness, you can hear the join.

Suddenly that lovely warm personality falls flat and dead. It is as if they have been replaced by a robot. They gabble through the script, clearly trying to get it over with as soon as possible. As a listener, you're left to pick up as best you can the sense of what they're saying, because they're certainly not thinking about helping you by using their intonation to point up the key ideas in it. Words get stressed totally arbitrarily, and you know immediately they are reading something, not talking to you. In fact, they have totally forgotten you – all they're thinking about is that piece of paper.

So in this chapter I want to concentrate again on the difference between reading and talking. In an ideal broadcasting world, we should not be able to hear the 'join' where you stop ad-libbing and start a scripted piece. Everything you deliver on air requires what some broadcasters call a 'conversational' tone.

SO IS BROADCASTING A 'CONVERSATION'?

Broadcasting is only a 'conversation' in that you are *talking* to somebody – *to* them, remember, not *at* them. You want them to feel you are being 'conversational' in the sense that you are aware of their presence.

A conversation implies something that is two-way. Sometimes, of course, broadcasting will be literally that – two people conversing on air, either as an interview (on which the listener eavesdrops) or a phone-in where the listener can directly participate. But when you pick up a script and start addressing the listener or viewer, when they are 'silent' in the process, can that still be said to be a conversation?

Well, yes. There are plenty of conversations in which one participant is listening rather than contributing. Indeed, your listener at home might even be answering you back – it's just that you can't physically hear their responses. (Don't you ever shout at the radio or TV?)

But enough of this philosophical hair-splitting. The point is that 'conversational' is a word that a lot of broadcasters use to describe the effect they are aiming at. For some people, that is a really helpful idea. But it is a word that can also sometimes conjure up the wrong kind of picture in your mind.

Conversational is not a tone of voice, but a state of mind

Sometimes when I ask a client to be more 'conversational' in their approach, the results are disastrous. They imagine the wrong thing entirely – that I am asking them to mimic a conversational tone of voice. They start to put in a lot of 'Wells' and 'umms' and 'ers', and break up the flow of information in a strange and jerky way, imitating the kind of hesitations you might hear in someone who was feeling their way with difficulty through what they were trying to express. They complain that the kind of words in a broadcast script are not the way they would put it if they were in fact chatting to one of their friends. (Ideally, of course, broadcast writing is much closer to normal speech than writing for the page, as we'll see in a later chapter, but nonetheless it is often more formal than a true 'conversation' in that it is prepared and expressed succinctly, especially if it is a news broadcast where it is important to be precise.) They don't understand that I am not asking them to be less fluent. In fact they are thinking only about the sound, and not about the *sense*.

Being 'conversational' is an attitude, not a speech pattern. You can be conversational without using a single 'well' or 'um'. All I am asking you to do is shift your mind-set so that you remember there is someone listening to you, and concentrate as you do in normal conversation on the ideas you want to express to them.

LIFTING A SCRIPT OFF THE PAGE: THE DIFFERENCE BETWEEN READING AND TALKING

Other broadcasters use a different phrase to describe the same effect. They talk about 'lifting a script off the page'. Doing that is not just a matter of physically lifting your head, though as I have suggested that helps. It is also a matter of altering the way you think about the written words.

So let me suggest one further idea that may help you. It's going to sound a bit odd, coming from a voice coach.

Stop thinking about how you sound.

You probably weren't expecting that. After all you bought or borrowed this book to help you improve the sound of your voice. But it is the best single piece of advice I can give you to help you become a good broadcaster.

Don't worry: you have already laid the foundations of a good voice if you have absorbed the chapters on physical work. The way you use your body to produce a strong sound will become instinctive if you continue to practise the advice on posture and breathing. Later on – much later on – you can maybe allow yourself a tiny corner of the brain to analyse what you sound like as you are actually speaking. But for now, thinking about how to make a good sound is part of your preparation *before* you go on air. At the moment when you are actually broadcasting or recording yourself, you should NOT be thinking about the sound of your voice. Wait to assess that when you listen back afterwards, because worrying about the sound as you speak is a distraction from the task at hand – communicating.

When you are talking to someone, do you think much about the sound of your voice? I think not. You have much more important things occupying your mind. First, you are thinking of the ideas you are trying to get across. Second, you are weighing up whether the person listening to you is receiving those ideas – how they are reacting to them. Those two things fill most of your conscious mind. If you get distracted you will lose your thread.

You don't even think very hard about the words you are choosing. In fact if you think too hard about the words – when you're trying to find the exact turn of phrase, for instance – oops, that's the moment it just seems to disappear from your head. People talk most eloquently and fluently when they concentrate on the *ideas* they are trying to get across, rather than trying to discover the 'mot juste', the precise word.

So if we are trying to create the impression of talking, rather than reading, what we must do is ditch all those distractions. Stop worrying how you sound – let your body take care of that, instead of your conscious brain. Concentrate on what you're saying – the story you're telling – and how your 'imaginary' listener is likely to be receiving it.

The analogy I find helpful here is to think of yourself as about to cross a river via a rather narrow plank bridge. If you were to worry about the process as you did it – how to walk, step by step – my guess is your knees would lock, you'd wobble and possibly even fall in. If on the other hand, you think about your *aim* – getting to the other side – and take a deep breath and concentrate on that instead, your balance miraculously improves because you have let your body instinctively look after the walking process while you are thinking about your destination. That's what you must do with a script: concentrate on your main objective – what it's about, and whom it is directed to, not how well you are performing. The words and the sound are less important than the *story* and the *listener*.

The only way to test out how this works for you is by trying it.

Exercise 6.1: Telling the story

You're going to have to make a recording as you do this exercise, because I don't want you to give the sound of your voice a moment's thought while you are actually reading – no, TELLING the script – into the microphone. Pick one of the broadcast scripts you have written for your course – or if you are a working professional, borrow one from the newsroom or a programme department. Look it over first to make sure you understand it. While recording, firmly ignore everything except the story and the urge to communicate it to your listener. Then listen back to hear how you sound.

Better?

Using the imaginary listener's reaction

This is where the imaginary listener could be helpful again, to distract you from worrying about the sound of your voice. Remember I said that your listener or viewer is reacting at home to what you are telling them?

Use that. When you look over your script before reading it aloud, imagine what their likely reaction is going to be to the story. Will they be angry, delighted, moved?

And here you can push the idea of your imaginary listener just a bit further. While you should only ever be talking to one person at a time, let the face of that person change as you read the story, to a different person who may be reacting differently.

Suppose, for instance, you are reading a script about the British foot-and-mouth crisis of 2001. The disease led to the slaughter of millions of farm animals, and the closure at the height of the tourist season of much of the British countryside.

The crisis provoked many different reactions. Farmers were angry with the Government for not responding more quickly. Some felt that their animals were being slaughtered needlessly; whole herds that they had spent a lifetime building up were wiped out in a day. Meanwhile those who worked in the tourism business were furious that their livelihoods were threatened, through no fault of their own. Some blamed the farmers for having allowed agriculture to become so intensified it could have contributed to the spread of the disease. Then a third group – townspeople being denied access to the countryside – saw it differently again.

The point is that your audience would have contained representatives of all these groups, and their reactions will encompass all shades of opinion. It is not your job to take one side or the other, simply to bear in mind that there will be different reactions within your audience to the story.

Of course, you will have your own opinions about a story. If you haven't, I would suggest it is time to assess what you are doing in broadcasting, because good broadcasters are thinking people who care about the information they are conveying to the listener – and if you *don't* care, I promise you the listener is going to know. Trying to disguise your total indifference to a subject with a false show of enthusiasm never really works. You have to make yourself understand why the subject is important to someone – if it isn't, why does it deserve a place on the air? I have often found that if you think about the kind of people to whom it might matter, and why – in other words, putting yourself for a moment in *their* shoes – it's a sure way of engaging your own interest in the subject.

A classic example is that standby of every local news bulletin – the story about a group of mothers who are protesting that a busy road needs a pedestrian crossing. At first sight, it seems hard to care about the story if you are a young broadcaster who doesn't yet have children yourself, living nowhere near the road in question.

But that crossing matters to the people who live in that area. Perhaps a child has already been injured or killed. Perhaps many of those mothers take a long detour in order to take their children to school. Perhaps more of them drive their children to school – clogging up the traffic and impeding *your* journey to work – because they are afraid to let their children walk. There are all kinds of ramifications to the story, if you allow yourself to think about it for a moment. If it wasn't worth reporting, why is it in the bulletin? If it is worth reporting, it is worth reading with some sense of interest and significance.

I am not suggesting you should deliver it as if it is the biggest story in the bulletin. Clearly it is unlikely to be that. But it does matter to a number of people, which is why it has a place on the air. So don't just skate through it, allowing your mind to wander to other things. Think about those people to whom it does matter, and you will stand a chance of making it interesting to other people as well.

ENGAGING YOUR BRAIN

I sometimes think there should be a notice on every studio wall, or attached to every microphone and camera: 'Before putting mouth in gear, please ensure that brain is fully engaged.'

Communication is a vehicle best NOT driven on automatic. The brain is the clutch pedal – by which I mean it is the connector of all those complex physical mechanisms that enable us to get our message across. If it is somehow absent from the process – because it is thinking about something else! – then communication becomes unclear.

Not for a moment would I suggest you would be so crass as to spend your time on the air thinking about what you're going to cook for supper, or how you are going to get beyond first base with that particularly attractive new Production Assistant. But even without such trivial distractions, there is plenty to occupy your mind in a broadcasting studio that could take you away from the sense of the words coming out of your mouth. The clock, for instance: you may be obsessed with whether or not you are going to finish what you're saying on time. Or malfunctioning equipment: is the next clip actually going to come up in the right place, or will that CD start when you want it to? You may be waiting for breaking news, or as I suggested at the start of the chapter, you may be worrying about the *sound* of your voice.

If any or all of these things are allowed to occupy your mind excessively, you might have a shock if you listened back to what you actually said on air. You would notice immediately that your voice was giving away your pre-occupation with something else. There might be, for instance, an inappropriately jolly intonation pattern on a serious story. If you are not thinking about what the story is about – and what it might mean to your listeners – you can sound remarkably unfeeling if you use rising inflexions on a sentence like 'Exeter Crown Court heard today how a six-year-old boy was battered to death by his stepfather.'

You think you wouldn't do it? Well, all I can say is that I've heard it – not once, but many times, when a broadcaster isn't engaging the brain.

The trouble is that we all have an 'autopilot' mode for those moments where we have to do several complicated things at once. For those of us who make a living from our voice on air, 'autopilot' is a set of familiar intonation patterns that make us sound a lot like functioning broadcasters – but unless we actually THINK about what we are saying, there is always the danger we could be using the wrong pattern on the wrong story. We are imitative creatures, and there is an unexpectedly good mimic in all of us – that was how we first learned to talk. With a little experience, we can all sound without too much difficulty like a seasoned on-air performer, but unless we engage the brain in the process it is all so much 'sound and fury, signifying nothing' – in Shakespeare's words, 'a tale told by an idiot'.

AUTHORITY

You will remember we briefly touched on this elusive quality in the introductory chapter, when we considered the attributes of a good broadcasting voice. But what do we actually mean by it? Some people consider that authority is a tone of voice. They might ask you to 'say it more authoritatively.' So you put on your deepest most impressive voice, and wonder why they are still not satisfied.

That isn't authority. Authority comes from understanding. 'I have it on authority ...' means you got the information from someone who knows what's what. If you know and understand what your script is about and are thinking about getting that across, you will sound more authoritative.

When it comes down to it, *authority is not a tone of voice; it comes from knowing what you are talking about.*

EMOTION AND EMPATHY

You need to care about what you are saying; you need to understand the information you are conveying, and in the process you may well develop opinions about it. What you should NOT do is automatically share those opinions with the audience at large. (The exception to this, of course, is if your job is to be an opinionated commentator, employed specifically to reveal what you think and jolt the audience with the force of your personal views.)

Broadcasters are human beings and, of course, we have feelings and opinions about the subject matter we broadcast on. But there is a long tradition in British broadcasting of balance and impartiality. The two are not the same. Balance allows us to put opinionated commentators on air, so long as we balance out their view with the opposing lines of thought. Impartiality, however, is a trickier matter. Journalists, in particular, are expected to present the news or current affairs in an unbiased way.

The question of broadcasting impartiality is a fascinating debate, but not one I intend to enter – except to look at how it impinges on your tone of voice. You need to have given thought to the content of what you are saying, but you should not let your own opinions and feelings colour your delivery. Your tone should remain as far as possible detached from emotion, while recognizing that the subject may arouse strong feelings in those who are listening to you.

It is something like the way you might decide to break bad news to one of your friends. 'While you were away on holiday, I'm afraid your cat died.' Most of us feel rightly that bad tidings are best delivered straight. It isn't going to help your friend cope better with the news if you either break down in tears while imparting it, or adopt a falsely hushed over-caring tone.

Of course, there are times when we want to see or hear that broadcasters are themselves shocked by what they have to report, but that feeling must be genuine, and as much as possible controlled. John Simpson wrote in one of his entertaining books on his life as a BBC correspondent that when he was starting out, an old newsroom hand told him there was no place for the word 'I' in the reporter's vocabulary. Sometimes you will have to use the 'I' word, but use it with care and moderation. And if, in exceptional circumstances, you are going to allow emotion into your delivery of hard fact, make sure it is real feeling, not gushy fakery. The audience will see through that immediately.

How can the audience tell?

We all have an automatic lie detector built into our heads. Some people are better at recognizing what it is telling them than others, but it is part of standard human equipment.

Deep inside the brain, the more instinctive part of our mental equipment helps us recognize that someone is not being entirely sincere. Some people assume that this works by helping us to recognize when body language is at odds with spoken language. The person may be telling us one thing, but their eye movements or muscle tension tell us another. That can be true, but there is another even more infallible give away, which seems to be equally beyond our conscious control – the sound of the voice.

Tension in the muscles of the body affects the sound of the voice. People talk of something 'striking a false note', and that can be literally true in the voice. A pitch that does not feel quite natural, as well as hesitancy, can give away that someone is not being exactly honest with you.

The BBC carried out an interesting bi-media experiment some years ago. They broadcast interviews on both radio and TV with various people, some of whom were lying, some of whom were telling the truth. The audience were asked to decide which were the liars.

What most people expected was that it would be easier to tell the liars from the TV interviews, because they would have both body language and the sound of the voice to give them clues. But quite the reverse was the case. People listening to the radio broadcasts had more success in deciding who was lying, relying on the sound of the voice alone.

Perhaps liars find it easier to control their body language than their voice. Perhaps the body language even acted to distract the viewers from detecting the 'false notes' in the voice that reveal a lie. Whatever the reason, it is a salutary lesson to all of us who use our voice in broadcasting. If you are being insincere, the listeners can hear it.

Actors' voices

Do actors make great broadcasters? Sometimes – but I would put my money on the 'ordinary' person every time.

The only advantage an actor has in broadcasting is that their voice has been trained to a state of near perfection, so that vocally they are extremely flexible. But a lovely voice is not enough. You need to be able to use it to communicate in a real way. That is why this book stresses the importance of your mind-set.

If you put an ordinary person with an untrained voice in front of the microphone for the first time, they will naturally feel self-conscious and that can make them sound stiff, or timid. An actor too will be feeling self-conscious on a first broadcast 'out-of-role', but although they are sufficiently trained to overcome the self-consciousness, it will still be there in the voice in the form of over-smoothness. It will sound very mellow and polished but somehow not quite real, because instead of being themselves and communicating, the actor has just adopted another imaginary persona – what he/she imagines a broadcaster sounds like.

I once co-presented a radio show with an actor. We had a great time, but it was a very odd experience. She has remained a good friend and I hope she won't mind me saying that I reckon she spent the whole of the series not presenting, but acting. I first got the clue when one of my friends said, 'You know, I can't tell the pair of you apart on air.' I listened back to the programme and saw what he meant. We had different voices, different accents, but we sounded somehow indistinguishable. The actor was doing what came naturally to her – picking up the intonation patterns of someone else and performing an ever-so-subtle parody – she was acting me.

Broadcasting isn't acting. It is something much harder than that. It's being yourself.

Can you be too nice?

The worst thing you can do, wherever you are broadcasting, is to be overly 'nice'. It is a sure giveaway that you are not being yourself, and far from making the listeners like you, it distances you from them.

I often tell the presenters I train that there is no place for politeness in broadcasting. Politeness is something we fall into when we do not know someone very well; and your listeners want to feel they have a closer relationship with you than that. The subtext of your voice is shouting 'Like me! Like me!' when it should be telling the audience 'This is me, take me or leave me.' Be real. Listeners enjoy it when you are cheeky. It implies you respect them and like them enough to show them your real self.

It *is* important to respect your audience. Suggesting you should not be polite is not necessarily the same as asking you to be rude or to insult them. While you will still be talking to your personal listener, who may not be the same generation as your actual audience (see Chapter 3), do spare a thought for the age and sensibilities of your real listeners or viewers. You can often go further than you think, but your station will have clear guidelines about where to draw the line.

Being rude, of course, is in certain circumstances just what the audience want to hear – and some broadcasters have made a successful career of doing just that. When I used to go to football matches every Saturday with my dad and brother, we always listened on the way home to a particularly aggressive fans' phone-in on BRMB hosted by a brilliant Brummie called Tony Butler. His catch phrase, when confronted by a particularly stupid caller, was 'On yer bike', at which point they would be cut off mid-rant. We loved it – far better entertainment value than the respectful after-match analysis over on the local BBC station at the time. Tame stuff now, when you compare it to some of the shock jocks, but very innovative in its day. We would never have dreamt of phoning in, but we effectively joined in, shouting back at the radio.

And that is what good radio and television should be – participatory, with a real feeling of banter and exchange between broadcaster and listener.

The great betrayer

It is not only insincerity that your voice will reveal. I sometimes amaze my clients with my apparent ability to read their minds by listening to them deliver a piece of script. I can easily tell when they are worrying about the sound of their voice and not thinking about the sense of it. Or if we have been trying to practice telling a script to an imaginary listener I might say, 'I know you weren't thinking about him.'

People imagine this impressive parlour trick is based on years of knowing how broadcasters think, but they are only partially right. I am not the only person equipped with an acute ear for the nuances of the voice. All of us have it; it is part of our evolutionary heritage. Your listeners have it, and you owe it to them not to let yourself be distracted from the sense of what you are saying. Engage your brain because the listener will know when it is not fully in gear.

SUMMARY

- If you think of yourself as 'reading' rather than telling, it will show in your voice.
- Don't think about the sound, think about the sense.
- Use the listener/viewer's likely reaction to help you find what is interesting in the story you are telling.
- Don't become too emotionally involved yourself.
- Always be sincere – the audience can tell if you are not.
- Engage your brain before putting your mouth in gear.

7 Signposting the sense (or how not to be a plonker)

Voice teachers have a mystifying language of their own which is largely impenetrable to the everyday broadcaster – words like 'intonation' and 'inflexions' are all very well in theory, but sometimes seem remarkably difficult to translate into practical broadcasting. All of us are capable of getting the intonation right and making sense without having to ponder which words to stress – we do it all the time in conversation. So why does it go wrong when we pick up a script? How you can use the five 'P's to get the message across; why it is wrong to think only in terms of 'emphasis'; and a way of preparing a script that will help you make better sense of it.

The human brain is an amazing organ. It is thought that our capacity for spoken language evolved about one and a half to two million years ago, even before modern humans, *homo sapiens*, appeared on the scene. Unlike other animals, we have specific 'language areas' in the brain, which are concerned with both constructing and comprehending speech, though many other brain areas are also involved in the act of communication.

No two brains are the same – we all develop individually, according to the genes we have inherited from our ancestors and according to the outside influences on us in childhood (and indeed, through-out our life) that shape the neural pathways as we learn. For those reasons, some people will be more musical than others, or find it easier to read aloud, partly because they have inherited those abilities but also because they were exposed to that kind of activity in childhood. We still have the capacity to go on developing and learning throughout our lives, though, so practising a skill will help forge the right connections in the brain to make it easier for you. If you don't practise, you might as well not have tried to pick up the new skill in the first place – use it or lose it.

Reading this book won't give you a better broadcasting voice. *Practising* what it suggests – over and over again – will. **Practice** is the first of several 'P's you will come across in this chapter.

HOW WE UNDERSTAND HUMAN SPEECH

Let's think for a moment about how the brain tackles the act of understanding human speech. What comes out of other people's mouths is a stream of sounds to which we as listeners have to assign meaning. How those sounds are combined gives us words. And as if that wasn't difficult enough, within a single language, there will be a whole variety of subtle alterations to the basic building blocks of speech – vowel sounds and consonants – depending on how the speaker uses their speaking organs, and the habits of speech – accent – they have developed by copying those around them. Although people talk about 'standard' English, or 'received pronunciation' (see Chapter 14), the reality of our language is anything but standard. Even in 'standard' accents, there will be a massive variation in the sounds – that's what gives each of us our own individual voice. Yet the human brain is fantastically good at sorting out the meaning of these different sounds, even when the voice is an unfamiliar one. How does it manage?

One reason is that meaning is not conveyed by words alone. There are several layers of 'subtext' in every spoken communication, which help the listener's brain sort out what the speaker intends. One is a layer of visual clues – while we are using our ears to take in the sounds, our eyes are also watching for extra guidance. We are all, though we often don't realize it, lip readers. Take, for instance, the sounds 'p' and 'b', as in 'pour' and 'bore'. They are very close in sound – yet a long way apart in meaning. How is it that we generally manage to tell them apart without too much difficulty? Part of the answer is that as well as the sound, the lip movements required to produce them are very slightly different. (Get someone you know to say 'Peter Piper picked a peck of pickled pepper' while you watch the movements of their lips, then ask them to say 'Beater

Biber bicked a beck of bickled bebber.' The difference is subtle, but it's there.)

We use other visual clues to help fathom the meaning – facial expression and movement being the most obvious. It is very hard to follow speech from someone who has a particularly blank and immobile expression – our attention tends to wander off. Body posture and hand gestures, thought by scientists to be the precursors of our spoken language, also help.

But the other sub-level of communication is one that *doesn't rely on visual clues at all* – which is good news for broadcasters, as so much of our job has to be done out of vision, whether it is in a radio studio or when we are doing a television voice-over. It's what we call 'intonation' – subtle shifts in the sound, which underline the meaning of the words we are using. If we don't use intonation properly, we become like the person with a blank and immobile expression, and people will dismiss our voice and what we are saying as 'boring'.

INTONATION – THE VOICE'S PUNCTUATION AND LAYOUT

When you are reading words like these I have written, on the printed page, you have time to take them in and absorb them. If I have written a sentence that seems difficult or obscure, you can go back and read it again. Yet even on the page, a writer uses tricks that are the visual equivalent of intonation to help you get the message. Punctuation, such as full stops and commas, divides the words into understandable chunks of thought. Paragraphs can show a change of direction. And if I want to *emphasize* a particular thought, I might use *italic type*, or underline the word, or even put it into CAPITAL LETTERS.

In spoken communication, intonation serves a similar purpose. It is all the more important because the listener really has only one chance of grasping speech; they cannot read it over and over again. In broadcasting, we also have to allow for the fact that the listener's primary attention might be directed to some activity other than listening. They are perhaps cooking or driving while they listen to the radio, and if they are watching television, a large part of their brain is busy processing the visual information in the pictures you are sending them. So if you want your viewers or listeners to understand what you are saying to them, intonation is clearly important.

Now pause for; a MOMENT and try *to* think about the difficulty of grasping. The sense of *something* where, the intonation IS wrong.

I have deliberately used misleading punctuation and type to give you some idea of the difficulty a listener has if you use the wrong intonation. Confusing, isn't it? It is not impossible to sort out the sense, but the process of understanding is made much more laborious. While your listener is still puzzling out your first point, they may be missing the second important thought you were trying to plant in their head.

So it is clearly vital not only to use some sort of intonation (without it your listener will find it hard to concentrate on what you are saying), but also to make sure it is not the *wrong* intonation.

Here is an example of a sentence that was written for a news bulletin:

> 'There are reports of protests against this morning's
> air strikes in Pakistan.'

Look at it carefully. What does it mean? Did the protests, or the air strikes, take place in Pakistan?

In fact, this is an example of poor writing. If I told you that the story was written at the time of the war in Afghanistan, you would realize with the benefit of historical knowledge that the air strikes took place not in Pakistan but over the border. The writer intended that you should understand it was the *protests* that took place in Pakistan. Ideally he or she should have written, 'There are reports of protests in Pakistan against this morning's air strikes ...'

However slipshod the writing, the newsreader has to deliver it to make the meaning clear. And you can do that even without changing the order of the words, but by altering the intonation. Consider these two different ways of reading the sentence, using a pause (phrasing) to help clarify it:

> 'There are reports of protests/against this morning's
> air strikes in Pakistan.'

> 'There are reports of protests against this morning's
> air strikes/in Pakistan.'

In the first example, the protests could be anywhere, but the air strikes are clearly linked with Pakistan, so the listener will misunderstand the story. In the second, by separating the air strikes from Pakistan with a tiny pause, the listener is more likely to understand that it is the protests that took place in Pakistan, not the air strikes. Ideally of course the sentence should be rewritten, but it is a useful example of how intonation can alter the meaning of the sentence.

So how do we get it wrong?

If you analyse the intonation in an ordinary conversation, most of the time most people manage to be reasonably clear in what they are saying – especially given that they are usually making it up as they go along and not even thinking about the intonation! Yet intonation is there, naturally and unconsciously, subtly signposting and underlining the meaning of what the speaker is trying to convey. It seems bizarre that when a broadcaster actually has a script with the words on it, they can so often make a complete hash of intonation so that it becomes arbitrary and misleading, fighting the sense.

Of course it is that script, or rather the *reading* process so many people fall into instead of *talking* the words, which is the problem.

As we've already discovered in earlier chapters, your mind-set can get in the way. If you think too hard about the act of reading words off a page, you will fail to let your natural instincts sort out the right intonation for you. Your speech will stop being 'conversational' and become mannered and artificial.

It follows that if your mind-set is right – if you are thinking of yourself as talking a set of ideas, rather than reading a set of words – you should theoretically get the intonation right.

But if it were that easy for everyone, I would be able to retire. It often happens that however many times I implore someone to free up their attitude to broadcasting, to think of the sense not the sound, they somehow cannot shake the notion that they are reading a script.

So for the duration of this chapter, I am for once going to ask you to 'think hard' not just about the sense, but also about the words, the sound of the voice as you say them, and how that relates to the sense. To understand where intonation goes wrong, it is necessary to spend a bit of time being analytical. Later, to stop you from delivering a script too deliberately, I will ask you to go back to the more instinctive approach – to liberate yourself from the notion of reading, and 'feel' the sense rather than be overly analytical.

SIGNPOSTING

You could think of intonation as a set of signposts that help your listener through the sense of what you are saying.

That is not the only way of thinking of it, though it is the one I prefer. Many broadcasters call this 'getting the emphasis right', though as you will see later that is a somewhat misleading way of describing the process.

In order to find out where these 'signposts' lie, you will need to think hard about the *ideas* you are trying to convey and the groups of words that carry them. Making sense of a script involves rather more than just grabbing a bit of copy and arbitrarily underlining a few words that for whatever reason leap out at you.

So I am going to introduce you to what will seem at first like a rather laborious process of analysing which words are carrying the ideas. It is going to take some time until you get used to it, but it is the same basic process I, and many other broadcasters, use *whenever* we pick up a script. The difference is that because we are using to looking at words this way it takes us a fraction of the time it is going to take you at first.

But don't try to run before you can walk. For the time being, I want you to take your time over this process, to make sure you are getting it right. You are probably going to find that there are many more important words and phrases in each sentence than you thought at first – and each of those important words or phrases needs some sort of special intonation to make sure your listener is picking them up.

There are all kinds of different names for this process of working out what is important. A broadcaster I know refers to it as 'underlining the sense groups' and others describe it as 'finding the who, what, where, when, why, and how'. I prefer to think of it more simply as sorting out the *signposting*. (Privately, I call it 'key phrase analysis', but that sounds too much like jargon for everyday purposes.) I don't care what you choose to call it, so long as it helps you to grasp the underlying principle: *we are looking for the words and phrases that carry the ideas and the meaning.*

Exercise 7.1: Sorting out what to signpost

We are going to look at a piece of script and work out what are the important points in it that your listener must hear clearly to understand the sense of it. But first, I would like you to record a base-line version of it, which you can compare with how you later approach it when you have analysed the sense of it.

Today, Avebury in Wiltshire is part of a World Heritage site.

Hundreds of thousands of visitors flock there each year to see its ancient stone circle.

But how many visitors realize what they're seeing is a reconstruction – the vision of a rich and gifted archaeologist?

Some say he was a genius who saved one of our greatest prehistoric monuments. To others, he was a wealthy egotist who destroyed a community. He changed forever the village and the lives of those who lived there.

Last year, a group of villagers gathered in the Red Lion pub in Avebury to watch a piece of remarkable home movie footage ...

This script is part of the opening to a television documentary, but it could as easily have been the lead-in to a radio package. I've chosen it partly because it does have pictorial qualities – it was designed to explain the pictures the viewer was seeing on the screen, but as a radio piece you could think of it as attempting to create pictures in the head of a listener.

Now you have recorded your base-line version, I would like you to spend some time working out which are the important words and phrases your listener/viewer has to hear in order to understand it. Every spoken communication contains words and phrases which encapsulate the ideas behind it – the building-blocks of meaning – and other words which are the 'filler' between those blocks, like mortar between bricks, useful for joining the whole thing together but less essential to the meaning.

Mark up the script so you can compare the conclusions you've drawn. How you mark it is not for the moment important. You could use a highlighter pen or – if you plan to let someone else use this book after you – light pencil markings circling the important words. (We will discuss script marking later.)

This is by no means an exact science. Your conclusions may not exactly correspond with mine, just as no two broadcasters will deliver a script identically. I may include a word or two more in a phrase than you do, or vice versa. But ideally the ideas we have highlighted – for that's what these groups of words represent – should be broadly the same. You will perhaps notice that this process is rather similar to the way you might take notes of relevant points if you were jotting down the gist of the information someone was giving you. You would pick out not just individual words, but whole phrases that strike you as important.

Now check your version against mine.

What you should have highlighted

Today, **Avebury in Wiltshire** is part of a **World Heritage site**.
Hundreds of thousands of visitors flock there each year to see its **ancient stone circle**.

But **how many** visitors realize what they're seeing is a **reconstruction** – the **vision** of a **rich and gifted archaeologist**?
Some say he was a **genius** who **saved one of our greatest prehistoric monuments**. To **others**, he was a **wealthy egotist** who **destroyed a community**. He **changed forever** the **village** and the **lives of those who lived there**.
Last year, a group of **villagers** gathered in the **Red Lion pub** in Avebury to watch a piece of **remarkable home movie footage** …

Perhaps you arrived at much the same conclusions as I did. If not, let me explain my thinking about what is or is not important in the script.

Today, **Avebury in Wiltshire** is part of a **World Heritage site**.

This first sentence contains just two ideas – *where* we are talking about, Avebury in Wiltshire, and *what is special* about the place. You could also argue that the idea of 'today', as opposed to thousands of years ago, is important in setting the time-frame. But you might reason as I did that it is obvious in the first sentence that we are talking about the present day – the listener can work that out for themselves. The word is there to add to the overall picture, but it doesn't have the importance that the other two ideas have. Is the fact that it is only 'part of' a World Heritage site also important? I would argue that the exact boundaries are not so important as getting across the concept that this place is a very important part of our cultural history. It doesn't matter whether or not the listener understands entirely what is involved in granting the status of World Heritage site – the key idea here is that this place is recognized as having a special status.

Hundreds of thousands of visitors flock there each year to see its **ancient stone circle**.

In this sentence, there are two main ideas – that there are many visitors to Avebury (the *who*), and *what* they come here for. There's no need to highlight 'flock', which is simply another way of saying there are many visitors – we know that already from the 'hundreds of thousands'. Nor do we need to highlight 'see' – visitors generally 'see' things, and what is more interesting here is what they have come to see.

> But **how many** visitors realize what they're seeing is a **reconstruction** – the **vision** of a **rich and gifted archaeologist**?

I've highlighted four ideas here, the last three of them quite closely connected. 'How many' poses the question in this sentence, suggesting that probably very few people realize what lies behind the façade of what they are looking at. 'Reconstruction' tells you *what* it is that is actually there, and signposts ahead to the story the whole documentary is going to tell. 'Vision' and 'rich and gifted archaeologist' give you more information about *how* the reconstruction came about. You could have seen these two ideas combining as a single phrase, 'vision of a rich and gifted archaeologist'. Alternatively, you might choose to ignore the word vision, and simply highlight the idea of *who* brought the reconstruction about. It depends on how much emphasis you might want to put on the archaeologist's visionary approach to his work. (This is what I mean by this analysis being far from an exact science, and open to personal interpretation.)

> **Some say** he was a **genius** who **saved one of our greatest prehistoric monuments**. To **others**, he was a **wealthy egotist** who **destroyed a community**.

Here I've picked out both 'some say' and the word 'others' to encapsulate the idea that there are different ways of seeing the archaeologist's achievement. The rest of the highlighted words and phrases tell us *what* is the gist of those two different views.

> He **changed forever** the **village** and the **lives of those who lived there**.

This sentence is about the conclusion you might draw, whichever side of the argument you might be on. 'Changed forever' is *what* he did, and 'village' and 'lives of those who lived there' explains *what* he changed.

> Last year, a group of **villagers** gathered in the **Red Lion pub** in Avebury to watch a piece of **remarkable home movie footage**...

Again I think when this event took place is less important than the event itself. 'Villagers' tells us *who*, and the other two ideas highlighted give us the *where* and the *what*.

Incidentally, you may find that for a television voice-over the ideas that need to be signposted are slightly different from those you would signpost for a radio version. In the documentary, we showed a picture of the pub sign, so there would be less need to point up *where* the event took place.

When you first approach scripts in this way, it seems a rather laborious process. I have asked you to take time over it so that you can understand the principles we are applying. But the more you get used to it, the faster you will become. It can even become the basis for sight-reading, and this is the way I scan a script that I haven't had time to read in advance, pausing for only a millisecond at each full stop for my eyes and brain to take in the sense-groups before my mouth opens for the next sentence. (We will look in detail at sight-reading in Chapter 11.)

Not just one word

Please note that I have been talking about both words and **phrases**. Very often an idea is expressed not in one word alone, but in a group of words, a phrase. A 'red bus' is not really two ideas but one, even though the colour and the nature of the vehicle might seem at first to be two separate notions. Thinking of it as a picture might help. Red alone is not enough to convey the image; nor will bus suffice.

> He was travelling in a **red bus**.

Because in this sentence we are trying to create a picture in the mind of the listener, both words are equally important. You should not stress one at the expense of the other. Think of it as a phrase where equal weight goes on both words – a balanced phrase, like a see-saw with someone sitting at each end.

It would, of course, be a different matter if the whole script had been about buses.

> Tim's hobby is travelling on buses. Today, he's
> taking a **red** bus to Clapham.

In that case, as we have already introduced the idea of bus earlier in the script, it is not so important in the second sentence. The colour is the new piece of information, so only 'red' gets stress. The phrase is not balanced, and the seesaw has all the weight at one end.

This may seem like stating the utterly obvious, but you would be surprised how many times people get a simple stress like this wrong.

Does it matter? If I were directing you on a recording, I would make you do a re-take and say it right, because to get it wrong shows you are not really thinking about what you are saying. It handicaps the listener/viewer's understanding by misdirecting their attention to the less important word. On the other hand we all make mistakes occasionally, even in 'natural' conversation. On a live broadcast, you might be allowed the odd slip. To do it as a matter of habit, however, is just sloppy broadcasting.

Exercise 7.2: Signposting as you broadcast

Now that you have thoroughly analysed the important words and phrases in the Avebury script, try delivering it again (recording it, of course, so you can listen back).

Compare this version with the one you did before. Does it sound better? If so, what makes it better?

Did it 'feel' better to you as you did it? Did you feel as if you understood the story more as you spoke? Did it feel more like 'telling' than 'reading'?

Just in case you think it sounds worse, decide why you think so. Is it perhaps over-deliberate? If so, you could have another go, trying not to be quite so heavy-handed in your delivery – perhaps a little faster and lighter.

You may also find that the next section helps – looking at ways of **varying the kind of intonation you use**.

MORE THAN EMPHASIS

For people who are supposed to be good with words, broadcasters can be astonishingly lazy. We all like to simplify. It is part of the nature of our job. But sometimes we over-simplify, and an example of this is the word many broadcasters use to describe intonation – 'emphasis'.

For many years, editors, producers, and trainers have been bandying about the term 'emphasis' as a kind of shorthand to describe how you should use intonation to get the meaning across. But it is a misleading way of describing a far richer, more varied set of processes than you might expect.

Emphasis suggests weight and force – stressing a word by pushing out a greater volume of air, and therefore a greater 'volume' of voice. But simply saying a word louder is by no means the most effective way of expressing its importance, just as thumping the table every time you want to make a point can actually reduce the force of your argument, making you sound strident and over-emphatic.

Unfortunately, emphasis is the single most over-used tool in the broadcaster's kit of vocal techniques. Listen to almost any news broadcast, and you will hear young reporters thumping away with their voices to get their points across. It sounds strangely unconvincing, when you compare their delivery to the smoother, more experienced voices of the newsreaders. I am afraid that broadcasting trainers have a name for this particular kind of over-emphatic delivery, especially when the reporters in question keep over-stressing the *wrong* words, the ones that make no particular point in the sentence. We call it **plonking**. And, therefore, anyone who sounds that way is, logically, a plonker.

So it is important to realize that rather more than just 'emphasis' – the stress or weight of the word – is involved in intonation. For a broadcaster to use only 'emphasis' would be rather like only painting in black and white. Intonation actually gives you a whole palette of colours to mix and use in many different, subtle shades to enhance the meaning.

Before I start describing these other 'colours', I would like you to see how many you can work out for yourself. Think about the kinds of things you hear other people do with their voices when they are speaking, which help you understand the meaning. Write a list, and then check it against mine.

THE FIVE 'P'S

When you listen to someone speaking, you will find they employ several different vocal techniques to keep you listening and under-standing.

These fall broadly into five groups, conveniently all beginning with the letter 'P'.

- **Punch.** This is what most people think of by the word 'emphasis' – pushing the word out with extra breath, so it feels 'heavier' and more stressed. As I have said already, it is the vocal equivalent of thumping the table – useful sometimes, but best used in modera-tion. Sadly, it is the most over-used (and misused) technique by novice broadcasters. Punching words takes a lot of breath, so if you find you are frequently running out of breath when you broad-cast you may be over-emphasizing.

- **Pitch.** Voice coaches often describe the changes in pitch of the voice as 'upward or downward inflexions'. The voice rises up or comes down on a particular word or phrase. Like all these tech-niques, you are probably not conscious of doing this as you speak, and many people seem to think that shifting the pitch of their speaking voice is difficult, whereas in fact we do it all the time in conversation. A classic example is in the phrase 'On the one hand *this*, on the other hand *that*, where *this* will tend to go upwards and *that* downwards.

- **Pace**. Have you ever noticed how a speaker will slow down over a phrase they want you to take particular note of? Normal conversational speech never goes at a constant pace. As a general rule (though like all rules, this can be occasionally broken), we speed up over the parts that are less important, and *slow down* over what we want to give the listener extra time to absorb. This is a very useful technique when it comes to a long phrase that needs to be signposted, such as **remarkable home movie footage** in the piece of script we analysed. All of the words in the phrase are equally important. To stress each one (using punch) would take a great deal of breath. So a simpler way of making the phrase stand out in the sentence is to take it comparatively slowly.

- **Pause**, sometimes also known as **Phrasing**. These are actually two related but slightly different techniques, but they both make use of the spaces between the words. If you pause *after* a particularly important word or phrase, the message you are passing on to your listener is: 'What I've just said is particularly important. I'm giving you an extra moment to take it in.' Phrasing involves separating off the groups of important words so that they stand out.

  Some say/he was a genius/who saved one of our greatest prehistoric monuments/. To others/he was a wealthy egotist/ who destroyed a community.

  These pauses are subtle, however. If you take too long over them, you will sound laboured and staccato. They are rarely as long as a comma pause, and sometimes no more than tiny breaks in the flow of the sentence, just making sure that one word is finished before the next begins, instead of eliding the two together as we often tend to do in speech.

  When you use pause or phrasing, you must be careful not to sound like one of those automated announcements on the train. Because these are constructed by recording someone repeating a set of stock phrases and place names, which are then edited together, you get an unfortunate mechanical effect. 'We shall shortly be arriving at – Newport. Newport – is the next stop.' The problem is not just that the pause sounds artificial because it is too long; it is that because it is edited, there is no natural **elision** between the two words. In normal speech, your mouth is already preparing to shape the next word before the one you are saying is finished, and so the sound of the next word will 'colour' the end of the one before it. If you don't allow this to happen where it would naturally, you will sound clipped, staccato, and **over-enunciated**.

- **Projection**. We've talked about projection as something you need to do in order to reach out beyond the microphone to your listener, and you have probably been imagining it as a constant. But there are moments when you can 'drop' the projection (in the way that people talk of 'dropping your voice') as if drawing your listener towards you, becoming more confiding. I sometimes refer to this as 'varying the intimacy and attack', and if you analyse the sound, it is a mixture of altering both the volume and pitch of your voice simultaneously. However the way to think of it is NOT to say to yourself, 'I am going to get quieter and go down' or 'I am going to get louder and go up', because you will almost certainly overdo it. Much better to think of helpful words like 'intimate' or 'attacking', 'soft' or 'hard', which convey a feeling. Your brain, which responds best when it is acting at a subconscious level, will then automatically find the tone you are looking for.

These are the five basic 'colours' of intonation on your broadcasting palette. Like any painter, you will want to mix them, and produce yet more variations. You can hear examples of the five 'P's on the accompanying CD-ROM, in the section on **intonation**.

MARKING SCRIPTS FOR INTONATION

I am not an advocate of script marking in general, except as an exercise to help you in the early stages of your career. I rarely mark scripts these days. If I do, it is because I am having a particular problem getting the intonation right on a tricky sentence. (In which case I might ask myself why I wrote it that way – sometimes it is better to change the script!)

But I do think it is worth going through a period of script marking if you are trying to correct something about your delivery. It will help remind you of your particular 'fault', and how to remedy it.

Somewhere in my archive of career memorabilia is a tattered article, clipped from a magazine, which is there to remind me never to get bigheaded about how I sound. It dates from about twenty years ago, when I had my first job on national network radio, hosting the *You and Yours* programme on Radio Four. I was already an experienced local radio presenter, and naturally I was nauseatingly smug about having landed on such a prestigious job. I was so pleased with myself I snootily turned down the opportunity to go on a presentation course – I thought there was not much they could teach me. (How I would like to give my former self a good slap now!)

Strangely, my performance on *You and Yours* at first did not win me quite the praise I imagined I deserved. The Head of Department kept muttering about me sounding 'rather newsy'. I hadn't a clue what he meant. (Actually, he meant 'not very good'.)

I only discovered what was going wrong when I was having a drink with a colleague. 'You have a very nice voice...' he began. I preened. 'But you keep EMPHASIZING your words in a heavy-handed way', he went on. 'You're thumping them all the time. Haven't you ever thought of going up or down, or altering the pace?'

I hadn't. But the point came home when someone handed me a copy of a satirical magazine of the time, which had the spookily appropriate name *Punch*. It contained an article spoofing *You and Yours*, taking the mickey out of its occasionally nanny-ish tone. 'Does *custard* cause *cancer*?' the article began. 'In *today's* edition *we* look at the *truth* behind...' And so on, italicizing words all the way through to indicate that the presenter, named as me, over-stressed them.

I was flattered to be the butt of satire – fame at last! – but it was also enough to make me realize whoever wrote it was right. I was a bit of a plonker. So I began marking my scripts in the hope that if I had some form of notation on the page, I might occasionally remember to go up and down, or vary the pace. I can still be over-emphatic, particularly when I'm tired, but marking scripts helped me break the habit.

I think the best form of notation on a script is one you develop to suit yourself. But this is the way I chose to do it:

- Upward and downward inflexions can be marked with an upward or downward arrow through the word.

- Key phrases to take more slowly can be underlined with a broken line. This is for two reasons – a solid line draws the eye too much and leads you to over-stress the words, which might be the fault you want to correct. (For the same reason, you should not use CAPITAL LETTERS for a word you want to emphasize – it will make you shout it.) A dotted line is less obtrusive, and I associate it for some strange reason with the succession of yellow lines marked on some roads leading up to a roundabout, designed to make you slow down. These visual metaphors are well worth adapting. If you can find the ones that work for you, they will trick your brain into producing the vocal effect you want.

- Pauses and phrasing can be indicated by a slash/after the word.

So for example:

Today Avebury in Wiltshire/is part of a World Heritage site.

You may find a similar system of marking useful for a time as you try to broaden your use of intonation. It can be very helpful if you are getting used to the way of analysing the script for 'signpost' words and phrases, especially if you have up to now been emphasizing the wrong words.

In the long run, though, I don't recommend becoming too dependent on script marking. Many programmes no longer use paper scripts, and it is not very easy marking up copy read from a computer screen. It is also unfair to impose your scribbled markings on anyone else who might have to read from the same script later, in a hastily collated news bulletin, especially if you have inadvertently marked up the wrong words! Finally, reading from a marked-up script can make your performance over-deliberate – perfect, maybe, but strangely mechanical.

Exercise 7.3: Script marking

Have a go at marking up the script we looked at earlier, so you can see what intonation you might use to signpost the 'key phrases'.

Remember that although there is a 'wrong' way to use intonation, by signposting the wrong words (those which are not carrying the ideas), there is no single 'right' way. The idea is not to turn you into a set of broadcasting clones, all using exactly the same intonation on a script. It is up to you to find the best use of it for your voice and the ideas you are trying to convey.

Today, Avebury in Wiltshire is part of a World Heritage site.

Hundreds of thousands of visitors flock there each year to see its ancient stone circle.

But how many visitors realize what they're seeing is a reconstruction – the vision of a rich and gifted archaeologist?

Some say he was a genius who saved one of our greatest prehistoric monuments. To others, he was a wealthy egotist who destroyed a community. He changed forever the village and the lives of those who lived there.

Last year, a group of villagers gathered in the Red Lion pub in Avebury to watch a piece of remarkable home movie footage...

After you have marked your copy, have a go at recording the Avebury script again. You may find that you become over-deliberate, reading off the marks on the script as if it were musical notation. If so, discard the marked script and return to a clean, unmarked version – you should find that you automatically remember how you planned the intonation to work. Trust your subconscious to sort it out for you rather than trying consciously to remember it.

Does it work better for you with or without the markings? (There is no 'right', infallible technique; it is up to you to find the way that works best for you individually, though it is worth giving any technique a fair try before you discard it as unhelpful.)

Individual interpretation

To get a feel for how someone else might make use of the different varieties of intonation on the Avebury script, listen to the CD ROM. This should show you that there are as many 'right' ways of delivering the script as there are wrong ways. We all need to find our own, individual voice.

What not to stress – prepositions

One of the most annoying vocal mannerisms you can slip into is the habit of unnecessarily stressing prepositions. Prepositions are joining words, which indicate one idea's relationship to another: the cat is *on* the bed, the door led *into* the house, the best *of* the bunch, today *in* Parliament, the time *before* this. Very occasionally they need stressing because they indicate a contrast to something you have mentioned earlier. An example might be if you are giving precise instructions about placing something: 'Make sure you put the key *under* the mat, not *on top of* it.' But this is very rare. Usually, to stress a preposition is not only meaningless, it is also distracting for the listener/viewer.

Ask yourself if stressing the preposition adds to the meaning or not. For instance, would it help you understand the previous sentence if you stressed the word *to*? If it doesn't, it shouldn't be stressed.

Of all the mistakes in intonation, this is the one that you will hear quite frequently in ordinary conversational speech. If normally we get the intonation right when we talk, why does this mistake occur so often? The answer usually is that it is a distraction tactic, a habit that the uncertain speaker adopts because he or she hopes it will make them sound more positive and definite. (It doesn't.) It also sometimes happens when the speaker subconsciously realizes they have forgotten to stress the preceding word, which is usually far more important to the sense than the preposition. In the sentence 'Ask yourself if stressing the preposition adds to the meaning or not' the word that should have been stressed is *adds*. Unfortunately, if you stress *to* instead, this is too late to help the listener grasp the sense of what you are saying. Stressing prepositions is both irritating to the listener, and unhelpful.

Boring or 'flat' voices

When people describe a voice as boring or flat, what they often mean is that the speaker is either *not using sufficiently varied* intonation, or that it is the *wrong* intonation. It may also be that the person has allowed their intonation to slip into a rhythm or a predictable pattern, which doesn't help the sense of what they are saying. We'll look at why these rhythms are wrong and how you can avoid them in the next chapter.

In the meantime, if you have been accused of having a boring, flat, or monotonous voice, be careful that in trying to correct it you don't make the mistake of over-punching your words, or going up and down in a meaningless sing-song way. You should aim for more *effective*, more *varied*, and more *meaningful* intonation, rather than simply 'more punch'.

Over-deliberate intonation

Beware of over-using a single technique, and be subtle with them.

- Too emphatic a punch, and you'll be over-labouring the script, as well as running short of breath.
- Too extreme a use of upward inflexions, and you will sound like an irrepressibly cheerful twelve-year old.
- Too slow on long phrases, and it will sound like *Listen With Mother*. (I doubt any of you has actually heard that long-defunct programme, but we can all guess what it suggests – a patronizing delivery.)
- Too many obvious pauses, and you will sound staccato and jerky.
- Too many changes in projection, and you will sound too dramatic.

This is why I suggested earlier that although in this chapter we are being deliberately analytical in looking at how intonation works, the best thing you can do to put it into practice is not to think about how you are going to use it, but – armed with the knowledge that it exists in several varieties – return to what I asked you to do in Chapter 6. Think about *what* you are saying, not *how* you are saying it. If you are focused on the sense, your brain will automatically help you find the right sound.

SUMMARY

- Without intonation, a speaker cannot successfully convey the meaning of the words. It is the vocal equivalent of body language, or punctuation and typography, and it should reinforce the sense.
- Analyse each sentence for the words and phrases that are carrying the ideas.
- An idea is more often carried in a whole phrase rather than a single word, so beware of only emphasizing single words.
- Intonation is more than just 'emphasis' or punch.
- Think of using all five 'P's – *pitch, pace, pause/phrasing, projection*, as well as *punch*.
- Marking scripts may be useful for a time to help you get the hang of varying your intonation, but don't come to rely on it.
- Beware of over-deliberate intonation. Analysing how it works is useful while you are learning to fine-tune your delivery, but at the end of the day the easiest way to sound natural is to think of the sense of what you are saying, rather than to be overly concerned with technique.

8 Rhythms and patterns: where intonation can go wrong

Sometimes a broadcasting voice will sound strangely unnatural. It may be that listeners will describe it as 'boring', 'flat', or 'monotonous'. This is the moment to consider whether you have dropped into a predictable intonation pattern, which is fighting the sense of what you are saying. In this chapter, we look at how to spot rhythms and patterns; why it may be a mistake to imitate other broadcasters; and how to break a rhythm or a pattern if you have fallen into one.

I *wan*dered *lone*ly as a *cloud*
That *floats* on *high* o'er *vales* and *hills*,
When *all* at *once* I saw a *crowd*,
A *host*, of *gold*en *daffodils*...'

Poets like Wordsworth strove to give their verses rhythm, carefully choosing and arranging words to give the sound a pattern. It's a long and noble tradition – but it has no place in broadcasting.

It is all too easy to slip into rhythms and patterns when you have a script to read. They may not be quite as easy to detect as Wordsworth's rather obvious ti-TUM-ti-TUM-ti-TUM-ti-TUM, but, nonetheless, they may be there – and getting in the way of the story you're trying to tell.

So what's so bad about a rhythm or a pattern?

First of all, a rhythm in speech is hypnotic – it tends to send the listener into a light doze. Second, it draws the attention to the words you are stressing rhythmically, and they may not necessarily be the words that are conveying the sense of what you are trying to communicate.

Good poetry – which is actually much more difficult to write than most people think – arranges words so that the stresses fall on those that are most important. If you look again at those lines from Wordsworth's 'The Daffodils', you'll see that it's actually cleverer than you might have realized. The stressed words are those that create the picture. The poet is *wandering* – it's by chance that he comes across the daffodils. He's *lonely* (poets do tend to revel in their isolation) like a *cloud* – the last word in the line drawing your attention to the metaphor. In the next line, he adds to the image of the cloud, which *floats* over the *vales* and *hills* – that tells you where he is, too. Then *all* at *once* – he wants you to appreciate how sudden the revelation was – he sees a *crowd* – another image, this one designed to contrast with his loneliness – a *host* (the point being there were an awful lot of them) of *gold*en (lovely colour, painting the picture in your mind) *daffodils.*

Now look at the words and syllables that aren't stressed. They're the joining words – the ones that you could fill in for yourself. The actual story is carried simply in the stressed syllables, and the poet's skill is in arranging the words so that the stresses fall only on those that matter.

The same rule applies in any piece of good poetry. 'Shall I *compare* thee to a *summer's* day? Thou art more *lovely* and more *temperate...*'

Now take a look at a piece of broadcast scripted material. Unless you're an unwitting Shakespeare, the chances are you have written it in prose – you won't have arranged the words deliberately in a pattern so that a rhythmic stress falls on those that need signposting. Instead you've chosen the most simple and direct way of telling the story, so that it's easy for the listener to follow. (Or at least we hope you have.)

If, however, you try to impose a rhythm on those words, you will see that you end up stressing the wrong ones. You won't be making the best use of intonation to get your meaning across.

So rhythms and patterns fight against the sense, and obscure the meaning. They are to be avoided. But first, you need to be able to recognize when you are slipping unconsciously into a rhythm.

HOW TO SPOT RHYTHMS AND PATTERNS

The chances are your rhythm or pattern will not be quite so obvious as Wordsworth's was in 'The Daffodils'. Rhythms are the lazy way of broadcasting. They give you the feeling that you are getting some sort of intonation and authority into your delivery, without having to think too hard about the sense. Usually, they come about because you are trying to sound like other broadcasters, and you've picked up a single pattern of intonation from them and are imitating it slavishly and repetitively. You think it makes you sound authoritative, but in fact the opposite is true. It makes you sound like you don't know what you are talking about.

One of the most common patterns that people pick up is what I call '**end word stress**'. Never mind the main part of the SENTENCE, the word you pick to stress is the last word before the comma or full STOP. A further refinement on this not-to-be-recommended technique is that you pitch your voice on the word before the comma UP, and the word before the full stop DOWN. If you are really predictable, you'll be hitting almost exactly the same note on every up, and likewise every down will be an identical note to all the other downward inflexions.

As you'll hear on the accompanying CD-ROM, in the section on **Making sense of intonation**, end word stress sounds both bored and boring. Your mind is clearly not on what you are saying. In fact, the brain is not engaged in communication at all.

We can all do this; it's easy. It's *lazy*.

Where rules go wrong

Most people like a set of rules to work from. It makes us feel safe – if I do this, I will be on the right road. I'm afraid that learning to use your voice is not always quite so simple. Sometimes what works best is letting go of the idea of rules.

When I began teaching voice, I rather hoped I might find a set of rules from which I could teach. But I quickly discovered that the act of applying a rule could be the very thing that was spoiling some-one's performance. For instance, someone I worked with recently claimed she had been told by another voice coach that the way to make yourself sound authoritative was to make your voice go up at the beginning of the sentence, and down at the end. It seems unlikely that an experienced trainer would have said something quite so crass; perhaps he said something rather less categorical which she misinterpreted as a fail-safe rule. And she was applying it, rigidly and doggedly, to every sentence. Consequently she had fallen into a pat-tern of delivery that sounded extremely unnatural.

Every
    sentence started high and finished
                                  low.

If you
    try that for yourself you will quickly see it sounds
                                  odd.

Because
    when we speak naturally we don't speak to a
                                 pattern.
See what I mean?

Other typical patterns

There are other patterns that you may fall into. For instance, there is a common fault amongst inexperienced newsreaders. Every new story in the bulletin starts on exactly the same note, goes up in exactly the same way, then comes down again just as the one before it did. There is an example on the CD-ROM, in the section on **Making sense of intonation**. It is particularly easy to fall into this trap if the person writing the bulletin always tends to construct their sentences in a similar way – for instance, they might make them all the same length, pausing at a similar point some-where in the middle with a comma. But even if the writing is at fault, it is still the newsreader's job to *break* the pattern, to keep the audi-ence awake and listening. News isn't supposed to send the listener to sleep, it's supposed to wake them up to what's happening in the world.

You might also have a pattern problem on weather forecasts or travel news. The trouble with these is that they tend to be broadly similar, day after day. It's all too easy to switch off the brain and deliver it to a predictable pattern. But what you must never forget is that for someone – stuck in a traffic jam on the motorway, or trying to decide if today is the day for a long bracing walk on the hills – travel news or weather reports actually *matter*. You owe it to them to read with some intelligence, varying your intonation pattern so that your listener stands a better chance of picking up the piece of information relevant to them.

It is very often the scripted material – your reads rather than your ad libs – where the patterns will develop. But nevertheless I have heard record requests delivered as if the presenter couldn't care less. 'And here's one for Mrs (*voice goes up*) JONES, on your golden wedding (*voice goes down*) ANNIVERSARY. Specially for (*voice goes up even higher in vain attempt at sincerity*) YOU, Chris de BURGH sings Lady in RED ...' Easy to mimic; harder to avoid, if you're not really thinking about Mrs Jones and how much that record might mean to her. It sounds like a tired old cliché, but you could really be making her day by playing it. You've got to make that moment special to her, and that doesn't mean that you should *pretend* sincerity – think about her as if she was your Mum or your Gran, listen to how you are saying those same old words you say every day, and *make them different*. I know it's not easy, especially if you hate the song and find it deeply depressing that people's tastes are so predictable. But that is no reason to put on your syrupy voice, and be as predictable as the track.

EMOTIONAL TONE

How would you deliver these two headlines?

Thirty people died today in a coach crash on the M4.

Thirty people today shared a lottery win of twelve million pounds.

When you absorb the sense of them, they are very different in the kind of emotional response they should evoke in your listener or viewer. Yet in terms of grammatical construction they are remarkably similar.

If you imagine how someone might say them, you will probably hear that the 'good' news has an upward feel to it, while the voice on the bad news tends to go downwards.

Certain intonation patterns are associated with specific emotional responses, in much the same way as particular facial expressions are indicators of a particular emotion.

According to psychologists, facial expressions cross cultural boundaries. A smile indicates the same emotion in Peking as it does in Preston or Paris, while an angry face on an Eskimo will be immediately recognized by a European. I believe the same holds true for some of the common intonation patterns. I worked for a while at the BBC's World Service, as a technical operator on foreign language transmissions, and though I understood not a word of most of the broadcasts I was helping to put on air, it was often possible to get the gist from the intonation used. The BBC famously is impartial, yet you will always know whether what is being broadcast is good news or bad, serious or light. In countries where the broadcasting organizations do take sides, you will easily recognize whether the broadcaster is announcing a violent coup or a joyous liberation, however scanty your knowledge of the language.

As broadcasters, we should use these tones not to tell our listeners and viewers what *we* think, but to prepare them for their own likely emotional response to an item. As a very general rule, bad news feels downward, good news upward, because we are likely to use more upward inflexions to impart something that is cheerful, and more downward inflexions on a serious story. The more extreme these inflexions are, the more we are colouring the story emotionally, and there comes a point where the speaker ceases to be the impartial bearer of good or bad tidings and appears to be responding emotionally themselves to the content. So the amount of 'upwardness' or 'downwardness' in any broadcast speech needs to be moderated with some thought.

All this is pretty obvious, and I apologize for labouring the point. But if you have allowed yourself unconsciously to imitate what you imagine are the appropriate rhythms and patterns of a broad-caster, you may be shocked to discover that sometimes you can make the most appalling gaffes in the emotional tone of your delivery.

I have heard people read headlines about fatal crashes with exactly the sort of jolly upward intonation that would be appropriate for a lottery win or the creation of hundreds of new jobs. The trouble is that when you start to fall into a pattern of any kind, not only does the listener start mentally to tune out, the broadcaster's brain tunes out too! And before you know it, you are halfway into a story of death and disaster heading cheerily upwards.

It comes back once again to that process I keep harking back to in these pages: *Before opening mouth, engage the brain.* After all you are hoping to engage your listener or viewer's brain. You cannot do that unless you are *thinking* about what you are saying.

Air-check yourself

Are you convinced you don't fall prey to patterns and rhythms, indig-nant at the very suggestion you might? Before you stamp off in a huff, check it out. Get some ROTs – recordings off transmission – and listen to yourself for those patterns. Remember all those syrupy broadcasters you've heard, the ones you think seem insincere. Do you think they have any idea how they sound?

Air checks are the best way to find out how you *really* sound, as opposed to how you think you sound while you are in the euphoric state of broadcasting. Much as we all dislike listening back to our actual performance, it can lead to some ear-opening moments.

Some years ago, I was asked by a producer to be an occasional reporter on a business programme. What I knew about commerce and industry could have been engraved on the back of a very small business card, but I persuaded myself that it is the job of a reporter to ask ignorant questions because often they are the very ones that reveal what the audience want to know. However it's fair to say I knew I was out of my depth, and as I plodded round different com-panies comparing management styles, I kept worrying that some-one would find me out. Perhaps that was why I felt the need to put on a 'business reporter's voice' when I came to record my packages. I thought it would somehow lend my pieces credibility.

I'm not quite sure where I got that 'business reporter's voice' from. I must have been imitating something I'd heard other business reporters do. And while I was sitting there in the studio pre-recording my links, I was very pleased with it. I really thought people would take me more seriously.

Nobody said anything, because they never do. The horrible moment of truth only dawns when you really listen properly to yourself. The following evening I was driving down the motorway and the programme came on the radio. Feeling particularly smug about the report I'd made for that week's edition, I decided to listen – and was horrified. Far from sounding credible and serious, I heard a voice – my voice! – that sounded bored and flippant. It bounced its way rhythmically through the script, plonking every third word or so irrespective of the sense, and every sentence ended with a fine FLOURISH. While I was actually recording, I had thought that I was really hammering my point HOME. Instead I must have been sending my audience to SLEEP.

HOW TO KEEP IT INTERESTING AND EXCITING

The best way to make yourself sound interesting and exciting is to be interested and excited about what you are saying.

For example, one of the most demanding jobs in broadcasting is reading the news so that it remains understandable yet also exciting. Commercial stations in particular like their news to sound upbeat and urgent – quite rightly so. On a music station, the news should be in keeping with the pace of the music and the overall sound of the station. But that doesn't mean you allow yourself to adopt a rhythm just like the music – meaningful speech must be meaningful, and the news should be read with intelligent intonation, or it won't communicate the sense to the listener. The best newsreaders in independent local radio deliver with an excitement that truly engages the attention of the audience, because the newsreaders themselves are engaged and excited by the news. To do anything else is to insult the intelligence of the audience. People genuinely want to understand what is going on in the world around them.

The only place for rhythm in broadcasting is where it is intended to be a *part* of the music; a DJ may want to make his delivery match the pattern of the music he or she is playing. But like good poetry, it works best if the words where the rhythm forces stress are also the words that should be stressed to communicate meaning. That's how good rap works, and if you're clever you can apply it as a broadcast DJ.

However, for most broadcasters, rhythms and patterns should be an enemy. Your aim is to break them, to keep the audience awake rather than entranced!

HOW TO BREAK A PATTERN

Patterns, like any habit, take some effort to break. Once you have recognized that you have acquired a characteristic pattern, you are going to have put some work in.

The first step is to mark out what really needs to be stressed, and concentrate on stressing that. (See the previous chapter for script marking.) For a while, you may find that this makes you rather over-emphatic, but at least we hope you will be emphasizing the RIGHT words. (As opposed to the wrong WORDS.)

There is an exercise you can try that often helps you gain control over your intonation. I call it **headlines technique**. Although it sounds as if it's a technique for news broadcasting, you will find it flexible enough to apply to other kinds of scripts too.

Exercise 8.1: Headlines technique

This is actually a way of breaking a pattern by using a *different* pattern, but I have found it to be remarkably effective in persuading people they can easily get more variation into their delivery. We are all familiar with the way a set of headlines should be read. While there are no firm rules, we can tell by listening to good news-readers that if you start the first headline on a high note and work your way down, it will be more effective to start the next with a lower approach and then go up, to show that this is a very different topic. For the third, you will try for a different approach again.

A colleague of mine once likened it to a range of hills and slopes. You can start at any point on the gradient, high or low. The idea is to start at a different point each time, and go in different directions, up or down, so that each headline has a different 'tune'. You are aiming to surprise, and get as much variety into the headlines as possible (without of course sacrificing the sense or the appropriate tone if the news is sombre).

Try it on this set of headlines:

- The Government has announced a change in the laws on sex offences.

- Another terrorist bombing has killed eleven Israelis in a Jerusalem café.

- The British Prime Minister is flying to Washington for talks with the American President.

- At the World Trade Summit, protesters have again run riot in the streets of Rome.

- Twenty pensioners are injured in a Midlands coach crash.

Now try the same technique on a full script – reading only the first sentence of each story, or the first sentence of each paragraph. As usual, record yourself and listen back. See how much variation you can get into those first sentences, as if they were a set of headlines. (You will find that most are slightly longer than a real headline would be.) It may take several attempts to free yourself up from predictability, but when you have practised it several times you should realize that in fact it is not that difficult to gain control over where your voice is going. If it sounds rather mechanical and stilted at first, keep practising until you feel it flows better.

Big tax cuts could be on their way for working parents in today's Budget. The Chancellor is expected to announce a new allowance to help families with the cost of childcare.

A teenage boy has been jailed for seven years for killing an elderly woman when he crashed a stolen car. Kevin Wilson, aged 17, was joyriding in a Ford Sierra when he lost control and ploughed into a bus queue in Elmesley, Greater Manchester.

In Turkey, thirty-four children died when a landslip of mud hit a village school in the province of Anatolia. Rescuers have been working through the night, and say there is now very little hope of finding anyone else alive.

The car company Nissan have just announced they're to open a new manufacturing plant on Tyneside. It's expected to create at least four thousand new jobs for the area.

Thirty people today shared a lottery win of twelve million pounds. The syndicate, from Batley in Yorkshire, all work in the same call centre, dealing with tax inquiries for the Inland Revenue.

And as headlines:

- Big tax cuts could be on their way for working parents in today's Budget...

- A teenage boy has been jailed for seven years for killing an elderly woman when he crashed a stolen car...

- In Turkey, thirty-four children died when a landslip of mud hit a village school...

- The car company Nissan have just announced they're to open a new manufacturing plant on Tyneside...

- Thirty people today shared a lottery win of twelve million pounds...

Once you feel you have made changes in the ups and downs of your voice, experiment also with varying the **pace** of each opening sentence. You can also try varying the **projection** – the 'intimacy or attack' of your voice, which we looked at in the previous chapter. You can hear how this can be done on the CD-ROM.

Engage your brain

Finally, you must always remember to *engage your brain in the business of communicating*. It may help to bring your imaginary listener into play – concentrate on what they need to know, and how they are reacting to what you are saying. If you can make that mindswitch from reading to telling, it can break a pattern as effectively as the more deliberate techniques you have practised.

SUMMARY

- Avoid imitating what you imagine are the 'rhythms' of broadcast speech.
- Never automatically stress the last word in a sentence unless it contributes to the sense of what you are saying.
- Air-check yourself regularly to make sure you are not slipping into a predictable rhythm or pattern.
- Make sure your *emotional tone* is appropriate.
- Practise 'headlines' to get the trick of varying your intonation.
- Always engage your brain.

9 The words – and the pictures

Writing for the voice – some simple guidelines for broadcast grammar and language that should make you sound better on air. How the choice of words can influence your relationship with the listener/viewer. Script layout for easy delivery; reading scripts from a computer screen. And is there a difference between the way you use words in TV and radio?

No manual on the broadcast voice would be complete without some space devoted to consideration of how the way a script is written influences the ease with which it can be delivered. It's not just the words you choose – their structure is important too. (Which of the two preceding sentences is easiest to read aloud?)

I am not going to embark on a full guide to writing for broadcast. There are already many excellent textbooks that cover the subject. But there are some basic principles that need reinforcing, because they have a direct effect on how easy it is for your voice to transform words on a page into a convincing broadcast.

A broadcast writing style is fundamentally different from the way you would write for print. One is for the ear; the other is for the eye.

The reader of a newspaper or book has more than one chance at understanding what the words convey. They can go back, over and over, until they pick up the sense. But in broadcasting, the listener or viewer only has one chance at grasping the point, at the instant of transmission. Even if they are so dedicated as to record a broadcast, or revisit it through the Internet, they are most unlikely to shuttle to and fro using the rewind and pause buttons. The moment comes and is gone. They have either got it, or missed it.

So it follows that the language and grammar you use, in both radio and television, must be simple enough for them to 'get it'. Unfamiliar words that they might need to look up in a dictionary are out. So are convoluted grammar and sentences so long that they have forgotten the point made at the beginning, by the time you laboriously struggle to the end.

WRITING FOR THE EAR AND VOICE

When writing for the ear, short sentences and simple words work best. They give the listener/viewer the best possible chance to follow what you are saying.

But you should also think of yourself as writing for the *voice*. By now you will be superbly in control of your breathing, if you have worked through Chapter 4. But you will also recognize that where and how often you can fill your lungs is an important consideration for the broadcaster. If you write short simple sentences, you are making it much easier for yourself to breathe.

Simple words

It is a good idea to avoid unfamiliar words, however much you want to show off your impressive vocabulary. You probably haven't often heard that word spoken aloud. Are you sure you know how to pronounce it correctly?

Let's take for instance two words which mean broadly the same thing: 'emaciated' and 'thin'. There is a subtle difference in the meaning. 'Emaciated' means *abnormally* thin, conjuring up an unhealthy, skeletal image, and there will be times when you want that extra layer of meaning. But many people misuse 'emaciated', when the word 'thin' would do perfectly well. Thin has one syllable, but emaciated has five. That's five times as much breath, five times as many different sounds to get your lips and tongue around. And do you really know how it is pronounced – 'ee-may-ciated', or 'emm-ass-iated'? (If you don't know, go and look it up.) You're going to sound pretty stupid if you get it wrong.

Here's a simpler example: 'however', and 'but'. Both mean exactly the same thing. As a general rule, always use 'but', because it's shorter. Less breath is required, so you can maintain a stronger sound.

English is a particularly rich language because it has developed from several different sources. After the Norman Conquest, three different languages were in use: upper-class French, the Anglo-Saxon spoken by ordinary people, and an administrative/Church language, Latin – the language in which learned people wrote. All three began to mix, so we often have several different words that can do pretty much the same job, though sometimes with subtle shifts in meaning – 'emancipated', 'liberated', and 'free', for instance. The traditional advice is to avoid 'Latinate' words – words that came originally from Latin – and use instead words with good old Anglo-Saxon roots, which tend to have less syllables. Nowadays, when Latin is rarely taught in schools, I doubt if many people know how to spot a word with Latin roots. But broadly the principle is you shouldn't use a long word, when there is a shorter one that will do the job, and you shouldn't use a posh one when there is a better word in more common use.

It's a hard lesson for those of us who are proud of our command of language, and like to show it off. But you can still be creative with language, while restricting yourself to simpler words with fewer syllables. Take the word 'recognize'. Could you replace it with 'grasp'? You can still make good broadcast writing rich, even when it's crisp.

Here's an example of how *not* to do it. You can hear this, and other examples from the text, on the CD-ROM, in the section on **script problems**.

Beneficial tax concessions have been announced for working parents. The new allowance, payable to families whose offspring are under school age, is designed to assist with their expenditure on childcare. The Chancellor of the Exchequer gave it as his opinion when he addressed the House of Commons today that this would make it economically feasible for more family units to avoid being entrapped in the benefits system.

Simple grammar

Grammar is not much taught in schools today. I am genuinely glad today's pupils don't have to go through some of the tedious torment my generation suffered, parsing sentences to mark up the subordinate clauses, and looking for the correct use of the subjunctive. But a basic understanding of grammar is useful to grasp how words hang together.

You don't need an intimate knowledge of grammar to be able to write for broadcast. No one is going to actually care if you split an infinitive, as I have just done, apart from a few old fogies who have a bee in their bonnets about it. On the other hand, don't you dare say 'different to' in my hearing – it's 'different from'! We all have our particular grammatical obsessions, but many of these are so frequently ignored in everyday speech that it really doesn't matter if you break some of the supposed rules of written English – like starting a sentence with 'but' or 'and'.

But what you do need to know is what to avoid – over-complicated constructions.

Subordinate clauses are the main peril. You are trying to cram so many facts and ideas into the sentence that you end up with an impossible long and tottering structure, full of little asides hanging off each other like branches and twigs on a tree, with a new thought here, which is meant to reinforce your main point, that is followed by a particularly striking metaphor that just occurred to you, another aside there (not to mention the odd phrase in brackets) that makes the whole thing so difficult to follow that ... So where *was* I going with that train of thought?

Here are two versions of the same story. You can hear and compare them on the CD-ROM, in the section on **script problems**:

1. The Chancellor of the Exchequer today announced in the House of Commons new tax concessions for working parents, which are designed to lift more people out of the benefits trap,

if they have children under school age, and have to pay for child care, though it is not intended, the Chancellor said, to cover the cost completely, but rather to go some way if they can towards helping poorer parents who would otherwise have to stay at home rather than work when they would actually prefer to have a job and not be a burden on the state.

2. Working parents will get a tax cut to help with the cost of childcare. The Chancellor of the Exchequer today announced a new allowance for families with children under school age. He said the cut would lift more households out of the benefits trap.

Don't ramble; it's too difficult to follow. And it's too hard to say in one breath. Keep it short. If it's a new thought, start a new sentence. Avoid too many 'whichs' and 'thats'. They signal the beginning of the dread subordinate clause, which is what this is – often a clumsy construction. Put in a full stop instead.

Computer grammar checkers, which operate by rules known only to themselves, will not help you greatly. When I write for broadcast, they tend to pop up saying 'Fragment, consider revising.'

But isn't it 'conversational' to ramble?

It's true that some people speak conversationally in long sentences, and include many different thoughts. It is possible to get away with a long sentence in real conversation, because your listener has the opportunity to interrupt and ask you to explain what you mean if they have lost your drift.

In broadcasting, we create only an illusion of conversation. (See Chapter 6.) You must make sure that your listener/viewer can follow easily, so you must keep sentences and thoughts short, simple, and clear.

Contractions and apostrophes

In everyday speech, we often contract or elide words that would more formally be separated.

- *It is* becomes *It's*
- *It is not* becomes *It isn't*
- *will not* becomes *won't*
- *did not* becomes *didn't*
- *I have* becomes *I've*... and so on.

I've been writing for broadcast so long that it's now become remarkably hard to write without contracting. It should become an automatic process for you, too. If you don't remember to write contractions in from the start, you and anyone else who has to deliver your script will have to make an extra effort to remember to contract as the words are spoken aloud.

HOW SIMPLE LANGUAGE HELPS YOUR RELATIONSHIP WITH YOUR LISTENER

It is obvious really. Using big words and complex grammar has a distancing effect for the people you are talking to. It makes you sound as if you are over-keen to impress, or unnecessarily formal. When you use everyday words, the sort you would use while talking to friends, it becomes easier to visualize yourself talking to one person, and reinforces your own sense of connection with the listener/viewer.

I don't mean that you should talk down to your audience. You don't want them to think you are using words of one syllable because you believe they are not capable of understanding anything more complex. Longer words are not utterly forbidden, so long as you think you would use them in everyday conversation.

Even Radio Four, the last bastion of the intellectual in broadcasting, encourages its presenters not to use over-clever words, unless there is a good reason for it. Most of its listeners probably understand what 'hegemony' means. But it's an academic word and not often used in ordinary conversation. On some programmes, like *Analysis*, you might use it to convey a very specific meaning. On the *Today* programme, which attracts a wider audience, you would be more likely to say 'leadership'.

LAYOUT – HOW IT LOOKS AFFECTS HOW YOU SAY IT

Most people don't consider the layout and typography as they hammer their script into the computer. But what you see on the page can have a big influence on your ability to read it fluently and intelligently.

Punctuation

Punctuation is the written equivalent of a set of instructions for the voice. A full stop says 'breathe here'. A dash or a comma tells you either to breathe, or to pause, because it separates two thoughts.

If you are writing scripts for other people to read please remember to include some intelligent punctuation even if you think you can get away without it.

Or preferably: If you are writing scripts for other people to read, please remember to include some intelligent punctuation, even if you think you can get away without it.

The second version is much easier for a broadcaster to pick up and read aloud. They know immediately where they can breathe, and it is much easier to absorb the sense at a glance. Including punctuation makes a script much safer to deliver if, for instance, the broadcaster won't have a chance to look at the script beforehand, and has to sight-read.

I also get, irrationally mad, with people, who put commas, in the wrong, places. Or ... people who decide to use dots instead ... thinking that this makes it easier to read ... because it doesn't.

As a print-literate species, our brains have learnt to pick up messages from typography. Dots don't work as substitutes for commas, because ... conveys a subtly different message. It tells you a long pause for thought is in order ... a trailing off ... and so your voice may trail off too ...

If you have some allergy to using commas, try the humble dash instead. It doesn't convey quite the same message to the brain as a comma, but it's near enough to work. It says: 'Short pause – you can breathe if you need to.' Personally, I'd rather have a comma in most circumstances, because I think a dash indicates a breaking off, and it can make your spoken style a bit jerky and staccato. If I am writing a script for myself, I use dashes when I want to indicate a change of gear, but I use commas more frequently. A dash for me is close to being the modern equivalent of a semi-colon; most people have forgotten how to use these, but they indicate two thoughts that are connected, yet could almost be separated by a full stop.

I would advise against using semi-colons and colons to punctuate scripts. They are less common even in print, and most people aren't sure how to use them. Besides, they are harder to see than a dash or full stop.

Avoid upper case

It isn't only punctuation that sends subtle signals to the brain. Consider what happens if you see something written in CAPITALS. We are used to reading printed material where upper case either indicates a heading or a shout. So the temptation is to SHOUT the word at the listener.

There is a worrying trend in some Independent Local Radio (ILR) newsrooms either to print the whole script in capitals – MAYBE THEY WANT THEIR NEWSREADERS TO SHOUT THE WHOLE BULLETIN – or to print SELECTED words in CAPITAL letters, the selected words presumably being those that the news writer decided needed extra STRESS.

As I have already pointed out, you can emphasize without shouting. Indeed, it is better that you don't shout. There is also the danger that the sub, perhaps a desk journalist who has never read a bulletin on air, may have picked the *wrong* words to emphasize. You should work out for yourself what needs stress and signposting rather than have it dictated for you.

Underlining

Underlining a word has much the same effect. It makes you want to thump it, which is why I try to avoid heavy underlining, even if I am marking up a script for signposting.

If you must mark a script in some way, use instead a broken line. It doesn't draw the eye quite so insistently, and doesn't lead the voice into stridency.

Page layout

The way you lay out the **page** can have an effect too. This is worth remembering, especially if you are prone to stumble.

If you try following a line across the whole width of an A4 page, your eyes will have to move to reach the end of the line. Unless you have truly extraordinary peripheral vision, you won't be able to see the beginning of the next line at the same time; you will have to flick your eyes back to find it. As you do this, you may accidentally slip a line. Your brain will spot that you've skipped over a line before your mouth starts to speak, and your eyes will shift up quickly to the right line before you have even consciously registered that you almost made a mistake – but it can be enough to distract you into a stumble without realizing why it has happened.

So the shorter the lines of type, the easier they are to read. Breaking a solid mass of text into short paragraphs also helps. You should allow margins of at least one and a half inches.

In 1988, the quiet Cornish town of Camelford was at the centre of Britain's worst ever water poisoning.

On Wednesday 6th of July, a driver from a chemical supply company set out for the Lowermoor water treatment works, on the moor just above Camelford. His job was to deliver twenty tons of aluminium sulphate solution, a chemical used in small quantities to clean water.

He was a relief driver and had never been to Lowermoor. There was no one on duty at the works, no signs to tell him which tank to fill, and the key opened all the padlocks on the site. Twenty tons is a

month's supply of aluminium sulphate. He dumped
the lot into the wrong tank.

In the days before computers (when in some departments there
were actually secretaries who typed out the scripts for you!) it
was common practice to set up the margins on the typewriter so
that the script only occupied a relatively narrow portion of the
page, usually about half its width. With the advent of computers,
this ceased to be standard practice. Because computers tend
to start from a standard layout, perhaps people weren't sure how
to alter the margins and tended to go with what the computer
dictated.

Television-style scripts are often easier to work from. Because they
contain information about pictures too, they are often laid out with
the visuals down the left side of the paper, the words on the right.
There are many variations on this theme, but you can set up a table
to lay out the script in this way.

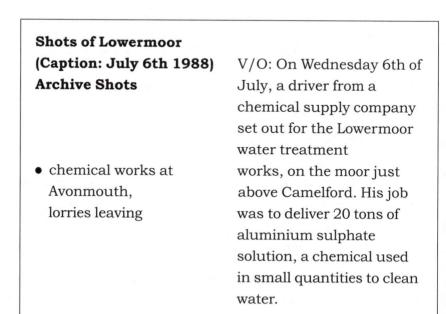

Shots of Lowermoor	
(Caption: July 6th 1988)	V/O: On Wednesday 6th of
Archive Shots	July, a driver from a
	chemical supply company
	set out for the Lowermoor
	water treatment
• chemical works at	works, on the moor just
Avonmouth,	above Camelford. His job
lorries leaving	was to deliver 20 tons of
	aluminium sulphate
	solution, a chemical used
	in small quantities to clean
	water.
	(See next page)

• padlock, manhole covers, pumps, aluminium sulphate tank	He was a relief driver and had never been to Lowermoor. There was no-one on duty at the works, no signs to tell him which tank to fill, and the key opened all the padlocks on the site.
Water Treatment Shots Diagram of System	Twenty tons is a month's supply of aluminium sulphate. He dumped the lot into the wrong tank.

The above is an extract from a working script for a retrospective documentary. During the edit it underwent many transformations, to improve the script. When it came to the voice-over, most of the visual information was removed from the left hand side, to make it less distracting. But the shorter lines of a script laid out like this make it much easier to read.

Spacing

I also increase the line spacing for a script. Single spaced text is much harder to read aloud. Use double line spacing, and a large clear font.

The print should stop well above the bottom of the page, so that you won't have to look down and go off-mic. Don't split sentences between two pages.

Computer screen layout

Increasingly, broadcasters have to get used to working on air from computer screens. In television, autocue has been in use for so long that the system has become refined and easy to use. Unfortunately in radio, reading from a screen is still relatively new, and sometimes not enough thought has gone into the layout on the screen. You may not even be able to make changes to it.

You can always lobby for changes in the system to make it easier for you to read from a screen. Increasing the type-size may help, and can stop you from leaning forward to peer at the screen. A different font can improve your performance. If possible, make sure that the lines on the display are not too long and the screen is not cluttered with other unnecessary information.

Reading from screen is a useful tool in getting last minute changes or new information direct to the presenter, although there have been some teething troubles with new systems, causing them to crash on air and leave the presenter wordless! Many presenters in radio still prefer to work from a paper script, which they can scribble on if they need to make a sudden change – even those who are used to working from autocue in television.

Corrections

If you have to make last minute additions or corrections, make them clearly. A script that has been changed at the last minute by scribbling all over it can be difficult to read and is often the cause of stumbling. When you make lengthy corrections to a paper script, it is often better to rewrite the whole section on a new sheet, rather than making corrections over the lines and in the margins.

WRITING TO PICTURES

Is there a difference between the way you write for television and the way you write for radio? For both, the general principles hold true: short sentences, simple language and construction.

But because television relies on pictures as the primary information carriers, writing for television is subtly different from writing for radio. In radio, you write to *create* pictures in the mind of the listener. In television you write to *explain* the pictures that are in front of the viewer.

So generally, television writing needs to be more sparse and economical than radio. You don't want the words to distract from the pictures. They must be utterly to the point, and as simple as possible, because the viewer's brain is processing information from two sources – visual and aural. The eyes tend to take precedence over the ears, so less than half the viewer's attention is going to be on your words.

In the television documentary script we have already looked at, for instance, it would be no use writing a long discourse on precisely how the aluminium sulphate at Camelford reacted with the minerals already present in the water and pipes to form a cocktail of highly toxic chemicals, then deliver it over a picture sequence of a woman walking through the daffodils in the town park. The words need to complement the pictures, and vice versa. Your voice-over will be lost to the viewer if it goes over strong visual images that do not match, and draw attention away from the sense of the words.

Nor should you use a flowery voice-over crammed with adjectives to describe a picture the viewers can see for themselves. Your task is to supplement the pictures with a few well-chosen words.

This is not easy to do. I love words, and have to forcibly restrain myself when writing for television. I go through my scripts ruthlessly slashing out adjectives. Adjectives create pictures, and you don't want to create a picture to muddle the viewer, who is already looking at one on the screen. Give them facts, simple unadorned facts, as Mr Gradgrind from Dickens' *Hard Times* might have said, had he been a TV producer.

Exercise 9.1: Writing to pictures

Here are two different versions of a piece of television commentary:

FERN SETT – CUBS PLAYFIGHTING	*V/O*: These cuddly cubs are doing what comes naturally – playing at fighting each other. Ouch! That was a nasty nip.

CU cub biting the other, draws blood	It's drawn blood. In this leafy glade, their mock battles will help them learn how to wade in with claws and teeth to
CU claws	ensure their survival. Badgers are fiercely
WIDE SHOT glade, large adult badger in mouth of sett watches cubs playing	territorial creatures – a male badger has to fight tooth and nail to establish his dominance in the hierarchy of the sett.

FERN SETT – CUBS PLAYFIGHTING	*V/O*: Badgers are natural fighters.
CU cub biting the other, draws blood,	Even as cubs, their play can get rough.
CU claws	
WIDE SHOT glade, large adult badger in mouth of sett	They're territorial creatures – a male badger has to fight to win his place in the sett.

Which do you prefer? Which do you think explains the pictures better? And which is easiest to read? Try recording both versions.

The second version, though sparse, gives all the information that is needed to understand the pictures. It is paced to allow the viewer time to absorb the visuals, rather than covering every second of the footage, as the first script does. And its plainness makes it much easier to deliver.

Now let's imagine the same subject in a **radio** documentary. No pictures except the ones you create with your words, and the judicious use of a few rustles and squeaks, which you recorded on your trusty mini-disc or DAT recorder on location.

> Amongst the rain-drenched ferns in an Exmoor wood, two badger cubs are at play. They look cuddly, but their claws are out. As they roll and tumble in the glade, sharp teeth nip, drawing blood and yelps of pain. One retires hurt to the cover of the bracken. Then he pounces, and chases his brother into the darkness of the trees. These mock battles prepare them for adult life. Badgers are territorial creatures, and fierce fighters. There's no place for weakness or timidity in the sett.

You can see how the radio version uses many more picture words – not only adjectives, but also active verbs like 'pounce', 'roll and tumble', and 'nip'. Even in a radio script, where the right adjective can create a picture, be careful how you use them. The more adjectives, the more breath you need! Sometimes a verb can create the same effect more economically.

In an earlier version of the script, I wrote '... chases his brother into the *steamy* darkness of the trees'. I wanted to add to the picture I was creating and convey the sense of a warm summer evening after rain. But in the final draft it came out. It was an unnecessary detail, and two extra syllables in an already long phrase, soaking up precious breath.

Notice also how none of the sentences exceeds two lines, and many are less than a line long, so they are easy to say on a single breath. Use a mix of sentence lengths, though, to avoid setting up a rhythm or a pattern in the writing.

AVOIDING RHYTHMS AND PATTERNS

In Chapter 8, I explained how important it was to avoid rhythms and patterns in your intonation. So you must also be careful that the writing does not unconsciously lead you that way.

I once taught a client who seemed totally incapable of lifting her delivery out of a rhythm. It was extremely monotonous. Seizing the script in a fit of frustration, I shouted: 'Here, let me show you ...' and instantly discovered that I could hardly avoid falling into the same trap. Every sentence was neatly constructed in two halves, and it was almost impossible to avoid going up in the first half, then down in the second.

> In a leafy glade, two badger cubs are at play. They look cuddly, but the claws are out. As they roll and tumble, sharp teeth draw blood. One retires hurt, and seeks the cover of the trees. Then he pounces, and chases his brother away. These are mock battles, preparing for adult life. Badgers are territorial creatures, fierce in war. There's no place for weakness, when they leave the sett.

Can you see how this altered version of the badger script sets up a monotonous rhythm for your voice?

Each sentence is a similar length. Each has two parts, with the pause falling close to the centre of the sentence. And almost every sentence ends on a one-syllable word. An unconscious writing pattern like this becomes monotonous and can lull the listener into a doze.

> Record a version of each of the badger scripts for radio. See which sounds best. Then – as you are by now an expert in the private life of badger cubs – write your own version.

SUMMARY

- Be economical with words, so you can be economical with breath when speaking them. Short sentences, simple language, simple grammar.

- Avoid too many subordinate clauses.
- Avoid long words when there is a better, shorter one you could use.
- Don't write yourself words you are not sure how to pronounce.
- Use punctuation to help your breathing and intonation.
- Lay out your script with care – shorter lines, clear type, open spacing, break it into paragraphs.
- Radio writing creates pictures, TV writing explains them.
- Be sparing with adjectives, even in radio writing.
- Avoid unconscious rhythms and patterns.

10 Ad lib

> *Not all programmes are scripted. A broadcaster who comes to rely on always having a script could one day run into trouble. Sooner or later the unexpected happens, and you find yourself having to make it up as you go along. As well as getting you out of a tight spot, learning to ad lib can make your delivery more natural.*

I want to start this chapter with an exercise. Before you read any further, since you should now know how to compose tight, well-honed scripts for radio and TV, I would like you to do some writing. Don't spend too long agonizing over it but jot down a minute's worth of scripted material. The topic can be anything you like – preferably something you know about, of course!

In the early days of broadcasting, the airwaves were stuffed with what were called 'talks'. They were an opportunity for worthy persons to pontificate on the subject of their choice, but they were always scripted, and that is what I want you to do now – write a short talk for radio.

You might occasionally hear a 'talk' on speech radio – *From Our Own Correspondent* is an example – but they are rare now. Their demise came about because the people who were invited to give them were often remarkably bad at delivering them. Some bright spark spotted that you actually get better results if you interview experts, rather than letting them drone on at length. You of course will not drone, because you know how to write well for broadcast and how to lift a script off the page.

Exercise 10.1: From script to ad lib

When you have finished writing your talk, sit in front of the microphone and record it. Don't play it back yet.

Now glance back over the script, and note in your head the important points you were trying to get across. The subject matter should be fresh in your mind, so you won't need to make written notes. Set the script aside, start the recorder going again and tell the same story, ad lib, off the top of your head. Don't try to reproduce exactly what you wrote. The point of this exercise is to get away from the written word, and give you practice in broadcasting without a script. If you try to remember exactly the words you used before, you will come unstuck. So concentrate instead on the ideas you want to communicate, telling the story in a fresh way.

At first, you may feel awkward but it is worth persevering. Have more than one go at doing it, if that helps, but don't cheat by starting to memorize the words. Afterwards, listen back to the two versions, the scripted and the ad lib, and assess their relative merits. Which do you prefer?

This exercise I have stolen unashamedly from a wonderful voice coach called David Dunhill, who taught me when I began to broadcast. It is a really useful one, because it teaches you a number of different things. It may have revealed to you, as it did to me when I first tried it, that you actually sound better ad lib than scripted. Paradoxically, my ability to communicate *scripted* material also improved dramatically, because I finally realized the difference between reading and talking, and how it affects your voice.

It may also have revealed that your broadcast writing is not yet as good as it could be. When you hear the freshness of the way you express the story without the script, you may realize that you are still over-writing or using non-conversational language.

Or it may have shown you that dropping the script is a wonderful liberation. You might be a little hesitant at the moment, but with practice you can see it is possible to broadcast without that safety net.

Of course, I may be a little over-optimistic here. You may have hated every moment of the exercise, muttered and stumbled your way through some rambling load of old codswallop, and be all the more convinced that you are never, ever going on air without a proper script. In which case you have still learned a valuable lesson. Maybe you are just not one of nature's ad libbers, and you should never attempt that more modern staple of broadcasting, the two-way. But I doubt it. You just need more practice.

WHY YOU MUST OVERCOME YOUR FEAR OF AD LIBBING

Technology fails, and the computer screen goes blank. Fate intervenes, and a passing whirlwind snatches your script out of your hand and scatters the pages. The unexpected happens: as you are on air, delivering a carefully prepared voice-piece live into the programme, a man across the street goes berserk and starts shooting passers-by. Do you run for cover? Well, yes, but you carry on broadcasting, live and ad lib.

There are many situations in broadcasting where you would sound completely wrong if you were scripted, or where it is impossible to script. Today, people would laugh at a DJ who scripted his or her entire music show. (Yet so nervous was I as a fledgling presenter that this is exactly what I did with my first record request programme. It sounded terribly stilted.) Local radio presentation is generally ad lib, though there may be written lead-ins to cue in interviews and packages. In both television and radio, breaking news sometimes means you must depart from the script and wing it.

Live, your ad lib broadcast should capture the flavour of the event as it happens. You cannot commentate on a sports match or a Royal visit with a script in your hand. By all means make a few notes. It helps, for a start, when you have to remember who the goalkeeper is and which team he used to play for, or the name of the small girl presenting the bouquet to the Royal Personage. I remember one of my colleagues, tasked with commentating for radio on a Royal visit to Bristol. In suitably hushed tones, he described the youngster making a graceful curtsey: '... and now she is handing Her Majesty a bouquet.' (*small pause*) 'A bouquet...' (*longer pause*) ' – appropriately enough ...' (*very long pause*) ' – of flowers.'

Yes, it is helpful to make a few notes.

PLANNING AD LIBS

When restaurants advertise 'coffee ad lib' at the bottom of their menus, they don't actually mean that you can go on all night drinking the stuff. Nor should you imagine that talking ad lib means you can go on waffling endlessly.

The best ad libs are almost always planned in some way. There are a very few gifted people – I suspect the comedian Paul Merton is one – who can genuinely come up with brilliantly funny remarks, totally spontaneously, over and over again. But most of us aren't so lucky. We need a framework and a bit of advance planning before we can sound relaxed, concise, and witty.

I am not suggesting you should rehearse your jokes to the point where they come out so pat the audience suspect you have learned them by heart. Really funny remarks often are spontaneous, and as unexpected to the person making them as they are to the listener. But there is nothing worse than listening to a broadcaster in free fall, going on and on and on, rambling and tumbling through the skies of his or her imagination and basically never saying anything except the first inane thing that floats into the head.

Get a parachute. Get some control. Plan what you might say.

You can always diverge from the plan. But if you know at least what you could say, you have a framework to fall back on if you get in a tangle.

Planning for live commentary

There is a sod's law for live commentaries. The more momentous the occasion, the more likely you are to screw up.

If only my poor colleague at the Royal visit had thought to equip himself with a few more details about the presentation of the bouquet. Jotting down the name of the flowers might have helped, given that he was so horticulturally challenged. But he could also have provided himself with some background about the youngster curtseying to the Queen. Where did she go to school? Why had she been chosen?

In fairness, live commentary on a Royal visit is not an everyday task, and is a difficult one. In the nature of such occasions time-tables fall to pieces so that you may find yourself having to talk for far longer than anticipated. So it is always wise to prepare much more material than (you hope) you will ever need. Write down names, because they will inevitably fly out of your head. Keep your notes in a handy form – index cards are useful – where you won't have to scrabble through them to find a fact or name.

For any live commentary, your job is to give people a flavour of the occasion. On radio, you must describe what you see. You are the listener's eyes and you must paint pictures for them. On television, it would be tiresome to be so descriptive, because the viewers can see for themselves. Your job instead is to tell them what they can't see: what's about to happen, or background details of the event. The good commentator arms him or herself with an encyclopaedic knowledge of related trivia: from the entire career history of the people taking part, to how many tons of manure will have to be cleared up after the horses in the procession have passed by. If it is a sports match, you need to turn yourself into an instant expert on the players or competitors. Any detail, from the striker's goal average to the imminent birth of his first child, can come in handy when there is a lull.

If all else fails during a live commentary, there is always the good old standby: 'So let's pause, for just a moment, to absorb the atmosphere of this awe-inspiring occasion...'. In fact, whether it is television or radio, it pays occasionally to let the pictures or the sounds of a live event speak for themselves.

But be warned. We all make gaffes under pressure, and inevitably one day you will too. The trick is to recover as if nothing had happened, continue with aplomb, and not beat yourself up while you're still on air over whatever crass remark you happen to have let slip. The editor will do that for you once you return to base.

On the same Royal visit, another colleague was positioned on the roof of the railway station to wrap up the live broadcast as the Queen's train left for her next destination. In the excitement of the moment, he began his summary of the day's events with the words: 'And as the Queen slips slowly away from under me...'.

Is that a treasonable offence?

Planning for ad lib in the studio

Ad lib has to sound spontaneous, and it may look that way to the outside observer. We've all seen presenters who wander into the studio two minutes before the show begins, carrying nothing but a pile of discs and a running order scribbled on the back of an old envelope.

But this nonchalant ease is not quite so effortless as you might imagine. Before the mic opens, they know what they are going to say. While each piece of music is playing they are not only setting up for the next item, but deciding how they will introduce it, sometimes scribbling a note or two, more often just fixing the ideas in their head.

The better ones always keep it simple. Each link will be no more than a couple of pithy thoughts, to keep up the pace. If they decide to talk about, say, last night's television, they will do it in no more than two or three sentences. 'Did you see that documentary on the couple who moved to Spain? What were they thinking of, starting a pet's beauty parlour? I give them a year – then they'll be back with their tails between their legs ... Ten past four, the lines are open, call us on ...' And within half a minute, the phone lines will be flashing, the text messages flooding in, giving them more fresh material.

Those little broadcasting mantras, the oft-repeated phrases like the time-check, the phone-in number, the address of the web-site, can really help. You know them by heart (or you should) and they give you thinking time as you move on to the next topic. They carry you through the gear changes of the programme.

Of course, you must be careful not to over-use them or they become irritating. During the normal course of the day, resist the temptation to time-check between every item. I have even heard nervous presenters managing to do it twice within the same link. The only programme where you should be really generous with time-checks is the breakfast show, when many of your listeners will be using the radio as a clock to keep them on time as they stumble blearily through their getting up routine.

I discussed in Chapter 6 how the critical moment for the ad lib presenter is when he or she has to move seamlessly from ad libbing to reading a scripted lead-in or cue sheet. If you have not read this chapter yet, go back and do so now. It is important not to spoil the flow of your programme by sounding as if you have just picked up a piece of paper to which you have given only a cursory glance. The audience should not be able to tell the difference between your ad libs and your reads, so if you really cannot manage to lift a script off the page it is better to dispense with it and talk from notes. But you should keep it at least as concise as the script, and you will waffle unless you work it out in advance.

Taking a deep breath – a pause for thought – is often a better way of moving between two items than trying to compose a convoluted link. I always cringe when I hear a presenter beginning a sentence with the words: '... And talking of...' I know that some horribly torturous connection is about to be made between two topics that are almost certainly not related. It is not necessary. When you change the subject in ordinary conversation, you can almost always do it by just taking a beat – then launching into the new topic, changing the inflexion of your voice rather than wasting words trying to make a spurious bridge.

You could think of it as the way a newsreader moves between items in a bulletin. You will never hear the words: 'And talking of financial matters, today the Chancellor launched his new Budget...' or 'And since we're on the subject of war, last night there was a border skirmish between India and Pakistan...' What the newsreader does is use a pause, then a change in the intonation pattern either to indicate it is a related story (which will often begin low then move up in pitch) or a wholly new subject (which may begin high then come down). You can use the same economical voice technique when you are ad libbing.

I hope as you ad lib you will be mindful of the invisible presence of your personal listener or viewer. Remembering to talk to them will actually make it easier, because it relaxes you and stops you worrying so much about getting the words out.

THE PIECE-TO-CAMERA

You may be surprised to find advice on the piece-to-camera (PTC) in a chapter on how to ad lib. Many broadcasters imagine that the only way to do a good PTC is to write a short script and memorize the words.

I can promise you there is a better way, if only you can bring yourself to be brave enough to try it.

A PTC is the TV reporter or presenter's chance to shine. It is the moment when you stamp your presence and personality on the package or programme. You look the viewer straight in the eye through the channel of the camera lens and assert your ownership of the piece. Careers are made and broken during PTCs, so even if you loathe doing them it is worth taking the trouble to find out how to make them better.

Paradoxically, it is the urge to get them right that is often the presenter/reporter's undoing. The more you worry, the worse it gets. And so on for twenty or so takes.

Filming a PTC can be a fraught business. First, the director (if you are lucky enough to be working with one) may spend ages dithering about where you should stand, whether you should walk and talk, changing his or her mind several times. Then the cameraman or woman starts shoving their oar in, and almost invariably positions you so the sun is blazing straight into your eyes. Finally all is ready and you begin. Three words in, you stumble. 'Still rolling.' So you begin again. This time you are half way through and the sound recordist shouts 'Plane!' So you have to stop while some idiot in a microlight weaves his way across the sky. Finally he disappears, and you start again. 'Oops, my fault', says the camera. 'Got the focus wrong.' Next time the director's mobile phone rings. Then a lorry starts grinding its gears in the distance. Then the sun goes in half way through so the exposure is wrong. After many, many takes, you get right through to the end, but the director looks unhappy. 'I think you could do it...' You wait expectantly for guidance. 'Well, sort of ... *better.*' And so on.

But as they say, that's television – the process of winding a relaxed presenter up until he or she is a mass of jangling nerve fibres. You might as well get used to it. Unfortunately, if you add to the mix the responsibility of trying to reproduce a script word for word, you are only increasing the possibility of failure – and with failure comes loss of confidence, and with loss of confidence the ability to perform naturally flies out of the window.

Memorizing words is a knack that can be learnt by anyone. But although a skilled reporter can get quite good at it, the act of retrieving words from your memory can get in the way of a truly direct and fresh performance in front of the camera.

Tony Robinson is an actor who became a TV presenter. He has an actor's trained memory, so he should be able to remember the lines of a script better than most of us. But if you watch Tony doing a PTC, you will find that he rarely bothers to memorize the words. He concentrates on the ideas he wants to get across, and improvises, so each take will be subtly different. And indeed because of that there are far fewer takes needed, because he doesn't keep tripping himself up.

Directing a different presenter, I made the great mistake of writing the PTCs for her. Although she scribbled down a few changes to make the piece her own, our starting point was words on paper. Every time we filmed it took at least six or seven takes to get it right, always supposing there were no other interruptions like aircraft or small boys shouting 'Hello Mum!' (Once someone actually dropped his trousers and mooned in the background of the shot.)

On the third day, we were filming a sequence of walking shots, no words required. Suddenly my presenter stopped. 'Look at this!' she said with great excitement, pointing at what looked to me like a perfectly normal stretch of dry stone wall. 'Those are stones which have been shaped – they're probably from a Roman villa!' She was an archaeologist so she should know.

'Why don't you do a piece-to-camera?' I said. 'Right now – off the cuff.' She stood for a moment in thought. I could see her mentally ticking off the ideas, working out what she needed to explain. Nothing got written down. The camera rolled, she crouched by the wall and did a perfect first take, speaking for nearly a minute, explaining with great clarity what we had found and why it was so exciting.

It is often much easier to do a good PTC if you have not written down the words. Instead, simply run through a mental checklist of ideas. It also helps if you have something to do as you explain those ideas: something to point to, something to demonstrate. Those actions, if you rehearse them through once or twice as you speak (and you will have to rehearse the actions because the camera needs to know where you will be moving and pointing) will help fix the sense of the words in your head.

These 'spontaneous' PTCs will often prove to be the best once you get them back to the cutting room. They have a freshness that no carefully written PTC can ever reproduce. You should try wherever possible to avoid ever writing words on paper, because once the words hit the paper you will find it hard to stop yourself trying to learn them word for word.

Memorizing

Some people, though, refuse to be convinced that it is better not to learn a PTC word for word. So are there perhaps ways of improving your memory technique to make it easier to remember what you want to say, without getting that terrible, strained look of concentration on your face or doing umpteen takes?

As any old hand in the newsroom will tell you, the more you do it, the easier it gets to learn PTCs. But how successful you are may depend on how you go about activating your memory.

There are several different ways of committing something to memory. One used by many people is a process of 'seeing' the words, as if they were on a page in front of you. Although we imagine this is a trick that only people with a 'photographic' memory can pull off, in fact quite a lot of us use it to some extent. The true 'photographic' memory is one that can hold the image at a glance – one look and it is in the head. But if you learn words that are written on a sheet of paper, photographic memory or not, you will almost inevitably start to visualize the words on the page when you try to retrieve them from your memory.

The snag with this method is that effectively you are *reading* the words from a mental piece of paper. The effort of concentration involved can distract you from the act of communication, just as we saw earlier how *reading* from a script can distract you from *telling* the story.

A better way of memorizing words is by repeating them, preferably composing the piece without using paper to write it down. Here you will use a kind of 'muscle memory' to hold the words. Muscle memory is a way of retaining and retrieving actions without having to make a *conscious* effort to remember. You use this process when you 'remember' how to drive a car, how to ride a bicycle, or how to hold a knife and fork. You learnt those things by doing them over and over again, and you can achieve a similar effect by speaking the words over and over again. It is as if the speaking muscles of your lips, tongue and teeth subconsciously retain the pattern of movement. If you add other movements to the PTC – gestures, or stepping from point to another – it can help even more. But it is a process that can only work *if you don't think about it.* You must not try consciously to remember the words. You simply allow them to come back through the movements of your body.

A third possibility is to memorize by association. Once, in a mad moment that actually lasted for eighteen months, a friend and I set ourselves the task of learning the whole of Coleridge's poem *The Ancient Mariner.* (We thought it would be a good party trick, but strangely people seem to drift away when we offer to demonstrate.) We learned it as we hiked on Exmoor and the way I now remember the poem is by visualizing each of the places we walked, almost literally step-by-step.

To our surprise, we also discovered that the person who was *not* holding the book was the one who remembered each section most easily. I could probably work out even now which sections I learned by seeing the page (because I remember the look of the spelling and punctuation) and which I learned from the sound and feel of the words as I repeated them, and by associating them with aspects of the moody, bleak landscape around me. You can use the same technique when you do a PTC that involves demonstrating something, or talking about an object, by associating each line with a particular facet of the item or process. Giving yourself something to do in a PTC helps you remember what to say.

There's a myth among TV reporters that it is somehow more difficult to walk and talk. Not true: unless you are trying too consciously to 'remember'. The less conscious the acts of memorizing and remembering are for you, the easier you will find them. It doesn't matter if you change the words as you say them. That will make the PTC seem far more natural.

Focus

We have already touched on the point of focus for your voice. The more you can exploit that idea of the person *beyond* the camera, the more easily you will be able to lose your self-consciousness in front of it, and that will help you have the confidence to ad lib.

The worst thing you can do is let your eye get focused on the camera lens. That only serves to make you self-conscious – is my hair sticking up? Have I got lipstick on my teeth? Is the camera adding that mythical six pounds to my weight? One presenter once described to me her trick of talking to 'the little man inside the camera'. It sounded a shade whimsical to me – I've never been good at talking to elves – but it did the job for her, taking her *through* the lens to the person watching the programme. Others use the cameraman as their focus. 'If I can feel I've interested him, I feel I'm interesting the viewer.' For some people, the camera itself becomes a person. Or you can think of the camera as a doorway through which you walk into your viewer's living room.

The precise metaphor is not important; the **connection** is. Think of it as the same way that you look into and through a person's eyes to the intelligence within.

THE TWO-WAY

Two-ways – where a reporter on location chats live to the studio presenter to explain the background to a story – are used to get a more immediate, informal feel to the broadcast. They can bring a welcome freshness to news, and indeed to any live programme.

In principle, the reporter's role in a two-way is to ad lib, having thoroughly briefed him or herself on the subject. The studio presenter will begin by asking some pertinent question: 'So what's the atmosphere in Downing Street tonight, Sue?' and the reporter launches into an off-the-cuff description of events. The studio presenter will interject two or three more questions, and then the reporter wraps up with some suitably challenging thought for the viewers or listeners to chew on: '...but no matter what the outcome of the by-election, the Prime Minister may tonight be a worried man'.

The idea is that by speaking ad lib the reporter sounds more informal. It sounds more relaxed than the usual PTC, though the reporter may be using very similar words. The programme as a whole feels more like a team effort, with reporter and presenter interacting. It also offers the opportunity to explore a subject in more depth, and the viewers or listeners feel that they are privy to a back-ground briefing, the kind of real discussions that go on behind the scenes in news production offices or in the corridors of government. This is of course almost entirely an illusion.

For a two-way to succeed, there should be a considerable degree of advance planning. Not only must the reporter have at least some idea of how long they are expected to talk, they must also collabo-rate with the presenter (probably through the programme's producer) to make sure he or she does not spring on them an unexpected question to which they don't know the answer. The easiest way of arranging this is for the reporter to tell the presenter what questions to ask. 'You ask me what the Minister can do, and I'll say precious little, or words to that effect, then you come back and ask if the Government could fall, and I'll wrap it up.'

So the reporter can largely dictate the shape of the two-way. Some annoying presenters do like to chuck in a question of their own, but after a while you will learn to predict what those are likely to be and fence them adeptly: 'Well, John, I can't say whether the Prime Minister has approved the changes yet, but I can tell you that the Chancellor went into Number Ten earlier this evening and hasn't yet come out, so perhaps even as we speak those decisions are being made. But the real issue is whether or not the rest of the Party will go along with him ...'

It is essential to plan your answers thoroughly. The better you know what you must say, the more easily it will emerge from your lips. If time allows, and you are unused to two-ways, you may find it helps to write the whole interview down as if it were a scripted PTC or voice piece, with questions. But you should not work from this script, or you will lose the freshness that ad libbing gives the two-way. Instead, reduce your script to a set of headings, on a single sheet of paper, and work from those. You can even clutch them in your hot little hand, out of vision, to refer to if all else fails. It is won-derfully comforting to feel the notes are there as a safety net even though you will probably never need to look at them.

The real benefit of this technique is that writing it out, then reducing the script to note-form, is a way of fixing the ideas in your head. It helps you concentrate on the logical order of what you should say and takes some of the tension out of the process. You won't need to learn it off by heart, which would again put some of the formality of the PTC back into your delivery. You are simply focusing yourself so you can remember the gist of your piece.

Even if you work in radio, resist the temptation to work from a script. The point of a two-way is to get a fresh feel to your delivery and however good you are at reading from a script, there will still be a difference. You will also enjoy it much more if you ad lib. There is a wonderful, dangerous thrill to working live like this and getting it right.

But you must also consider the implications of getting it wrong. The real danger with the two-way is that in the heat of the moment, you do not always weigh carefully the words you are using. More than one reporter has lived to rue the day he or she decided to cover the story as a two-way, and inadvertently used a less than exact phrase that subsequently landed the broadcasting organization in trouble. Unless you are rock-certain of your facts and your phrasing, you should not risk doing a live ad lib two-way where there are likely to be legal or political ramifications to an injudicious use of words in the story.

TALKING TO TIME

Finally, a chance to try out a knack that has come to be regarded as one of live broadcasting's essential skills. If anyone were to compile a list of Great Scary First-Time Moments In Your Early Broadcasting Career, I would bet that somewhere near the top would come the first occasion you have to talk to time.

It isn't actually very difficult to talk to time, but there is something about the anticipation of it that brings you out in a cold sweat. So much seems to hang on getting it exactly right. But that's ridiculous. Will heads roll because you came out of your live report one second late? Is the world going to end because you crashed the pips or the news jingle? Of course not.

But broadcasters need to be perfectionists. Nearly right is never good enough. You could wait until you actually have to do it to discover whether you can or not. Or you could get in a bit of prac-tice now.

This is an exercise I devised for an experienced radio presenter who was nervous of getting it right on a national network – it's not just newcomers who suffer a terror of the process. 'I know I can do it, really', he said. 'I used to do it all the time on local radio. But the trouble is so many people listen to this programme, and I never know exactly when my co-presenter is going to finish speaking, and how long I will have to fill. Sometimes you have to go on for nearly a minute, and sometimes you only have five seconds before you hit the pips.'

The pips are an institution in British broadcasting. You don't hear the Greenwich Time Signal, as it is more properly known, so often on the airwaves today, but on Radio Four it still precedes most news bulletins on the hour. Some BBC local stations use them too. In the unlikely event that you have never heard the pips, tune in to Radio Four, because they have a part in the exercise. They consist of five short bleeps, marking each of the five seconds up to the hour, and a sixth long one on the hour itself.

You may never have to talk up to the pips. But if you work in TV, where timings of live programmes are exact, you need to get used to talking up to a predetermined 'out' point. In radio, you may have to hit precise junctions where your station joins another for shared news. DJs have to talk over the instrumental opening of a track without crashing the vocal. So talking to time, ad lib, is a useful skill to acquire.

The secret is preparation. Arm yourself with material that you can fill with. Let's suppose you are aiming for a junction. You need something like a written trail or weather you can sub-edit as you read, or the web-site address, or information on what's coming up after the news. Plan in advance your concluding sentence, the for-mula of words that will take you up to the junction (it may be a sta-tion ident and a time-check, or the name of the programme) and *know how long it will take you to say it*. Make sure you time it at an average, comfortable speed, so that you can always go a little faster or slower to stretch it to time.

When you have gathered all the material you need, try this exercise.

Exercise 10.2: Talking up to the pips

For the exercise, you will also need two other items: a friend, and a large clock with a clearly visible second hand. If you have access to a broadcasting studio, use the clock on the studio wall.

It is actually better to talk to time using an analogue clock rather than a digital one, because your brain doesn't have to struggle to calculate how much time is left – you can see. A sweeping second hand is much easier to follow than a set of numbers. In television, you will be given a verbal countdown from the gallery in your earpiece, or if you work on a programme where there is a floor manager they will use a set of hand signals. These can be a little tricky to follow at first – there's a tendency to try and count how many fingers the floor manager is holding up! – but after a while you get used to the rhythm of it.

Sit where you and your friend can both see the clock. Your friend acts as the timekeeper and determines how long you have to talk for, but should not give you any inkling of this in advance. When he or she cues you, perhaps as early as forty seconds before the pips, perhaps as late as ten seconds before, you will begin speaking. You must talk up to the moment when the pips would start, where the second hand reaches five seconds before the minute. At this point your friend may wish to imitate the pips – 'Pip! Pip! Pip! Pip! Pip! Peeep!!!' – to rub your nose in it if you have crashed them, or left an embarrassing silence.

If you try this a few times – and it is only fair to take turns, so you can impress or humiliate each other – you will soon get skilled at talking exactly to time. You can practise a television variation of this exercise where your friend counts you down verbally, or uses hand signals. Or you can adapt it in a radio studio where your partner will play in the news jingle on the appointed moment, as if you were joining another station at a junction.

LIVE AND DANGEROUS

As well as planning, there is another thing that can help you when you ad lib – the adrenalin rush of being live on air.

Adrenalin coursing through your body is a wonderful sensation. It is one of the hormones released when your brain perceives some sort of danger, designed to prepare your body for 'fight or flight'. You can capitalize on that hormone rush, because it causes something rather strange to happen to your mental processes. Everything seems to become much sharper and clearer. Time itself seems to slow down, giving you the opportunity to size everything up in a flash – it feels as if you are able to think much more quickly. You will find that being live triggers the swift thought processes needed for ad libbing. You make fewer mistakes and recover more quickly if something goes wrong. You become, literally, quicker witted.

But there is a downside. When you come off the air, you may find it is at first difficult to come down off that 'high'. Then gradually the world seems dull and flat and you can even start to feel rather depressed. It doesn't help that often your bosses forget to tell you how good the programme was, which is why broadcasters sometimes end up feeling bitter and unappreciated.

Don't just slump; go and tackle something purposeful, or head for the gym. Physical activity helps to disperse the stress hormones and makes you feel much better. And do remember that just as you feel down after giving your all on a live broadcast, so will your contributors. Don't forget to thank your interviewees and make them feel they were part of something special too.

SUMMARY

- Getting used to ad libbing will not only prepare you for the unexpected, it can also help you improve your writing and your delivery of scripted material.
- The best ad libs are usually planned.
- Make sure you know what you want to say, and have spare material to fill with for commentaries or talking to time.
- Be concise – less is more.
- Try not to learn PTCs word for word.
- Plan two-ways carefully, and use with caution!

11 Right at first sight

Sight-reading a script is something you should in theory never do. But once in a while you may have to. This chapter takes the fear out of it by suggesting ways of improving your ability to sight-read.

Like most broadcasters I know, I occasionally suffer from anxiety dreams. Not for us that familiar scenario of finding yourself out in the street stark naked, or going into an exam with no clue about the subject. We plunge into a nightmare world of studios where all the music has unaccountably disappeared from the CD player, or the script starts melting before our eyes. The typical dream finds me with a long and difficult script to read sight unseen, stumbling my way through it while some famous broadcaster sits sneering across the desk, eventually grabbing it from me and saying 'For goodness sake, *I'll* read it.' Which he does, perfectly. Usually at this point, I wake up and find the clock radio has switched itself on to the *Today* programme, which has somehow penetrated my dream. No wonder I can't get a word in edgeways.

MYTH, MAGIC, OR SOMETHING YOU CAN LEARN?

Sight-reading is one of the mysteries of broadcasting. Some people can do it without turning a hair. Others find it almost impossible. It is also one of the great unexamined myths of radio and TV. Many people will tell you that unless you can sight-read, you cannot consider yourself a broadcaster. Because of this far too many people imagine they are good enough at sight-reading to do it as a matter of course, rather than regarding it as a technique to be practised *only in the most extreme circumstances.*

To me it is the broadcasting equivalent of insisting on always riding bareback when there is a perfectly good saddle hanging in the stable. It would be useful to know how to do it, but riding saddle-less increases your chances of a sore backside, not to mention actually falling off the horse. If there is one thing that is guaranteed eventually to lead to disaster, it is the blasé broadcaster who imagines that there is no need to take a look at the script before he or she goes on air.

So you've been getting away with it for years, because you've got the knack? One day, you'll be merrily sight-reading away when to your horror you glimpse an unpronounceable foreign name popping up in the text. Or a typographical error that you just can't make sense of on the spot.

Even without these looming pitfalls, it is undeniably true that you will give a better performance if you have looked at the script – and ideally, *properly prepared it* in advance, as we discussed in Chapter 7. You should be making the time to think through and round the content and context, looking for the nuances and implications of the story, changing the words if necessary, deciding which ideas need signposting, and working out where you can afford to take a breath if someone (God forbid!) has written you an impossibly long sentence without benefit of commas or dashes.

This is not to say you should over-rehearse. Some people are 'first-take artists'; they sound fresher on the first attempt. But to get that first take right, you still need a good look at the script beforehand to understand it properly.

On the other hand, Carolyn Brown, an experienced network newsreader, will tell you that to get her best performance she has to read the script *aloud* at least once before going on air. She doesn't always have the opportunity to do that, because sometimes the news arrives at the last minute, but she will still always quickly scan it through to check for sense, pronunciation, and pitfalls.

Even if you wrote the script yourself, I still recommend that just before you broadcast, you run an eye over it, to remind yourself what you're trying to get across, and why you chose those words. Very often you will notice something that you might have expressed better, and this is your last chance for a quick rethink.

BUT WHAT IF YOU HAVE TO SIGHT-READ?

I would like to say that you should never, ever, sight-read a script. But that simply wouldn't be realistic. There are times when as you are on air a late news flash comes in. Carolyn Brown was reading the news on the day the Queen Mother died. She had only seconds to prepare, and once she was on air new pages of copy were being thrust under her nose for hour after hour, with hardly a moment to relax. So it happens – and you wouldn't want to screw up on a day like that.

Before we get on to discussing ways of helping you sight-read, though, first let's dismiss some of those common excuses used to justify sight-reading when it really isn't necessary. Most of them, I'm afraid, come from news journalists, amongst whom the practice of sight-reading is almost a matter of macho pride.

Excuse number one: '*I come on shift at six o'clock in the morning and I just have to grab the news and get in there.*'
Rubbish. Get in at five forty-five and give yourself a few minutes to look it over.

Excuse number two: '*The news copy comes down from London and doesn't appear until just before I'm due in studio.*'
Tell London they're being unhelpful. Or get your editor to tell them. Your newsroom system clearly needs an overhaul, because someone somewhere is being unprofessional. Breaking news is the only time you can justify leaving it till the last minute – and breaking news is a relatively rare commodity. Most news bulletins consist of huge swathes of rewrites and updates from the previous bulletin, and there's no real excuse for London not to be able to send it in time to give you a chance to look it through.

The same is true if your colleagues in the newsroom are writing it – tell them you need it at least five minutes before transmission. Or sit reading it over their shoulder as they type it frantically into the computer. They'll soon get the message if you keep breathing down their neck (particularly if you make sure to eat an especially smelly curry the night before).

If all else fails, read at least the first couple of stories as you make your way to the studio – though preferably not as you negotiate the stairs.

183

Excuse number three: '*On our station we put out two bulletins simultaneously for different areas and I have to record one immediately before going live with the second, which leaves me no time to read them through properly.*'
Tricky, I admit, and I'm glad I don't have your job, but it can be managed, assuming that like most news bulletins these days yours contains a fair bit of recorded material – packages and voice pieces. While these are on air you will have time to look through the next couple of stories.

On the other hand you might also be very brave and suggest to your news editor that he/she would get a better performance out of the newsreaders if they didn't have to work this system.

Excuse number four: '*I'm a DJ and the people manning the phones come rushing in with requests or lead-ins for packages while I'm on air.*'
Easy. You read them through while the music's playing.

Excuse number five: '*Everybody on our station does it, and they say you're not a true broadcaster until you can.*'
That may be one of the most pathetic excuses I have ever heard. Are you going to let them bully you into performing at less than your best? Of course it is useful to be able to sight-read, but it isn't the be-all and end-all of broadcasting. Some people do find it harder than others and you shouldn't be intimidated by your colleagues.

Excuse number six: '*I sound better when I sight-read.*'
Then I suggest it's time you got voice coaching, or studied this book with more attention, because something must be going seriously wrong with your delivery if it's better when you sight-read.

But sight-reading *is* a useful tool on certain rare occasions, so it would be unfair of me not to include some suggestions to help you develop the skill if you are having some difficulty with it.

READING FOR PLEASURE

Let me repeat that some people find it much easier to sight-read than others. It helps if as a child, you were encouraged to read aloud as often as possible. People who were always being picked to read aloud in class, for example, have much more confidence in their sight-reading abilities.

So my first suggestion would be simply that you practise reading aloud, preferably to your nearest and dearest to give the activity some point. For once, please don't inflict broadcasting scripts on them – this time I want you to find something to read that will give both of you pleasure in the act of reading and being read to. If you have kids, go back to reading them bedtime stories. If you have a partner, every night before snuggling up to sleep, read them a chapter of an entertaining book. If you are single, try impressing the cat with your reading. Join a play-reading group. Do good works in the community and read to blind people. Or just read aloud to yourself – stories, poetry, the newspaper, anything you can enjoy. Do it often. Make it a habit. You will soon find that your confidence grows.

BEWARE 'INSTANT' SOLUTIONS

Many people experience some degree of reading difficulty in their early life. It is not uncommon even to find broadcasters who are mildly dyslexic, and for these people sight-reading will always pose a difficulty. For this reason, I am always wary of schools of broadcasting – the sort which advertise in the back of newspapers and claim to be able to turn you into a top TV presenter over a single weekend – who also boast they can teach infallible sight-reading techniques. I have occasionally come across people who have tried such techniques and failed miserably, because they can't perceive the words on the page in the same way that the people teaching these methods do.

One such technique requires your eyes to be one line ahead while your mouth is actually saying the previous line. To develop this, you are taught to cover the line you are saying to force you to look at the next line – it's a sort of memory training test. I have to say that I experimented with this and fell to pieces immediately, even though I am a pretty good sight-reader. I came to the conclusion that I sight-read in a completely different way.

Though I will happily share with you my own technique, I would stress that it is by no means the only way of doing of it and I would hesitate to claim it will work for everyone.

THE 'FLASH' TECHNIQUE

I absorb the meaning as I read not in words or even lines, but in blocks. On an alert day, I would claim I can absorb as much as a paragraph at a time, but you will need to build up to this by starting more modestly. The point is to read ahead not as you are speaking but in the tiny pauses between sentences and paragraphs. You have to let each sentence flash into your brain, not reading it word by word, but focusing on the signposts, the ideas it contains. Think of your attention as a hard, concentrated beam of light, rather like the flash bulb in a camera, instantly illuminating the meaning. Or you could imagine it is a torch beam, wandering across the page, picking out the key ideas.

Exercise 11.1: Sight-reading the signposts

You can try this for yourself by looking at a piece of text. At this stage, don't attempt to read out loud yet. Cover the whole of the script, then reveal it first in sentence chunks, then a paragraph at a time. (I've laid out the text to help you by making the first couple of sentences single paragraphs.) See how much of the sense you can absorb by 'flashing' on one sentence, then on a whole paragraph. Give yourself a beat to take in each chunk. To help you do this, think back to the way we analysed the key ideas in a script, looking for the phrases that carry the meaning. You are doing exactly the same here, searching out 'signposts', skimming over joining words. The only difference is you are doing it faster, almost instantaneously.

When you have gone through the whole thing, cover it up, and write down as much of the gist of the story as you can remember. It's not a memory test, where you are expected to regurgitate it word by word – we are just looking for key points. Check back on the text and see how accurate your recollection was.

There was no time like it, and there were no fans quite like the Apple Scruffs – the fans who camped out on the steps of the Apple offices in London, waiting for their idols, the Beatles.

Phil Spector called them the most faithful fans in the music business, and Paul McCartney said they were the eyes and ears of the world.

They were so dedicated they devoted their days and nights to waiting for the Beatles. Rain or shine, they were always there – and in the end, a curious kind of friendship grew between them and their idols, summed up in the song George Harrison wrote about them.

This is their story – a story that spans a few brief years at the end of the Sixties and beginning of the Seventies. The tensions that would lead to the break up of the Beatles were just beginning to show, as they began to record the Abbey Road album.

You'll need to keep practising this on fresh pieces of text, so here are two further extracts from the same script. It is adapted from one written for a music documentary.

1:

Although there had always been girls who waited outside the Beatles' homes to meet them, the friendship that grew between Jill and Margo was the beginning of an organised group. They were to become the Apple Scruffs.

Two others were Nancy Allan, an American from Ohio, who'd asked for presents of luggage every birthday to prepare for the Great Escape to England to meet her idols, and Londoner Wendy Sutcliffe – a motorbike-crazy rock and roller, but also a Beatles fan from the age of nine.

By 1970, the Apple Scruffs had fallen into the pattern of waiting out on the steps of Apple by day. By night, they were outside the recording studios – Abbey Road, Olympia, or Trident. They didn't need much to get them through the night. A warm blanket, a flask of tea, a strong bladder...and hopefully, a glimpse of their heroes.

2:

But finally, the days of waiting out for the Beatles had to come to an end. For some time, there had been tension between Paul McCartney and the other three, over who should manage the group.

On the tenth of April 1970, Paul announced to the newspapers he was leaving the Beatles. The Beatles were officially splitting up.

For a while the girls continued to meet, waiting to greet their idols, now busy on individual projects. But eventually, one by one they drifted away. Wendy went back to her motorbikes and rock and roll. Jill, like several other Scruffs, found a job in the music business, eventually working at Abbey Road Studios herself. Nancy went to college to study psychology and sociology.

Next, try it with sentences and paragraphs on a page from a book, or borrow some broadcasting scripts.

After a bit you may feel tempted to start reading aloud. I would resist this to begin with. Instead, keep practising the technique of 'flashing' on the text, sentence by sentence, then paragraph by paragraph. It takes a while to build up this kind of ability.

When you can resist the temptation no longer, take a fresh passage of unseen writing, a deep breath, 'flash' on your first sentence, then read it aloud. As you get to the last word of the sentence, 'flash' on the next and carry on reading. Don't attempt to read ahead while your mouth is forming the words in each sentence; save the reading ahead for the punctuation pauses. As you read, really concentrate on those signposts and sense groups in the sentence you are voicing. At first, your reading will probably feel stilted, with long pauses at the full stops, but this is a gradual method that requires you to keep practising to build up speed.

You are aiming for not merely an adequate, stumble-free read, but an intelligent one where your intonation helps signpost the sense to the listener. It takes a lot of concentration to get right. The minute the attention wanders, you will be lost. You are really alternating two processes: a quick overview of the meaning of the whole sentence (or paragraph) in the time it takes you to draw breath, followed by a much more focused phrase-to-phrase read.

Slow and gradual

Be patient though. For most people, this way of looking at a script takes some time and practice to get right. Like all broadcasting skills, confidence is the key. When you feel ready, try out your sight-reading skills on a friend or colleague – an honest but understanding one. Eventually you will feel bold enough to sight-read and make a recording of it, playing it back to yourself. There may be a few stumbles at first – just the fact of recording is enough to introduce some confidence-sapping tension into the process! But be patient with yourself. Convince yourself you can do it if you have to. And keep trying. Remember that it isn't your first stumble or fluff that is the problem – it is your failure to recover from it that will keep on tripping you up, once you let yourself lose confidence and concentration.

Keep practising

Good sight-reading takes practice. Even when you feel you've mastered it, you'll need to give yourself regular opportunities to remind yourself you can do it. But I would beg you not to practise it while you are live on air, broadcasting to the long-suffering listener. Sight-reading should only be regarded as a fallback skill for those occasions when there is no alternative. Like all the techniques I describe in this book, it is best practised off-air, little and often to start; say ten or twenty minutes every other day at most. Don't overdo it.

The well-rounded broadcaster needs a life too.

SUMMARY

- Never sight-read as a matter of course.
- To improve your skills, give yourself as many opportunities to read aloud as you can, outside the broadcasting context.
- Look for the 'building blocks' of ideas.
- Read ahead in the pauses, by 'flashing' on the next sentence as you reach the full stop before it.
- Concentrate hard on the sense of the words as you say them.
- Only sight-read when you really have to.

12 Learning to love the microphone

You don't have to be a technical genius to broadcast, but it is useful to be able to tell one end of a microphone from the other. This chapter aims to demystify how microphones work, to help you set up your own equipment and achieve a good balance on the voice without the aid of a sound engineer. How close do you have to be to the mic? Do some microphones suit some voices better than others? And can you position the microphone to disguise some of your voice's less appealing aspects, such as sibilance?

Learning to love the microphone is something every successful broadcaster has to do. It is not the same as being in love with the sound of your own voice. Broadcasters who think they are God's gift to the medium tend to be too self-obsessed to be truly great. But it's worth investing time getting to know and understand this miraculous device that carries your voice from studio or location to the listener. The way you use it can make a considerable difference to how you sound. If you respect its properties and quirks, it will respect and cherish your voice.

The first thing you need to understand is that although all microphones work according to similar principles, not all are the same. That is why you sound so ghastly on the little built-in microphones that come with most domestic-market audio equipment, or on your camcorder. The sound is thin and tinny because the microphone is cheap and basic, and does not respond to the full range of frequencies in the human voice. Broadcast microphones are designed to much higher standards. Yet these too differ from each other, depending on the job they are expected to do. A microphone built for a singer's voice belting out a rock song or rap will be different from a studio microphone designed for speech. Location sound microphones are different again, so that they will adapt to more difficult recording environments where there is more background noise.

This chapter will get a little technical at times, but it is worth learning some of the sound recordist's jargon so you can understand not only the right microphone to use in the right place, but also how to use it to get the best out of your voice.

HOW A MICROPHONE WORKS

There are many different types of microphone in use in broadcasting but broadly speaking, they all do exactly the same thing, converting sound waves into electrical impulses. It is remarkable how little microphone design has altered over the years. Some of the mics that were in use nearly fifty years ago produce a sound that rivals today's latest models.

Inside every microphone is a sensitive diaphragm. Sound waves are essentially the movement of air, and these movements vibrate the diaphragm. It then translates the vibrations as a series of electrical impulses, and in that form they are sent to the recording or broadcast equipment, which eventually converts them back into sound waves.

Microphones pick up two kinds of sound – *direct* sound, which occurs close to the microphone within its sensitive field, and *indirect* sound – 'noises off' or *background* sound. For the sound of your voice to be picked up clearly by the microphone, you must be within the microphone's sensitive field. You can think of this as an enormous bubble that extends outwards from the microphone. If you speak within this bubble, your voice will be the predominant sound on mic. If you speak beyond the range of the bubble, the sound can still be picked up, but will be more muffled and indistinct because it is now competing against other more distant background sounds, including the atmosphere of the room you are in. You will be 'off-mic'.

Room atmosphere is created by reflected sound waves bouncing off the walls. But there may be other background sounds too, which you are so used to hearing they hardly register on your ears – the hum of computer equipment, clocks ticking, central heating boilers, fridges, traffic noise, planes overhead, the rumble of tube trains, distant dogs barking, the neighbours' telly, feet in a room above ... The list is endless, and you'll be amazed what the microphone hears that you were simply not aware of at the time.

In a sound studio, you will not need to worry much about indirect background sound. The studio should be soundproofed, and the walls are acoustically treated to absorb sound waves instead of reflecting them back as indirect sound. So you don't have to work quite so close to the mic in a studio. But in a normal room, or especially out of doors, there will be a lot more competing indirect sound. The sensitivity of the microphone to direct sound is greater the closer you are to it. So the distance you choose between you and the microphone depends on how much background sound there is likely to be – and how much of it you want to appear on the recording. You should always try to maintain a high ratio of direct to indirect sound. If not, you will find that the sound of your voice is muddied by the indirect sound.

HOW CLOSE IS CLOSE?

The environment you are in, and the effect you want to create, determine how close you get to the microphone. You will of course need to set the right level, or gain, for your voice on the desk or recording equipment, but don't do that until you have first determined the right distance for the microphone. Putting up the level won't make you sound any closer to the mic – it's the physical distance that matters in getting the right balance of direct to indirect sound.

The best judges of the right distance are your own ears. You should always test the sound you are getting either by wearing headphones, or (even better) by doing a test recording and listening back.

In the studio

Studio microphones fall into two categories, **end-fire** and **side-fire**, and you need to know which you are working with before you can position it correctly.

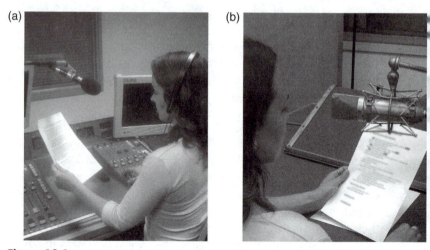

Figure 12.1
(a) End-fire mic. (b) Side-fire mic

End-fire mics, as the name suggests, have a sensitive tip, which you point towards you. Side-fire mics have a sensitive face, towards which you speak. Looking at the microphone, it is usually obvious which is which, but if there is a windshield – a foam jacket – around the mic, you may need to take it off first to be sure. When in doubt, make a test recording! If you are speaking 'on mic', towards its sensitive end or face, the sound will be clean and clear. If you are 'off mic' your voice will seem muffled and less distinct.

There is very little indirect sound in a studio. This means that studio sound is of the best quality, and puts you in a special 'neutral' space that is immediately recognizable to the listener as the conventional broadcasting environment. As a general rule, most **studio** mics pick up best when they are positioned six to ten inches (15–25 cm.) from your mouth. You can still get a decent result even when the mic is slightly further away, but you would be well advised to check the sound with a test recording.

The main problem to avoid in the studio is getting too close to the microphone. Inexperienced broadcasters often tend to work too close, perhaps because they have seen DJs or singers working this way. If you feel as if you are about to eat it, you are too near to it. Singers use a different kind of microphone, which is designed for working close, unlike your studio mic. Some broadcasters will claim

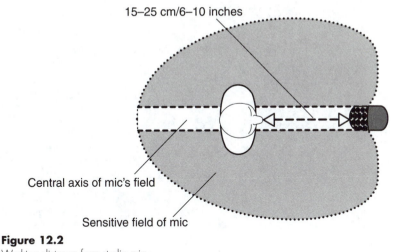

15–25 cm/6–10 inches

Central axis of mic's field

Sensitive field of mic

Figure 12.2
Working distance from studio mic

that the closer you work to the mic, the more it picks up your deeper bass frequencies, but this advice is sadly out of date as the type of mic that once produced this effect is now rarely seen. (If you want to make your voice sound deeper, go back to Chapters 4 and 5 on pitch and resonance.)

Getting too close to the mic can have some unfortunate effects. It will amplify all those tiny little mouth noises like lip smacks or saliva squelches. It will make you sound more breathy. And it can cause a weird effect called 'popping'. This happens usually on 'p' and 'b' sounds, the plosive consonants, which produce a strong puff of air. If you are too close, it hits the mic's diaphragm with such force that it cannot cope with the sound and produces a distinctive distorted bump. There is very little that can be done to treat this sound once it is on a recording, so it must be avoided at all costs. If you tend to 'pop' on the mic, try working further away, or slightly to one side of the mic, so the air stream is not reaching the diaphragm of the mic with such force. You can also use a foam windshield, or a pop screen. A good studio should be equipped with one or the other.

If you want a very intimate sound – as if you are in the head of the listener – work at the closer end of the range. You may even get as close as three inches ($7\frac{1}{2}$ cm) to the microphone, but do it with caution! Does your listener/viewer really want to feel as if you are part

Figure 12.3
Working with a pop screen

of their thoughts? You will only rarely want to achieve this kind of effect. It can feel unbearably intrusive, and is perhaps best reserved for drama work.

On location

Outside the studio, you will find you may need to work slightly closer, depending on how much atmosphere you want your recording to have. To allow you to do this, the microphones that are used for location work are different from studio mics. For radio work, in a **reasonably quiet room**, you might keep the distance roughly the same as the studio, perhaps moving the mic closer to you, between four and eight inches (10–20 cm) if there is a lot of background noise, or if you want a particularly intimate sound that doesn't place the recording anywhere in particular.

If, however, you are making a television programme, where the viewer at home will see that you are in a room, you will probably want to have the mic further away from you so that it doesn't appear in the shot, and also to allow some of the room's background atmosphere into the sound. Too clean and clinical a sound would strike the viewer as unrealistic! On location sound, television often uses different types of microphones from radio, designed to get a good sound with some general room atmosphere at a distance that gives the camera freedom to choose a variety of shot sizes. (We'll look in more detail later at the characteristics of television microphones.)

Out of doors, or in a very noisy room – such as a party full of people all chattering away – you will need to work closer still. Because there is much more indirect sound, you need to make sure the direct sound predominates by moving the mic nearer to you. But don't move it so close that you lose the background sound altogether – you may want some atmosphere to colour the sound. The balance of direct to indirect sound is again best judged by listening to a test recording.

A windshield helps you to work closer to the microphone, and I would recommend you use one in any noisy environment so that you can work closer to the mic without 'popping'. If I were standing in the middle of rush hour traffic to do a broadcast, I might be working with the microphone as close as two to three inches from my mouth. I would also make sure the mic was pointed away from the source of the background noise, or that I was using my body to shield the mic from the background.

You must *always* use a windshield when you are working outside, as the slightest hint of breeze can cause bumping noises on the

Figure 12.4
Working closer to the microphone in a noisy location

mic. Because the diaphragm is so sensitive to the movement of air, a howling wind that sounds so atmospheric to your ears will be picked up as thunderous rumbles and thuds by the mic!

LIP MICS

There are some specialist microphones called 'lip mics', designed for use in very noisy environments. Commentators at football matches use them so they can be heard over the roar of the spectators. They work by cutting out most of the bass frequencies, so that the rumble of the crowd is hardly heard at all, though a little is picked up by the back of the mic to create atmosphere. To make the voice sound as close to normal as possible, even though it will have lost its lower frequencies, they make use of an effect called 'bass tip-up', which occurs if you work very close to an old-fashioned ribbon-type microphone like this one, and this puts back some bass into the voice. (This is the effect that I mentioned some broadcasters try for when they work very close to a studio mic. Studio mics no longer work in this way, but the lip mic is designed to make use of it, as a compromise to make your voice sound less tinny.)

Television reporters sometimes use lip mics to record commentary over pictures when there is no proper dubbing booth available.

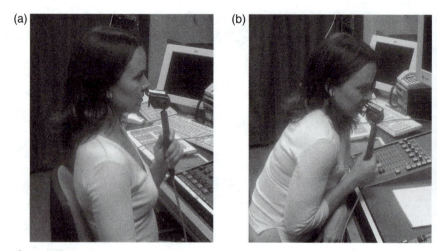

Figure 12.5
(a) Using a lip mic the right way and (b) the wrong way

The lip mic cuts out background sound from noisy computer equipment or busy newsrooms. Unfortunately, the effect it produces on the voice can sound very unnatural, especially on some female voices. Worse, because the reporter is required to hold the microphone right up against the mouth, it can make you forget all those tips about posture and relaxation that help the voice to sound its best.

If you have to use a lip mic, try not to hunch over it. Sit tall and straight, with your feet firmly on the ground. Keep the arm holding the mic as relaxed as possible, and don't be tempted to prop your elbow on the desktop! You need to make your breathing as easy and relaxed as possible so that the lip mic won't pick up too many gasps and mouth noises. You will have to accept that your voice won't sound its most beautiful, and if I were you I would lobby to get a proper soundproofed booth instead, but in some places the lip mic is a compromise that is unavoidable.

Sports reporters using lip mics would be well advised not to hunch over them either. You need a good strong voice and plenty of breath to compete with the sound of the crowd, and if you hunch you may strain your voice. If you find yourself hoarse after a broadcast, this may be the reason why.

TELEVISION MICROPHONES

When I worked in radio, we would always refer rather sniffily to the poor quality of television sound. Certainly it is true that if you took a TV interview and played it on radio, it would probably sound as if it had been badly recorded. A radio recording is generally done with the microphone close to the speaker, to minimize distracting background atmosphere and noise. But television sound is designed to match pictures, so the microphone must almost inevitably be placed further away to avoid it appearing too obviously in the shot as a visual distraction.

Background atmosphere, where there is a visual explanation for it, actually helps to enhance the way picture and sound work together. On the other hand you may find yourself coming back with an unusable interview if you failed to notice the lawnmower buzzing away unseen in the neighbour's garden, thundering but invisible traffic in someone's living room, or even – as once happened to me on a very important interview – leaves rustling in a light breeze, when I had failed to instruct the cameraman to make sure the trees appeared in the background of the shot!

In the dubbing booth, where voice-over commentary is recorded, the microphones will be very similar to those in a radio studio and their positioning will be identical. But for location filming, television uses two other types of microphones, and their use is often hotly debated between directors and sound recordists.

The best sound is usually produced by a **boom** microphone. This is the one we always associate with TV crews, the shaggy creature on a long pole. (Indoors its shaggy coat, which is a windshield, should be shed or the sound will be muffled.) It is a highly directional microphone, connected into either the back of the camera or the sound recordist's mixer by a long curly cable. Its sensitive field is like a long beam, so to pick up a good sound you must make sure it is pointed directly at whoever is speaking. Get as close as you can, and check you know the right end to point! For static interviews, it can be mounted on a stand.

Most cameras also have the facility to mount a microphone on the top of the camera itself. This is likely to be a smaller version of a similar directional microphone. This type of mic is NOT recommended for getting good sound on speech, as the camera will almost always be too far away from the speaker. But it can be useful for picking up background atmosphere if you are working in a small crew without a sound recordist.

If you are planning to film using a very wide shot, or the reporter or interviewee needs the freedom to move at a distance from the camera, you will be using a small '**personal**' microphone, probably via a radio link.

Personal mics work rather differently. They are *omnidirectional*: that is, they pick up sound from any angle and do not need to be pointed in a particular direction. This means the mic can be attached to clothing somewhere on the chest of the speaker and will easily pick up the voice. A personal mic is very convenient to use, will work through a layer of clothing so it can be made invisible in the shot, gives the speaker much greater freedom of movement, is easier to forget for the self-conscious speaker, and provided it has been positioned correctly the sound recordist can relax and give his or her arms a rest!

But personals do have their drawbacks. Because they are omnidirectional, the quality of the sound is less pleasing – some people describe it as rather 'metallic'. Their sensitive field has to be small, or they would pick up too much background sound. As a result, what they pick up often has a rather reverberant quality that sounds odd. If you position them where clothing can rub against them you will get a lot of extraneous noise, and if they are operated via a radio link, there can also be interference so you may waste time having to change channels. They can also be very sensitive to wind noise.

There are two useful tips for working with a personal mic. The noisier the surroundings, the closer you should position it to your neck. And men especially should be careful about which way up they set the mic. Men's nostrils let out big blasts of air downwards, so it is best to turn the microphone upside down. As it is omnidirectional, it will pick up sound whichever way it is facing, but this will save those huge gusts hitting the diaphragm head on! A personal mic usually looks rather like a very small pepper pot, with holes in the top, so make sure the holes are pointing downwards.

If you are working with a crew that includes a sound recordist and a director, you won't have to decide which mic to use – it is someone else's headache! But if you are out in the field as a lone reporter with a camera operator, you need to weigh up which will produce the best effect in the circumstances. For speed, and a good sound, use the boom. For freedom of movement, go for the personal, and if possible hedge your bets by persuading the camera operator to get background atmosphere through the camera mic.

Static pieces-to-camera using the boom

If you don't plan on moving around during a piece-to-camera, you will often find the best way to record your voice is by holding the boom yourself just below the level of the shot, pointing it upward towards your mouth. You will need to detach it from its pole; it has a handgrip. I suggest you hold it with only one hand. Gripping it with both hands tends to drag your shoulders down. This will make you look tired and depressed in the picture and will also have a corresponding effect on your voice. Keep your arms relaxed, and your head and shoulders high.

This is a useful way of recording your voice if you are working as a **video journalist** – a lone wolf who shoots the pictures as well as reporting. It gives you good sound and is relatively quick to set up. Make sure you set the frame fairly tight, though, or you will have trouble keeping the mic out of shot!

Video journalists have one of the toughest jobs in broadcasting, because they have to do everything. Often their voice is the last thing that they are thinking about as they scramble to get everything done. But please remember that a bad voice or a thoughtless delivery can wreck an otherwise brilliant piece. It is worth taking time to get your voice in shape so that you will always instinctively use it well, because there's precious little time to spare for retakes doing your job!

GETTING YOUR VOICE BACK TO THE STUDIO FROM A DISTANCE: TELEPHONE LINES AND ISDN CIRCUITS

The microphone is not the only part of the equipment to consider in getting the best from your voice. If you are sending your contribution back to base via a line, you may need to ask yourself what the quality of the line itself will do to your voice.

Everyone sounds different on a telephone line, because the microphone in a telephone is the most basic type possible, and the circuit does not carry the full range of frequencies in the human voice. When I began in broadcasting, the only quick and easy way to get your contribution into the studio from a distant location was by way of an ordinary telephone line; but more recently technological advance has brought us the ISDN line, offering a much superior sound without crackles and carrying a much wider range of frequencies. Most people imagine that all ISDN lines are the same, but in fact they are classified by various standards, which determine their frequency response. If you book the minimum standard, you will get a thin sound that doesn't reflect the full range of frequencies in your voice. Do make sure that if you want the voice to approach studio sound, you book a better quality line.

CHEATING: USING EQUALIZATION TO ALTER THE SOUND OF YOUR VOICE

If you have ever used a studio desk to 'self-op' a broadcast, you will have noticed row upon row of little knobs above the faders. These are designed to alter the sound of each channel on the desk in various ways. You can add echo, or move the stereo position of the sound, compress it, or affect it by cutting or boosting various frequencies. The latter is known as EQ, short for 'equalization'.

My advice is – don't touch these knobs! You can mess up the sound horribly unless you really know what you are doing, and even though I am trained as a sound operator I would much prefer to leave that kind of fine-tuning to audio engineers who have years of experience using EQ. They will tell you that the less you have to do, the better the sound.

Nevertheless, there are some top presenters, particularly in radio, who have over the years determined what they feel are the best settings for their own voices. They have worked closely with engineers who are expert at 'painting with sound' to arrive at the perfect formula for their show. If you access the BBC's Intranet, you can download Terry Wogan's personal EQ settings – not that they will be of any use to you unless you are an engineer working on his show.

Is it worth trying to do the same for yourself, if you have a technical bent and a good ear? That has to be your own personal decision, but I'd advise you to get someone else to lend a hand to help you judge whether you are really improving the sound or just messing it up. A touch of bass cut can help remove blasting or popping on a recording, but mostly you'd do better to concentrate on making your voice sound better by natural means, improving your breath support and your control of pitch.

But there are also ways you can use the microphone itself to improve a less than perfect voice.

MICROPHONE POSITIONING

A microphone cannot work a miracle. But just as clever camera angles can sometimes enhance the appearance of a face, subtle changes in the angling of the mic can make a difference to your voice.

We have already mentioned 'popping', and if you are the kind of speaker who ejects great blasts of air on the plosive consonants ('p's and 'b's), you will find by angling the microphone sideways so that you are not talking directly along its central axis, you will reduce the force of the airflow hitting its diaphragm.

Working off the mic's central axis can be used to minimize two other voice defects: **mouth noises** and **sibilance**. Ideally, of course, if you have relaxed your jaw and are opening your mouth properly, you should not be making lip smacks and tongue clicks and slurps (see Chapter 4). But we all have our off-days, and sometimes the pressures of broadcasting are such that you go into the studio so tired it becomes almost impossible to make those fine muscular adjustments required for clear speech. If you absolutely have to broadcast under such circumstances, angling the microphone so that you are speaking *across* it, rather than directly into it, will help to minimize the worst of your sins.

Figure 12.6
Angling the microphone to cut sibilance and popping

Sibilance is a high, whistling quality to the sound of a voice, typically in the 3–4 kHz range, which is a long way above the frequencies of the normal speaking voice. It is usually caused by a combination of too much breath and the incorrect positioning of the tongue in relation to the teeth. Some people with gaps in their teeth are prone to it; another common cause is a badly fitting plate of false teeth! Again, speaking *across* rather than along the central axis of the mic will help cut sibilance, because the microphone's frequency response is different as you move towards the edge of its sensitive field.

You will also find changing the position of the microphone can help in other ways. If you position the microphone high, pointing downward towards you so that it is less obviously in your eye line, you will make it feel less as if you are talking to the mic itself. It becomes easier to think of yourself as talking to a person *beyond* the microphone.

I also prefer this position to make the best of lighter women's voices. By directing the central axis towards the chest, rather than the mouth, you will ensure you pick up more of the chest resonance. Provided your mouth is still well within the sensitive field, though off the central axis, you will retain the clarity of the voice but enhance its deeper notes.

DO DIFFERENT MICS SUIT DIFFERENT VOICES?

Many radio presenters who are justifiably proud of their voices will swear blind to you that a particular mic suits their voice better than others. One presenter, who shall remain nameless, always insists that he uses an AKG414 in the studio, because he reckons its clarity best enhances his rich and resonant bass voice. I'm slightly embarrassed to confess that when I was regularly presenting radio programmes, I too was one of this vain fraternity. In my case, it was the Neumann U87, an expensive but much loved mic; it has a particularly warm intimate sound.

However, this discussion has to be largely academic, because most of us have to put up with what we are given in the way of studio equipment. It is a joy to walk into a dubbing studio that has been equipped with valve mic amps, because they give a wonderfully warm tone to any voice. Because you notice you sound so utterly lovely in your headphones, you relax and enjoy yourself, so you become even better. A good mic has a psychological effect on performance; poor studio equipment does nothing for your self-esteem!

If you are ever in the position of equipping a studio, you would do well to remember that here, as in most situations, you get what you pay for. It is worth investing time and money to get good mics and amps, as well as decent soundproofing and some comfortable and adjustable chairs.

In the meantime, count yourself lucky if you find yourself given a choice of microphones. When you reach the big time, you can do your prima donna act and insist on your favourite mic. Until then, get on with the job, and make sure you aren't blaming the mic for defects in your voice you could remedy yourself, by using better posture and breath support to increase the resonance.

SUMMARY

- The distance you position yourself from the microphone depends on the balance of direct to indirect sound you want to create.
- In the quieter atmosphere of a studio, you can be six to ten inches from the mic.
- Work closer to the mic on location to minimize background noise.
- TV mics can be used at a greater distance.
- Avoid lip mics for voice-overs if you can, but if you have to use them, be careful not to hunch.
- Experimenting with EQ is only for experts!
- Angle the microphone to minimize mouth noises, popping, and sibilance, or to increase the amount of chest resonance it picks up.

13 Help!

Some of the other problems voice coaches are often asked to 'fix', and how to look after your voice to get the best from it. If you have a problem not mentioned in this chapter, it will probably have been discussed elsewhere in the text; refer to the index.

VOICE CARE

We use our voices every day and rarely give thought to how to take care of them. Only when problems emerge do we begin to wonder what we are doing wrong. It is worth reading this section even if you haven't encountered these problems yet – it will give you some tips for looking after your voice.

People always seem to want advice about what to eat and drink before a broadcast, and I have included some suggestions based on the collective wisdom of other voice specialists and broadcasters. Please do not imagine though that we are all so saintly that we never allow diary products to pass our lips, never sip a glass of wine, or have never taken a puff on a cigarette in our lives. We may know that these things are not good for our voices, but we are after all human.

My own belief is that most voice problems are caused by poor posture and tight breathing, so the best way of looking after your voice is to look at the way you are using your body to produce it, in the widest possible sense. Changing your diet may help solve some problems for some people, but it cannot strengthen a weak voice in the way that changing your posture can. You should never feel that you have to push your voice to give it power – power comes from relaxed body use and deeper breathing. Forcing your voice leads only to vocal cord damage. So please bear in mind the advice in Chapters 2 and 4, if you want a healthy voice.

Why do I get croaky in the morning, and what can I do about it?

The first thing to ask yourself is what you were doing the night before. If you were sitting in a smoky pub, puffing your way through a packet of fags, trying to make yourself heard over loud music, it's not entirely surprising that your voice is not in tip-top shape.

But there may be other reasons why you find yourself croaky in the mornings. Croakiness is often caused by over-production of mucus (phlegm or catarrh). Some people are more prone to this than others. Many voice experts suggest you avoid dairy products, which are thought to increase mucus production. It may seem hard to start the day without that milky cup of coffee or tea, but I know many people who swear that their voices are much improved if they keep off milk, butter, cheese etc. There is certainly no doubt that plenty of water, which lubricates the vocal passages, helps.

I would find it hard to get out of bed without a cup of tea to look forward to, but I drink it black. This is not because I am particularly good at taking my own advice – I prefer it that way! There is also some recent research suggesting that black tea kills the bacteria that cause bad breath, so it may have the secondary advantage that you won't be causing your early morning interviewees to swoon. You may want to rethink your breakfast and avoid cereal with milk, or butter on your toast. Life's too short to deny yourself every pleasure, but wait until after the broadcast to have that big frothy cappuccino.

Smoking certainly is not going to help your voice. In the long run it will damage it. If you are a smoker, at least don't start your day with a cigarette. And try not to smoke heavily the night before you are going to use your voice for broadcasting.

Warming up

If I have a morning voice job (and as the years go by I find that gunge in the vocal cords becomes more of a problem rather than less!), I try and warm my voice up before I go in front of the microphone. Like most broadcasters, I feel a bit of a fool doing actor-type voice exercises in front of anyone else, so my routine tends to take place in the car on the way to work, or in the kitchen before I leave home. At its most basic, it consists simply of remembering to use my voice before I get to work. You can talk to your partner, to the cat, or to the radio – just make sure you get those vocal cords working.

Opening up your mouth and throat is good practice to prepare for a broadcast. Take in a few deep breaths through an open mouth, arching the back of your mouth to free the soft palate as we have described in Chapters 4 and 5, and relaxing your tongue. Try saying 'aahh' very gently, whispering it at first, then gradually increasing the volume, being careful not to tighten in the throat. Then bring the lips together and start to hum quietly, gradually increasing the power. Part the lips on the final mmm sound, and repeat it a few times, to get more flexibility into the lip muscles. Finally alternate the 'aahh' and 'mmm' sounds until you feel your voice is more free.

This is only a very basic voice warm up, but it may help to clear the croakiness from your voice.

Husky voices – sexy or damaged?

Everybody envies the person with a sexy, husky voice. There's something attractively vulnerable about that cracked sound. It's a turn-on because it reminds you what happens to people's voices when they are having sex – they get deeper, rougher, and breathier. But it isn't an over-active love-life that makes you that way.

Husky voices are often, though not always, a sign of vocal cord damage. They can indicate misuse of the voice, which has put strain on the cords so that they may even have become scarred with small growths called nodules. Singers or actors who force their voices at volume may get them, but you can also develop nodules if you have simply been producing your voice wrongly over the years in ordinary conversation or shouting too loudly on the terraces in support of your favourite football team.

The kind of postural techniques I described earlier in the book are intended to improve your body use so you don't put a strain on the vocal cords. Avoid thrusting your head forward as you speak, and try not to tighten in the neck, shoulders, or chest. Give up smoking, drink plenty of water, and never force your voice.

But if after following this advice you still have a noticeably husky voice *all the time*, combined with regularly getting sore throats, I would suggest you go to your doctor and ask to have an appointment with a laryngologist. The examination you will be given is not a pleasant procedure, but it could save your voice in the long run. If there is vocal cord damage – and there may not be, this is just a wise precaution – he or she may recommend either speech therapy, or in very severe cases surgery to remove the nodules. Surgery should only be a last resort. You might want to get a second opinion because in most cases the nodules should clear up once you change the way you use your voice.

If your cords are damaged you must do something about the way you are producing your voice, because eventually it will reduce the effective range of your voice. What was so attractively sexy in your youth will become progressively more cracked and unpleasant.

Why do I sound like Melvyn Bragg – the problem of 'bunged-up' voices?

One of the most common problems I get asked about is the 'bunged-up' voice: the voice that sounds as if it has a cold even when it hasn't. Ironically most people describe this as a 'nasal' voice, when strictly speaking it is the very opposite. Something has caused the nasal passages to block up so the voice lacks any nasal resonance, and can sound thick and clotted, particularly on 'm' and 'n' sounds which require some air passage down the nose to emerge clearly.

It is a common problem because the nasal membranes are very sensitive and many factors can cause them to swell up and block the nasal passage. Some of these might be:

● cigarette smoke

● drinking alcohol, particularly some of the white wines

● food sensitivities, especially dairy products

- dust mite allergies

- pollen allergies

- a dry atmosphere, such as an air-conditioned studio.

The first three are fortunately within our control. Don't smoke, don't spend a night on the booze before using your voice on air, and try to avoid dairy products because they can cause the body to produce too much mucus and catarrh.

The last three are more difficult to manage. Of course you can live your life in a hermetically sealed bubble, or at least make sure your own home is as free as possible from whatever might trigger the sensitivity for you. But out in the big wide world you are at the mercy of whatever is in the atmosphere. As most studios have some form of air conditioning, if you are sensitive to dry atmospheres you will have a problem. All you can do is try and minimize the problem by taking steps to counteract its effect. You may not be very popular, and indeed you may even look like a terrible prima donna, but it is worth it to sound better and feel more comfortable.

So here are my top tips for bunged-up voices – a problem I share with you.

- Drink lots of water.

- Try and find a way of getting some moisture into the air. I used to persuade the studio manager to 'mist' the atmosphere by spraying water droplets into the air, but as studios are also full of electrical equipment this should only be done with care and the permission (and supervision) of studio staff! There is no point in humidifying the studio if you then electrocute yourself. But even a bowl of water in the room, carefully placed away from electrical equipment, can help.

- Take frequent breaks and leave the studio to get out into the fresh air. I find that on a rainy day even two minutes outside is enough to reduce the swelling and de-congest my voice. (If you have hay fever this obviously will not work!)

- Find the kitchen area and boil a kettle, or wash your hands in hot steamy water. It can help clear the problem for a while. If things are really bad, you could prepare a bowl of hot water and inhale the steam with your head under a towel – not recommended though if you are making a TV appearance!

- Don't keep blowing your nose. The more you blow, the more you will produce mucus, so although you may have to get out the hanky occasionally to clear your voice, don't over-do it.

There are more drastic remedies for hay-fever sufferers – tablets and decongestant sprays. I am not a fan of either, as the tablets may make you sleepy, and decongestant sprays are often only a way of deferring the problem. In the long term, they may increase the irritability of the membranes.

For a few people, it may be worth a visit to a good ear nose and throat specialist. They can advise you if an operation would help in some rare cases where the nasal passages are constantly blocked. I once coached a woman who told me she could not recall ever breathing freely through her nose. It turned out that she had a damaged septum, as a result of which her sinuses were constantly full of mucus, and often became infected. But an operation cleared the problem and her voice was transformed.

There is one consolation – I once met a man who told me it was this very characteristic of my voice that he liked. 'It makes you sound warm and friendly', he said. I am not sure I will ever be able to bring myself to agree wholeheartedly – on bad bunged-up days I'd happily exchange some of that warmth for cool clarity – but he does have a point. There is a friendliness about such voices, and it doesn't seem to have done Melvyn Bragg's career any harm at all.

Broadcasting with a cold

What should you do if you have a cold and fear you might lose your voice? Ideally, stay at home. As a young broadcaster, I suffered frequently from heavy colds. I rarely felt really ill, so would totter into work streaming and spluttering – only to be told by my station manager to go straight home again. 'Think of the listeners', he exhorted me. 'You may feel well but you sound as if you're suffering. It's very uncomfortable to listen to.'

Unfortunately, not all bosses are so thoughtful as mine was, and you may not have the luxury of being able to take time off, especially if you are a freelance. Freelances don't get paid if they don't work, and they are always convinced nobody will offer them another job if they appear too weedy. They soldier on bravely and collapse in a pathetic heap at weekends.

If you must use your voice on air when you have a cold, never push your voice too hard, or you could end up losing it altogether. This once happened to me, when I was stupid enough to carry on working with a bad throat infection, and it was very frightening indeed. It took a week to come back – a week in which my doctor told me I must not speak at all, not even in a whisper. (Bizarre as it may seem, whispering can put even more strain on the vocal cords.) Although it is tempting to use throat sprays that say they will ease the discomfort of a sore throat, the pain is there to tell you not to push your voice, and numbing it may lead you to damage your voice without realizing.

A head cold, where the infection is concentrated in your sinuses, is more manageable. Try to clear your nasal passages as well as you can by following the advice in the previous section for 'bunged-up' voices. Take plenty of hot drinks too. You need to keep your vocal cords lubricated, and the steam from a hot drink helps to clear the head. Honey also seems to ease a rasping throat. Get as much sleep as you can, bearing in mind that medication to help you sleep may leave you feeling muzzy the next morning. If I have a heavy cold I do take decongestants, but only for a short period – otherwise they can prolong the period of recovery. In extreme circumstances, I will also use a nasal spray (one that was prescribed by my doctor), but only immediately before the broadcast. Sniffing menthol and eucalyptus capsules is a gentler solution.

Remember though that your colleagues will not thank you for sharing your germs with them. Sometimes, it is much fairer to cut your losses and stay at home.

Avoiding colds in the first place is difficult, though some people swear by a daily dose of Vitamin C. As far as I know – and I've been taking Vitamin C supplements daily for the last twenty years! – it has had no effect on the number of colds I have caught. But a few years ago someone suggested taking Echinacea as a supplement, and though

I have no way of knowing whether it is coincidence, I have suffered far fewer colds since. As with any dietary supplement, read the instructions on the packet. There is some evidence that you should not take it continuously, or the benefits will disappear, so the usual recommendation is to take it fortnight on, fortnight off. You should not take it if you suffer from high blood pressure, if you are pregnant, or breast feeding, and you should consult your doctor before using it if you are taking any other medication.

Why do I sound worse when I'm tired?

Tired voices often sound that way: unclear or dull. Making a good sound takes fine muscular control. If you are exhausted, it gets very hard to direct the tiny movements of tongue and lips and jaw that shape the vowels and consonants clearly. It is easy to slur, and while you are preoccupied with struggling to enunciate clearly, you are probably not thinking hard enough about communicating what you are saying.

Of course, your mother would tell you that you should have gone to bed early the night before, and that's good advice to remember if you have the choice! But you may be working night shifts or meeting tight deadlines – so what can you do to overcome tiredness once it has descended?

One way is to give yourself an energy boost. I try to manage my own diet so that I don't have blood sugar highs – there is always a corresponding low afterwards, and you can put yourself into a cycle of peaks and troughs which in the long run doesn't help your overall energy levels. But sometimes emergency measures are necessary, especially if you have been so busy working that you have forgotten to eat properly. Try to resist the easy temptations of caffeine and chocolate. (Chocolate often makes life more difficult by thickening the mucus.) Go instead for fruit and plenty of liquid. I bless the day some genius started bottling fruit smoothies, which are both lubricating and energizing. Plenty of water will also help keep you going. Often we don't realize we have become dehydrated in the warm dry atmosphere of the studio, and that can sap your energy too.

If you are working against a deadline, try and build in moments to get away from the pressure and calm down. Tension in your muscles drains energy; so try deliberately to relax every so often. It is important to do enough preparation to make sure the broadcast runs smoothly, but don't let panic overcome you. You need to control the work, not let it control you, so take it one step at a time and don't be afraid to delegate if there is anyone to help you. If you can, get outside into the fresh air at frequent intervals to wake yourself up. And keep moving; flexibility in your whole body is important to your voice. Two minutes outside can save ten minutes of retakes for a tired voice.

ENUNCIATION PROBLEMS

How do I stop stumbling?

There are a whole variety of reasons why people stumble on air. Tiredness, of course, as we have seen – but also tension. Nervousness ties knots in your muscles, makes it harder to breathe, and more difficult to control those fine mouth movements that shape words clearly.

At this point what I call the First Law of Stumbles comes into operation:

Stumble once, and you will probably stumble again.

Stumbling is a vicious circle. Once it has happened you become so preoccupied telling yourself what a hopeless broadcaster you are that your concentration slips – and hey presto, you've done it again.

The only way to avoid this escalation is to tell yourself firmly one slip isn't a problem, thus escaping the need to beat yourself up over it. Focus yourself all the more firmly on the task in hand – telling the story – and ignore the fact that you have stumbled. It isn't a hanging offence, provided you don't continue doing it.

You may also be able to cure your stumbling quite easily by finding out what it is that makes you trip up in the first place.

- You may be going too fast. Everyone has a natural pace, and you could be trying to make your mouth work faster than it can. Try going slower, allowing more pauses into your delivery so your eyes have time to read ahead and remind you what's coming up.

- Perhaps you didn't read your script through properly before you went on air. Are you trying to sight-read? Don't, unless it is an emergency. Sight-reading looks like a clever trick but nobody can do as good a job if they haven't looked at the script properly first.

- Perhaps you didn't check pronunciations of unfamiliar names or words. Or is your script a mass of crossings-out and handwritten alterations? All of these factors will make your job more difficult than it need be.

- You may be trying to read too far ahead as you speak, especially if you are unused to reading aloud from the printed page. A few broadcasters are even mildly dyslexic, which can make scripted broadcasting especially traumatic. Layout here is important. Don't be afraid to adjust and reprint the script to make it as easy as possible for you to read – large font, double spacing, and short lines (see Chapter 9 for some tips). Practice reading aloud as often as you can at home to give yourself more confidence. And use a trick from your childhood to keep your eyes focused on the words you are reading. Run a finger – or if that makes you feel embarrassed, a pen – along the line as you speak it. Broadcasters often hold a pen as they talk, so no one will think you look like a five-year-old learning to read.

Of course, you may also be what is colloquially known as a 'mush-mouth': someone who has trouble enunciating clearly whatever the circumstances. If so, you probably are holding your jaw very stiffly. It may even ache sometimes, a sure sign that you are not letting it work properly. And you are probably not opening your mouth widely enough to allow your lips and tongue free movement to form the words. Try opening up the mouth as described in Chapter 4.

Clear your head

Sometimes, when I find myself dealing professionally with a persistent stumbler, I find the problem is purely psychological. It goes deeper than nerves – he or she may have a deep-rooted insecurity about what they are doing on air.

I once worked with a superb broadcaster who had been on air successfully for many years in local radio. Stumbling had never been a problem for him there. But then he got a job on a national network. Suddenly he found himself questioning what he was doing. What right did he have to aspire to such a prestigious job, on a network with the scary reputation of being for clever people? The answer was, of course, that he had *earned* the right, because he was a good broadcaster with a great voice, warm, friendly, and personable. But as he saw it, his was the only Northern accent on the network. He felt, against all logic, that any day someone would suddenly notice his accent, announce they'd made a huge mistake and send him back to local radio. Terror set in. Every time he went on air he would stumble, curse himself for doing it (hadn't he just proved his point, he shouldn't be there in the first place?) and then go on to stumble again and again.

If this describes the reasons you think you stumble, the only way through it is to tell yourself you are doing the job because someone had the confidence in you to put you on air. They wouldn't have done that if you hadn't already proved yourself. You have to break out of the stumbling cycle, and you will only do that if you can let yourself believe in your own ability and your right to be on air.

Adopt a set of anti-stumble tactics:

- Make sure there is nothing in your script (or your programme, if you are working without a script) that you are not prepared for. Give yourself plenty of time beforehand to look things through. Try the signposting technique I described in Chapter 7 to help you focus on the sense of the script. I have cured several stumblers this way!

- Check tricky pronunciations and practise them beforehand. Ideally eliminate any words you are not sure of pronouncing correctly. Write phonetic or literal pronunciations of difficult names into the script in a form that will not throw you when you get there.

- Make sure your script is clearly laid out (see Chapter 9), using double spacing and short lines, to make it as easy as possible to read. Retype and reprint any corrections, rather than writing them in over the top or at the side by hand.

- Warm up your voice before going on air. Make sure in particular that your mouth is relaxed and working freely. Actors use tongue twisters to help them with this before going on stage, because they help the mouth become more flexible. But don't pick a tongue twister that you find so formidably difficult it will reduce you to a state of gibbering tension because you can't get it right! My favourite, because it's fairly easy but still stretches the mouth, is 'A proper cup of coffee in a proper coffee pot.' There are plenty of sites on the Internet where you can amuse yourself by downloading tongue twisters, or try writing your own. (Not so obscene, please, that it corpses you with giggles even before you get on air.)

- Follow the advice in the early chapters of this book about posture and breathing so that you minimize tension. Make using your voice as effortless as possible.

- Always go on air relaxed. Three deep breaths before the mic goes live – really filling then really emptying your lungs – are a good way to focus yourself and calm the nerves.

If none of these tactics work and you continue to stumble repeatedly, do get professional help. The cure for stumbling really lies within yourself, but it always helps to feel someone is working with you and offering encouragement.

Am I saying words clearly enough?

Although nobody expects you to sound as if you have just graduated from Miss Prim's Academy For Perfect Elocution, clear diction is important for a broadcaster, especially if you are working in news or other areas of speech-based programming where the sense must be plain. Remember the listener or viewer has only one chance to grasp your meaning. Opening your mouth properly helps (see Chapter 4). Watch out especially for the junctions between words. Many of us can be a bit sloppy in this area. 'An apple', for instance, may come out as 'A napple'. No problem with the meaning there, but what about a phrase like 'gets tough', if it emerges as 'get stuff'?

Here are some sentences to practise to sharpen up your diction. Record yourself saying them and check back to hear how clear the junctions are.

He's looking for an aim, I'm looking for a name.

A fine night, but a finite life.

You say Venice, I save Venice.

It was black at the spot where I saw the black cat.

You need to make them sound both clear and natural – over-enunciation will make you sound jerky and staccato. There's a side-benefit to practising clear diction like this, because it will also help you crisp up your pauses when you are using tiny breaks in the flow of the sentence to signpost the meaning by breaking it up into phrases. Try this technique on the headline we came across in Chapter 7:

There are reports of protests/against this morning's air strikes in Pakistan.

There are reports of protests against this morning's air strikes/in Pakistan.

I have a tongue stud – should I take it out when I broadcast?

Yes. Sorry to sound old-fashioned, but tongue studs get in the way of clear speech. And I don't mean just take it out when you go on air – I mean get rid of it. Your tongue will take some time to adjust to speaking without it, so taking it out five minutes before the programme isn't going to help.

There is also an appearance issue. If you are a DJ, you can pierce or tattoo any part of your body with impunity. But if you plan a career as a serious reporter or presenter, you need to conform to some extent in your appearance to have credibility with the kind of people you will be interviewing. Tongue studs are still associated with 'alternative' lifestyles, and although nobody is asking you to be a clone in a suit, you may find that your journalistic career will be severely limited if you don't accept some degree of conformity.

Lisps and weak 'r's

There are very few people who have 'perfect' enunciation, and it is the tiny differences in the way each of us forms sounds that gives a voice its recognizably different character. But sometimes, a voice strays just an extra step or two beyond the accepted norm in the way it forms a particular sound, and the result is labelled a 'speech fault' or – hardly more consolingly! – 'lazy' speech. The most common are *lisps* (making an 's' sound like 'th'); *sibilance* (a high, breathy, sweet whistling sound on 's'); and *weak 'r's* (where the 'r' sounds more like a 'w'). You may also come across a *mushy 's'*, where the sound is thickened, more like 'sh', because the air is spilling over the sides of the tongue.

The common factor in these is usually a tongue positioned just slightly out of alignment. Speech is made by the movement of air through differently shaped openings, so the tiniest difference in the shape of your mouth can let air escape in the wrong direction, changing the sound.

Sometimes the problem is identified in childhood, and lucky kids with sharp-eared parents get sent to a speech therapist to have the habit corrected or modified. The trouble is that even if you are diligent in following the therapist's exercises, it can be very difficult to make the fine adjustment needed in tongue position to alter the sound. In adult life, it can take months to effect a change.

So lisps or similar 'lazy' speech habits are not something a broadcast voice coach will be able to fix in the hour or so your employer is likely to pay for you to spend with them. Speech therapists and elocution teachers can offer more useful help over a longer period of time, but this will cost you money and involves serious hard work. Both therapist and client need a lot of patience. Sometimes I suspect there is some wishful thinking involved. 'I think my lithp thounds tho much better now!' clients have told me, after months of expensive therapy. I usually haven't the heart to contradict them, especially as I can't offer them anything better.

The sweet, breathy, whistling sound of sibilance is even harder to remove by re-educating your mouth. Unfortunately, microphones are particularly sensitive to sibilance, and will often make it seem more pronounced than it may appear in everyday conversation.

But there is fortunately a technical solution. If you angle the microphone *across* the airflow, rather than pointing directly into it, less of the breath will be hitting the mic's sensitive diaphragm (see Chapter 12 on microphone use). You will also be taking advantage of the fact that the mic's frequency response alters as you move off the direct axis, and is less sensitive to the very high frequencies involved in sibilance. Don't get too close to the mic either.

No such solution exists for the lisp, the mushy 's', or the weak 'r'. So is it worth even trying to make a change? If you have an otherwise confident voice, people notice its imperfections less. I would always advise working first of all on whatever else might be wrong with your voice – is it strong and well-supported by your breath? Are you using intelligent intonation? – before you start worrying about a lisp or a weak 'r'. It may not be nearly so noticeable as you think once you have improved the rest of your delivery.

You can also help yourself by practising tongue twisters, along the lines of 'Round the rugged rocks, the ragged rascal ran.' But before you do that, ask yourself – and your colleagues – how much of a problem it really is. Unusual 's' sounds and weak 'r's can be rather attractive characteristics in a voice. If they don't get in the way of understanding, they are not likely to be a problem. It hasn't hindered Jonathan Ross's career that he has a weak 'r'; it's become his trademark, just like Sean Connery's mushy 's'.

COMMON WORRIES

Am I too fast, or too slow?

This is always a difficult question to resolve, because often what appears to be 'too fast' or 'too slow' is neither – it is actually a pace that is *too regular and unvaried.*

Broadcasters often wrongly imagine that they should be aiming for a regular pace. Colleagues reinforce this misconception by telling you that the best broadcasting speed is so many words per second, or so many seconds per line. What you should bear in mind is that these speeds are *averages*, designed to help you calculate at a glance how long your piece of copy will take to deliver. Over the course of a forty second voice piece, or a two minute news bulletin, you may well find that your pace conforms exactly to the three words per second that the newsroom computer calculates for you. But within that time span – within every sentence even – you should not expect to be keeping to an unvarying, steady pace, as if reading to the beat of a metronome.

A monotonous pace sends the listener to sleep. Conversational speech rarely follows a regular pace, because changes in pace are part of the intonation that gives our words life and meaning. You should speed up and slow down within each sentence to signpost what is important for the listener to hear. You can also take whole paragraphs, or stories within a news bulletin, faster or slower depending on their content. It is this kind of variety that makes your delivery come alive.

Your overall guide to pace should be clarity. Can the listener follow you, or are you gabbling? Or is your delivery so portentously slow that the impatient listener will long ago have switched off?

Bear in mind also that different networks or stations have different stylistic conventions. Commercial stations like their news to be as upbeat as the music. Radio Four delivers news more slowly so that its listeners – older, and supposedly more thoughtful – have time to absorb and reflect on what they hear. BBC World Service recognizes that English is not always the first language of its listeners, so they require a still slower pace. The pictures often dictate the speed of television delivery, but you should be watchful that you are not trying to cram too many words in. Give the viewer time to absorb both the visual message and the voice-over.

The other complicating factor is that time runs differently when you are in front of the microphone. Because you are in a heightened state of awareness and your brain is working away at a rate of knots, you may sometimes think you are going slowly when you really are quite fast.

The only sure way of telling whether you are in fact going too fast overall, or too slow, is to record yourself and listen back. If it sounds like you are gabbling, you are too fast. If it sounds ponderous, you are too slow. Get a second opinion to clarify matters if you are uncertain.

Often it is the *pauses* in the flow that can make all the difference. Broadcasters sometimes are too terrified ever to pause in a quick-fire delivery, as if there was a danger the transmitter would shut down if they left even a millisecond of empty air space. Consequently, they don't allow themselves time even to draw a proper breath at the end of a sentence. As a long read continues, they become progressively more and more out of breath, and their voice becomes weaker and weaker.

Remember that a pause is the orator's oldest trick in the book. A pause in the right place engages the listener's attention, and keeps them hanging on expectantly. A pause can signpost a significant thought; draw quotation marks around reported speech; mark the end of one thought and the beginning of the next. You need pauses to indicate a change of subject – they not only tell your listener that you are moving onto the next topic, but they also give you time to draw a deep breath and change gear for the next subject.

I used a trick in my early days of broadcasting to get the hang of pausing long enough. I would use my foot (silently!) to tap out a beat for myself: one beat for a comma; two beats for a full stop; three beats for a change of subject, a paragraph, or news story; and four beats for a really tricky gear change from a tragic story to an upbeat one.

Get the pauses right and you can usually get the pacing right, no matter how fast or how slow you are aiming to be.

How can I avoid 'corpsing' – getting the giggles on air?

Is it any consolation to know that we've all done it – collapsed on air in uncontrollable laughter?

Some people are hopeless 'corpsers', and others take great pleasure in making their colleagues get the giggles. When I worked in local radio, it was never safe reading a bulletin in the evening when your colleagues had spent some time in the bar. There were occasions when someone would set the bottom of a script on fire to see if you could reach the last line before the flames did, and I once looked up to discover two particularly juvenile journalists had set the row of lights suspended above the desk swinging while they swayed rhythmically in the time in the opposite direction. Or there was the competition to weave a particular word into that day's broadcast – one broadcaster would set his on-air partner the challenge of some obscure or suggestive word, which they had to crowbar somehow into the programme, relevant or not.

Such childish pranks aside, it is usually the most ridiculous, meaningless and (to the rest of the world) *unfunny* thing that triggers on-air giggles. I once had to read out racing results when the winning horse had the extraordinary name of 'The Froddler'. For some reason, this struck me as unbearably hilarious and I got the giggles – made far, far worse by knowing that nobody in the rest of the known universe would find it amusing at all, as I made several breathless and strangulated attempts to explain to the listening thousands why I couldn't get the rest of the results out without collapsing again. It is that terrible tension – knowing you're being naughty, like children who can't stop laughing in front of a disapproving adult – that makes it so difficult to recover from corpsing.

Most of the time the audience love it. They may not actually see the precise joke, but they adore it when a broadcaster falls apart – the more serious the programme the better. You have the faint consolation that you are almost certainly going to make *Pick of The Week* on your particular station.

On the other hand, you have your professional dignity to maintain, and if you are working on a serious programme, at some point you are going to have to wipe your streaming eyes and start telling the audience about death, disaster, gloom, and doom in an appropriate tone of voice. That, of course, makes it much, much worse and impedes your ability to recover all the more.

The only solution I have ever found – and it is by no means guaranteed not to make things worse, if you have a particularly dark sense of humour – is to make yourself think of the most depressing and sobering thing that strikes at you personally. What that will be only you can determine, but it has to be something that you find really unfunny under all circumstances – the one part of your personal experience where you have a humour by-pass. Don't wait until you next corpse to call such a thing to mind, because you will almost certainly then pick something that will make your giggles even more uncontrollable. Decide what your sober-trigger is going to be right now so you are prepared.

And the best of British luck.

I still get nervous every time I go on air; how can I cure that?

Let me share a secret. Even the most experienced broadcasters get nervous, especially before a live transmission – and so they should. 'The day you stop getting nervous', one of the people who trained me said, 'is the day you should stop broadcasting'. In other words, it is the day when you will have become so smug and complacent you will have lost the ability to do your best.

The key is to control those nerves, rather than letting them control you. The pressure of performance releases the same hormones in your brain that are released whenever the body senses a threat. In this case, being on air is not exactly life threatening, but it is certainly stressful – are you going to screw up and look a fool in front of that huge unseen audience?

The hormones that are released are designed to help you overcome the threat – not just by giving you the physical energy to fight or flee, but by clarifying your thinking processes, shutting down unnecessary brain activity and distractions, so that time itself seems altered. You should embrace this clarity and focus – it gives you wonderful powers of concentration. It is also a fantastic buzz, and explains why so many broadcasters become addicted to the thrill of being live on air.

What gets in the way sometimes is another f-word – part of the same set of instinctive survival tactics, not fight or flight, but *freeze*. This is the rabbit's response to the oncoming headlights: do nothing, pretend to be dead and maybe the danger will pass you by. Helpful in fooling passing eagles, but not so clever if the danger is a juggernaut about to flatten you. And not so helpful in broadcasting either. The muscles lock rigid, which makes it extremely difficult to breathe deeply enough to support your voice. Not being able to breathe easily will start a subconscious sense of panic, and you lose control of the adrenalin response that would otherwise have been so helpful. Your heart rate rockets, your palms sweat.

This is the response you have to control, by rejecting the urge to freeze. You are not going to flee either – you are going to *fight*, and win. Deliberately unlock those muscles and make yourself breathe more deeply. That is why it can help to take three deep breaths before you start, really filling then emptying your lungs.

If you make use of the adrenalin of performance in this way, you will probably find that it gives you a real buzz. Personally I've always felt that the best mind-altering chemicals are the ones your brain produces entirely naturally, all by itself. If you feel stressed out or hyped up *after* a performance, go and do something physical, a run or a swim or a cycle ride, which will harmlessly disperse all those stress hormones you set loose.

The other thing to remember whenever you feel nervous before going on air is that a broadcaster's job isn't brain surgery. In the UK, broadcasting is not usually life threatening. Nobody is going to die if you don't get it absolutely perfect. That doesn't give you the license to stop caring about how well you perform, but at least it puts it into context.

GETTING FURTHER HELP

Some broadcasters will tell you proudly that they have never had a day's training in their life. They claim you don't need help to become a good broadcaster – you can pick it up by observing your colleagues at work. That may be true for a lucky few, but we all benefit from some objective assessment now and then.

Developing a voice's full potential is a life-long exercise. Many actors practise routines every morning, and religiously warm up their voice before performance. I am not suggesting that you should become obsessive about your voice. We broadcasters have microphones to help us and are not required to perform quite such extreme vocal gymnastics as those who work in the theatre. But a 'refresher' with a voice trainer can help everyone once in a while. Once you get a job in broadcasting, your employer should make it part of your ongoing training, though you may have to ask for it.

You should perhaps think of training your voice as you might think of training your body at a gym. It isn't necessary to belong to a gym to be fit; a brisk walk every now and then, or running up the stairs, can keep you in good shape. But you may find the gym enjoyable, and become fascinated by getting yourself to peak fitness. Of course it can cost money, but if you enjoy it, it's worth doing.

If you want to get further help with your voice, be clear before you start what kind of help you want so you can find the right trainer. For most common broadcasting problems, such as help with lifting a script off the page, intonation, or sounding more natural, you will be best off seeing a specialist voice coach who has background experience themselves as a broadcaster, as well as an understanding of how the voice works.

If you want help with breathing, or need more power in your delivery, or you want to lower the pitch of the voice – again you may be best off seeing a broadcasting specialist, but check first that they feel able to help in these areas. Voice coaches with a theatre background can sometimes be better qualified to work on the physical production of the voice, depending on the exact nature of the problem. Ask around among your colleagues, your bosses, or your college lecturers to find out if there is anyone they can recommend.

If you have a speech impediment of some sort you will need to seek more specialist help, and depending on its severity may even find that a speech therapist is the best person to see. Please remember that for this sort of problem there are no 'quick fixes' – it takes a lot of work on your part as well as the therapist's.

Voice coaching can be expensive if you bear the cost of it yourself. Your first step should always be to see what help you could get from the broadcasting organization you work for, or the college where you are studying. They should have expert voice trainers they can call on. Some broadcasting organizations also have informal mentoring schemes where a more experienced broadcaster will give you advice. These can be very helpful, but sometimes you will get a better result from seeing a trainer brought in from outside the department, who can give you an objective assessment untainted by office politics.

Don't be too proud to ask for help. The best thing about seeing a voice trainer is that it will almost always boost your confidence in your own abilities, and a good session should be fun too!

14 Does accent matter?

When I began voice coaching back in the late 1980s, one of the questions my clients would most frequently ask in those early sessions was 'Is my accent suitable for broadcasting?'

Thankfully it is far rarer these days for people to worry about their accent, but on the odd occasion when someone comes up with the same question I still answer in exactly the same way: 'So long as other people can understand you, *any* accent is suitable for broadcast.'

Regional accents are part of what gives broadcasting today its richness and texture. Broadcasting should reflect the diversity of national life, and thank goodness things have changed a great deal since I began broadcasting. Local radio, which started in the 1970s, was one of the major factors for change, even sometimes positively discriminating to encourage local accents onto the air. Inevitably, those local stations uncovered a pool of untapped talent who eventually moved on to national broadcasting, and so the stranglehold of the Home Counties BBC accent was at last broken.

It is almost unbelievable now to remember how tight that stranglehold once was. In 1974, I joined the BBC's World and External Services at Bush House, as a trainee sound technician. All trainees then were given a voice test, to discover if they had hidden potential as broadcasters. The voice coach at Bush House was a formidable woman called Fanny McCleod, who would listen as you read a short script, then grade your voice. I forget the precise nuances of the grading system, but basically we interpreted Grade One as a passport to future promotion: you would be considered good enough to try out for an announcer or newsreader's job. Grade Two suggested you had an acceptable voice and would be permitted to make the occasional on-air announcement, along the lines of 'This is London. ...' Grade Three implied you really were not suitable voice material and only in the event of a nuclear disaster, leaving just you and a cleaner with a cleft palate alive in the building, would you be allowed on air.

I was fairly proud of my voice in those days, having been the star in school drama productions. Plenty of people had told me I made a pleasant sound, so I expected to be instantly talent-spotted and labelled Grade One. Imagine my horror when Fanny McCleod scribbled a quick note on her pad, peered over her spectacles at me, and announced 'Grade Three'.

'*Three?*' I squawked somewhat unmusically. 'But why?'

'My dear', she pronounced with as much contempt as she could muster, 'you come from Birmingham'.

It transpired that the giveaway was the way I pronounced words ending with '... ing'. Midlanders tend to rather overdo the 'ng', especially on words like 'hanging' or 'singing'. To this day, it is the only trace of the Midlands in my voice and though it's not the prettiest sound, I have no desire to lose it. It was enough then though to disqualify me from announcing for the World Service.

Fanny McCleod is long gone, and nowadays if I fail to get a voice job the chances are it is because someone thinks I don't have *enough* of a regional accent! Regional voices are now hugely fashionable. First came a wave of Irish accents, snapping up some of the plum presenting jobs in national radio and TV. Next the Scots marched onto the airwaves, and became just as popular. (It is no accident that call centres are often located in Edinburgh or Dublin to capitalize on our fondness for those accents.) Then the compelling, anonymous voice of *Big Brother* sparked off a demand for Geordie voices. Welsh is still a bit of a slow burner, though a very soft hint of the Valleys has been always been considered exceptionally attractive in voices like those of Anthony Hopkins and John Humphrys.

So why are people still asking voice trainers 'Is my accent suitable for broadcasting?'

One possible reason is that myths about accent take a long time to die, even when the evidence is all over the airwaves that regional voices are now not only acceptable but also fashionable. There is in a few people's minds a vague unformed notion that maybe this is all a passing fad, and when it comes down to it, a sort of national standard accent is somehow best.

RP

RP stands for 'received pronunciation'. Language experts conceived the notion that there was a kind of national standard accent, a way of pronouncing English that every educated person might aspire to. For most of the last century, RP was considered to be aligned with Southern English pronunciation, and also identified with the 'Home Counties' accent. Because broadcasting was rightly considered to have an influence on the way people spoke, it was also often described as 'BBC English'.

The difficulty with the notion of 'standard English' is that language is not static. Not only do new words come into existence, and archaic ones fall out of use, but pronunciation itself changes over time. We would have difficulty understanding English as it was spoken in Shakespeare's day, not because the words are so very different, but because there has been a major alteration in the sound of the language, something known as the Great Vowel Shift. Before this, words containing the letters *er* for instance were pronounced with the sound of *ar*. So servants, to Shakespeare, were 'sarvants' – while for us the only relic of this archaic pronunciation is the odd word like 'sergeant', still pronounced 'sargeant' despite its spelling.

Although the Great Vowel Shift sounds like a cataclysmic upheaval, similar little shifts continue all the time. When I was at school – a private school where we were expected to throw off our local accents and speak as educated young ladies should in those days – there was shock and horror because my classmate Rosemary McConnell pronounced the letter 'l', when it came towards the end of a word, with a distinctive hint of a 'w'. *Little* came out as 'littoow', *well* near to 'wew'. Today, Rosemary's 'l' would fall easily within the bounds of RP pronunciation, because RP has shifted from Home Counties towards Estuary English. RP inevitably changes over the years, and the current speed of its change may well have been influenced by the recent openness of the broadcasting media to a diversity of accents. Perhaps before long the idea of 'standard English' will almost cease to have any meaning at all.

You can still be mocked for an accent, so it seems it is still the case that a hint of your origins in the voice is more acceptable than the full blown down-home variety of accent. But even that has begun to change.

This seems to be one area where we may be ahead of American broadcasters. I was intrigued to read in an American book on the voice that the preferred accent in most broadcasting organizations in the US is still 'Standard American English'. You can certainly find prominent broadcasters in the States who have regional accents, but it seems they are as yet the exception rather than the rule.

LINGERING PREJUDICES

But although the British airwaves are now open to a diversity of accents, there remain a few lingering prejudices.

It is still possible to find pockets of regional chauvinism amongst some local or regional broadcasting outlets. Their argument is that it is their job to reflect their area and encourage homegrown talent, so they may show a preference for local accents. I have some sympathy with the idea that local should sound local, especially where there are political sensitivities involved, as in the national regions – a Welsh listener might reasonably expect to hear more Welsh voices than English on Radio Wales, for instance – but it would be discriminatory to operate a blanket exclusion. Certainly it is possible for someone with an English accent to get a job at one of the national regions, even if they are unlikely to find themselves in the majority.

Nonetheless, there is some anecdotal evidence to suggest a non-local accent can tell against you when competing for a job at some local stations. Students on work experience placements occasionally report that it was made clear they would not be first in line for a job, because their accent didn't fit. There used to be a joke at Radio Bristol when I worked there many years ago that any accent was acceptable apart from a Welsh one – a reflection of the traditional hostility that was supposed to exist in the city towards any unfortunate Taff who ventured over the Severn Bridge. In fact the news editor at the time was Welsh, and sounded it – but he was the only one! These policies are rarely voiced openly, and certainly never written down, but even if they are more myth than reality they can deter some people from seeking jobs. Please don't let these myths stand in your way. We live in a mobile society, and it is time for prejudice to be broken down by able people who can do the job, no matter where they were born and brought up.

'Thick' accents

Far more common is the resistance to accents that are perceived as indicating a lack of education. It is, in our supposedly classless society, a hangover of class prejudice. Strong 'working class' accents like Liverpudlian Scouse, Brummie or Black Country, South London, and Glaswegian are still relatively rare on the air, because a few people consider that they sound 'thick' – unless you happen to be a comedian, in which case your accent makes you lovable. It is still felt in some quarters that the audience is not yet ready to hear news and current affairs, or serious documentary, delivered in an 'uneducated' voice.

It is worth pointing out that this is no more than cultural stereotyping. Why should someone with a Scouse accent, for instance, be dimmer or less educated than your average Brit? Some research was done a few years ago to canvass people's perceptions of a variety of English regional accents. The researchers played recorded examples to a group of English people. They asked them to rank the accents in order of preference and explain why. Bottom of the list, it turned out, was the Birmingham accent, upon which the English verdict was, roughly speaking, 'common, untrustworthy, and stupid'.

The researchers then played the same accents to a group of Canadians, who it seems were not blinkered by the same cultural prejudices. They ranked the Birmingham accent near the top of their list, praising it along the lines of 'warm, friendly, and quick-witted'. But sadly even Brummies themselves don't seem to like their own voices, infected with the national 'down' on their accent. 'It's ugly, isn't it?' said a friend of mine from the city. 'It's flat and whiney and boring.' But Canadians don't seem to think so.

'Posh' accents

The other area of prejudice is against accents at the other extreme of the class scale: upper class or public school accents. Particularly in regional broadcasting, these are considered to distance you from the audience. On the rare occasions I am now asked to help someone with an accent it is usually because it is felt they sound 'too posh'.

Breaking the bad news that their accent could hold up career progress can be a painful process, because the person concerned has probably grown up being told by their friends and family that they have a delightful voice. Twenty years ago, they would not have had the slightest difficulty getting a job in broadcasting. But fashions change, and the public school accent is now very definitely out of favour.

My usual approach (as it would be with any accent) is *not* to try and undo years of conditioning in the way people form vowel sounds and consonants. Broadcast voice coaches are usually brought in for one or two 'quick fix' sessions, and do not have the time to spend week after week taking a client through the kind of laborious vocal exercises practised by elocution and drama teachers. Nor is it necessary in most cases.

But to leave someone who has been criticized for having a 'posh' accent struggling on his or her own is unfair. They may do more harm than good, in the effort to make their speech fit in with what they imagine is the norm. For instance, many women with upper class accents have beautiful, clear enunciation – but trying to knock the cut glass out of their accent, they become deliberately sloppy in the way they form sounds. It rarely achieves anything useful – they simply sound like lazy speakers, pretending to be something they are not.

I try to persuade them that becoming a mush-mouth is not the solution. (Funnily enough, men with posh accents are frequently rather lazy speakers in the first place, drawling their words out of a hardly open mouth as if it is all too much effort to communicate.) Instead, I work with them not to change the accent, but to improve the overall sound of the voice and the effectiveness of their delivery. If you are a good communicator, the accent usually ceases to be an issue.

WORKING WITH AN ACCENT

The more a person with an accent worries about trying consciously to change it while they are on the air, the less effective he or she becomes as a communicator. Too much concentration is focused on the sound of their voice, rather than the sense of what they are saying.

Instead, you should work on the same kind of things we have already looked at in this book – relaxing the body, opening the mouth and chest, and *making sense of the words*. Frequently, this improves your delivery by taking the tension out of the process, and it gives you back the confidence you may have lost through criticism of your accent. The result is you will sound so much more authoritative on air that your accent ceases to be the first thing people notice about your voice.

Besides, you don't have to hurtle off to an expensive course of elocution lessons or make a great deal of conscious effort to knock the hard corners off an accent. There is a natural process that will do it for you. It is one we have all grown up with: the human talent for adapting to circumstances and changing our voice according to our environment.

Protective colouration

We all have a little of the Rory Bremner in us, the ability to mimic other voices. We use it mostly as protective colouration, and we often change our voices over the years according to where we live or work.

My brother and I for instance were both brought up in Birmingham. I went to a local school but he was sent away to boarding school, where you were likely to be mercilessly teased if you had a regional accent. Not surprisingly, his disappeared almost overnight. But after school, I left Birmingham never to return and headed south, where my voice became more 'southern'. He went back to Birmingham, where he married a Midlands girl, and he works in industry surrounded by people who have local accents, so he has reverted to a Brummie accent. But when we see each other, the distance between our respective accents is subtly eroded. He gets posher, I get more Brummie, and we meet somewhere in the middle.

If you have a particular accent, almost inevitably you will knock some of its hard corners off when you are surrounded by people who speak in a different way, unconsciously picking up some of their intonations and vowel sounds. This often happens to children at school if they have moved to a different part of the country – it is a reflection of our subconscious desire to 'fit in'. The more people travel around the country for work, the more we are becoming a nation of hybrid accents. Liz Barclay, a broadcaster on Radio Four's *You and Yours*, has what most people perceive to be a Scottish accent, after spending many years there. Yet if you listen hard, you can still hear Ulster in her voice from her early years in Northern Ireland. Meanwhile Huw Edwards came with a distinctive Welsh accent to read national news bulletins on BBC television. After only a few months in London, former colleagues in Wales had begun to remark that Huw sounded rather less Welsh than he had done when he was working in Cardiff.

This hybridization is likely to happen whether you intend it or not – the effort, perhaps, is in holding on to your original accent! Nor should you think of it as a betrayal of your roots. When you go back home to your family, your accent will begin to adjust back to the way they speak (though they will still swear you've got 'posher' if you've spent time down South, or more 'ee bah gum' if you've been working in the North). You should accept this as a natural way in which the voice adjusts to your circumstances. If someone where you work is prejudiced against your accent, you will probably find that the barbed remarks start to tail off after a while, not because you have made a complete change, but because you have unconsciously begun to soften its edges to an acceptable level by their standards. Of course, the other solution is to find somewhere else to work where the prejudice doesn't exist!

DOES 'ACCENT' MASK A DIFFERENT PROBLEM?

If one of your bosses criticizes your voice for an accent, make sure that there are not other ways you could improve it without trying to 'put on' a voice. Often criticism of an accent is just a way of suggesting that other aspects of your voice need changing. Some people don't have the vocabulary to describe exactly what it is that seems wrong about your delivery, so they seize on the most obvious difference from the norm.

For me, the issue is not your accent but how you use your voice. If you can deliver your words with clarity, intelligence, and warmth, sounding like a human being talking rather than a robot reading, it should not matter where you were born or brought up.

My hope is that if this book should ever be reprinted in a second edition, even the lingering prejudices against accent will have eventually disappeared so that I can cut out this chapter altogether – or keep it only as a reminder of our curious broadcasting history, along with announcers wearing dinner jackets, programmes recorded on vinyl discs, and splicing recording tape with razor blades.

15 A question of style

In the modern world of genre broadcasting, different stations, networks, or programming may look for very different vocal styles. How does Independent Local Radio (ILR) differ from BBC, for instance? This chapter also looks at genres outside the mainstream, including hospital radio and corporate video, and considers specialized voice techniques: how to deliver news with authority; how to make weather and travel sound interesting; how to make a TV commentary come alive.

When I was quite a young broadcaster, I remember sitting in the pub one night with one of my colleagues, staring into our drinks as we contemplated our future careers. 'The boss thinks my voice is awful,' said my friend gloomily. 'He said I'll never get an on-air job in broadcasting. My voice just isn't right for this station.'

'So what are you going to do?' I asked.

'Dunno. Go to London, I suppose – see if I can get a job there.'

So off she went. Two years later, she was reading the news on Radio One. She later reported for *Newsnight* on BBC2, made current affairs documentaries for ITV, was a presenter on BBC TV's *Top Gear*, and hosted a travel show on Radio Four. Which just goes to show how wrong some people can be – and how adaptable Janet Trewin's voice eventually turned out to be, working on a range of different networks and programmes.

When I look back now though, I can see the point our boss was making at the time. Janet then had a young voice and a rather breathless, breakneck delivery. It was at odds with the rather more measured style of our local speech-based station in those days, but perfect for the upbeat sound of news on a music network that targeted young people.

Over the next few years, Janet and I often used to run into each other in the corridors of Broadcasting House, she on her way to deliver rapid-fire news and hot entertainment gossip, I to dispense caring advice to the discerning consumer. I was always a bit envious – trivial soul that I am, I wanted to broadcast over a pounding music bed and banter with the DJs about the weather. But, quite frankly, I would probably have sounded ridiculous.

Are some voices more suited to particular types of programming than others? Or do we straitjacket ourselves into particular styles? Can you adapt? Should you adapt? Or when your face and voice don't fit should you simply pack up your bags and go, like my friend did?

There are no hard and fast answers. We have already seen that there is an element of personal taste that comes into our reactions to a particular voice, and if your boss hates your voice even after you have had some professional help, you might find you are both happier and more successful elsewhere. But there is also a perfectly legitimate question of style – how well a voice fits with the overall station sound or genre of broadcasting.

If you apply the principles you have learnt so far in this book, they should help you whatever kind of broadcasting you do – TV or radio, news or more general programmes. Whether you are a DJ or a journalist, a documentary maker or a weather forecaster, to get the best out of your voice you need to be aware of your posture, your breathing, and your mind-set. But if you want to move between genres you also need to be able to *adapt* your voice, which may not be as difficult as you imagine. Think of it as dressing in a different way for different occasions. You can still be as much yourself in a smart wedding outfit as in a pair of comfortable old jeans.

TUNING IN TO STYLE

Most of what you need to know about style comes from common sense and *listening* to the output. If you have chosen to work on a particular station or in a particular genre, you should immerse yourself in what others are doing on the same station or in the same genre. It is the best way to forge a shared sense of purpose and identity. That does not mean copying slavishly everyone else who broadcasts on your particular programme or station. You were hired to be 'yourself', not an on-air clone. Remember those keen-eared listeners and viewers with their built-in insincerity detectors. They will soon spot whether you are trying to pretend to be something or somebody you are not.

Of course, you must play to your strengths. You can love music, but still be a hopeless daytime DJ if you find inconsequential chatter... well, inconsequential. You would be better off finding a late night slot that lets you talk to other real aficionados of the music. And why try to be a news reporter if you find current events frankly dull? Get yourself a job on a celebrity gossip spot if that's what sparks your real interest.

But don't let yourself be pigeonholed. Broadcasting skills are often easily transferable from programme to programme, from station to station, from local to network, and from radio to TV and vice versa, despite what some of your colleagues might imply. Broadcasting is full of people who think they do a better job than anyone else. They like to look down their noses and claim that what they do on their station or programme is infinitely superior to what *you* have been doing in your previous job – but you should politely ignore them. Be ready to learn, but recognize you also are bringing something with you – perhaps something *new*. Style 'rules' are made to be broken; that is how broadcasting evolves over time.

GENRE STYLES

Imagine a world where every television chef felt they had to model themselves on Jamie Oliver. Yet bizarrely some sports departments seem to be stuffed with Des Lynam sound-alikes, and I sometimes find myself wondering if there is a specialist school of traffic reporters somewhere, urging their graduates all to use precisely the same weary intonation patterns. 'It's important to sound as if you *don't care* about temporary traffic lights', I imagine them telling their pupils. 'And a multiple pile up on the M25 – you can really be dismissive about that one.'

You should never feel you have to copy slavishly the sound of other broadcasters working in your chosen genre. Many years ago the comedy show *Monty Python's Flying Circus* satirized the style of a then famous broadcaster called Alan Whicker, whose particular intonation pattern was easy to imitate. His speciality was to travel the world making documentaries about the idiosyncrasies of cultures-within-cultures, rather like Louis Theroux has done more recently. In the sketch the *Python* team visited Whicker Island, an isolated community of broadcasters who all modelled themselves on Whicker – heavy-rimmed glasses, microphone clutched in the hand, strolling through their pieces-to-camera and all employing the same (*pause*) nasal delivery, the same (*pause*) signature pauses for effect, the same (*pause*) lists of carefully crafted wry phrases... It was very funny but – as *Python* often did – it made a serious point about television, and the way that broadcasters often unconsciously imitate a successful style rather than developing their own. I still hear Whickers today, but Louis Theroux, covering very similar subject matter, has had the wit to develop a sound and style of his own.

So it's worth examining the pitfalls you should avoid as well as the tricks you can borrow in some of the genres you may want to enter.

The news voice

Is there such a thing as a news voice, distinctively different from general programme styles? You would certainly think so, listening to news on both national and local broadcasting outlets. Many reporters assume an urgency and toughness to their delivery, which may be very different from their normal speaking voice. But is this necessarily the right thing to do?

Let's try to answer this question by looking at the audience's needs and expectations. First and foremost, your listeners or viewers are looking for *credibility*. They want to be able to believe that what you are saying is true and that you know what you are talking about. They also need *clarity* – to be able to hear and understand what you are saying. This is where that elusive quality we have mentioned before, **authority**, comes to the forefront. You will recall that I said authority is not so much a tone of voice as a state of mind – knowing what you are talking about, and engaging the brain in the process of communication. It is above all an *intelligent* delivery.

By all means, inject some power into your voice. You do need as a news broadcaster to sound strong, mature, and certain. But you must not adopt an unnaturally forceful delivery if that causes you to lose any of the clarity and intelligence of your voice.

Pushing the voice and over-stressing words – a common fault among reporters who are trying to adopt what they imagine to be a 'news voice' – does not give you authority. It undermines the credibility of your voice, especially if you happen to be stressing the wrong words.

Bulletin reading

For many years, there has been a debate in broadcasting over who is best qualified to read the news. Some stations prefer what you might think of as 'professional voices' – people chosen for the sound of their voice, no matter whether they come from a news background or not. Others prefer to use journalists as newsreaders, because it is felt their experience of news gathering gives them greater insight into the material and therefore lends extra credibility to their performance.

Ideally a newsreader has to have a blend of these qualities – both a good voice, and the background to understand and love news. Sometimes the pendulum has swung so far towards journalists reading the news that it has become just another job on the newsroom rota, and journalists have to do it irrespective of how suitable their voices are. Sometimes there has been a counter-swing back towards the 'professional' voices.

Whatever your background, a newsreader's voice must have those qualities of authority and credibility. To sustain a bulletin, you need both to understand the news and make a good sound. Because a bulletin can be a read of anything between a minute and half-an-hour, you will need to be able to support your voice with good breathing and intelligent intonation over a much longer period than a reporter usually has to.

When reading any news bulletin, the key point is to *vary* it. To keep your listener or viewer interested you must point up the difference between stories. If you start each one on the same note, following an identical intonation pattern on the opening words, they will soon switch off, mentally if not physically. A well-read bulletin requires texture. Some people describe this as *light and shade.* It means that both the inflexions and the pace should alter. Some stories can be taken faster; others you may want to slow down on because of their subject matter.

Think of the pauses between stories – and pauses there should be, however brief, however upbeat the bulletin, to let your audience know you are moving onto a new subject – as *gear changes.* They are an opportunity for you to get your head round the next story and change tone appropriately.

If you want to hear just how well some newsreaders manage to get texture into a bulletin, you could tune in to Radio Four at 6 PM. I am not suggesting you should copy the style, because Radio Four has a very particular audience and the measured pace reflects their perceived tastes. It would probably be far too slow for most local or regional stations and it is relatively formal. But what you can learn from it is how a single newsreader manages to sustain a half-hour read, albeit with inserts, and keep the audience engaged.

Balance your listening by then tuning in to a very different kind of bulletin – the breakfast news on Virgin Radio. You'll hear something with much more pace and excitement, but also the same sense of texture, varying the approach between stories. If you want to be a good newsreader, you should make an effort to listen to the different ways other stations and networks approach news, television as well as radio, ILR and commercial broadcasting as well as BBC.

If you are having trouble getting variety into your bulletins, refer back to Chapter 8. You will find some helpful pointers there for changing a monotonous delivery. Above all, remember to think about the stories as you read them. If you don't sound interested, your listener or viewer won't be interested.

BBC versus 'commercial' style

If there is any area where the debate over style turns into a battle, this is it. Because the BBC and the independent stations are rivals, even when they are not in direct competition for a particular type of audience, you may find yourself caught in the crossfire if you move from one to the other.

Commercial broadcasters characterize BBC style as 'slow and stuffy'. BBC broadcasters become defensively superior and the hapless new recruit will be told, 'You sound too commercial. Here, we deliver scripts with *intelligence*.' Ouch.

There are huge misconceptions on both sides about exactly what constitutes the opposing style. ILR does not simply require that you go fast and loud. Nor does the BBC demand you should necessarily be slow and sedate. Intelligence is not restricted to the BBC, nor is excitement only to be found on an ILR station or commercial TV.

BBC and ILR news styles

In radio, the most hotly debated question is how the news should be delivered. I listen to both BBC and ILR stations and for me the difference between the two is not a question of one being right and the other wrong. Each takes a different approach dictated by what they know about their individual audiences. Both are aiming to make news fit seamlessly with the overall station sound.

Bear in mind that most ILR stations cater for an audience who tune in for the music first, the news second. Station bosses have to make the news match the sound of the music or their listeners will turn off. Nevertheless, news isn't just there to fulfil the licence requirements, it is something that genuinely interests the audience.

Local BBC stations know that very often their audience is tuning in specifically for information – they like speech-based programming, with a more relaxed, less frenetic feel. A local BBC audience is probably older than an ILR audience and hearing the news may be what they turned on for in the first place.

These different approaches can be characterized by the *feel* of the news.

ILR news	BBC news
• Energized, it's happening right now	• Yes, it's happening, but stay calm
• Hot	• Cool
• Youthful	• Mature
• Exuberant	• Considered, thoughtful
• Excited	• Exciting (or at the very least, interesting)

ILR news is generally delivered with a faster pace than a BBC bulletin. This is not just to reflect excitement – you can still sound excited or exciting even when you are speaking slowly, and all news should be interesting and exciting – but to match the overall pace of the music on the station. But going faster is not a licence to gabble. You still need to be understood. You still need gear changes between stories, though they will be fast ones. Nor is matching the pace of the music any excuse for developing rhythms or patterns, which are the enemies of understanding (see Chapter 8).

It is your mind-set that will most easily help you achieve the right style. Remember what I said about using your personal listener to give you the key to your performance. This is where you need to invoke his or her help, by thinking of yourself as talking to a real person who is interested in the news, but who may be listening in different ways depending on whether they are tuned in to ILR or BBC.

Because of the common misconceptions, it is easy to make a mistake when you first try to adjust between the two. So you should also bear in mind what those individual styles are NOT:

ILR news	BBC news
• NOT gabbling, frenzied	• NOT slow and ponderous
• NOT rhythmic or predictably patterned	• NOT bland, uninflected, uninterested
• NOT stressing the last word in every sentence	• NOT monotonous, boring, turgid unvaried pace
• NOT shouted or powered by nasal resonance	• NOT wearing a metaphorical dinner jacket

In other words, in neither genre should the pace be tediously *predictable*. Sometimes it is hard to avoid these faults when you first arrive on a station. You may find that one or two of your colleagues have slipped into them, and merrily pass them on, like chickenpox. I think it is particularly hard for younger, inexperienced broadcasters (in either ILR or the BBC) who have not had much in the way of voice training, and who find that they are being asked to 'get more power into their voice'. Often they end up developing a false, over-projected, over-stressed delivery, which is actually the very reverse of powerful and authoritative. This is exactly the point at which you need some help from a trainer; and though well-meaning colleagues can pass on some useful tips, they are not always the best source of advice for how to increase the power of your voice (refer instead back to Chapters 4 and 5).

Music radio

There are so many different styles of music radio that it is almost impossible to generalize, and really the topic deserves a book to itself. But great DJ voices are unforgettable, often because they are unique and unafraid of sounding different. On good music radio, the DJ voice should be not so much an interruption to the music as seemingly a part of it. Your voice should be helping to create an overall sound to draw the listeners in.

It is the one area of broadcasting where you can get away with using rhythm in your delivery, and DJs sometimes do just that to keep the sense of beat and pace going. Used well, it is magical. Used badly, as a slavish imitation of another DJ's style, it is grim. In music radio you must find your own voice.

I may be old-fashioned here but I also think it is useful to know *when to shut up*. I am not suggesting you should restrict yourself to 'That was ... This is ...' – how terribly boring that would be. But people often listen to music stations because they like music, and not because they want to hear reams of chatter. There are notable exceptions – classic pairings like Mark and Lard on Radio One for instance – but they are genuinely funny. Be sure you are as amusing as you think you are. Perhaps a good rule of thumb for young broadcasters just starting out is to shut up at least two sentences

245

before you think you've said everything in your head. You can indulge yourself later in your career, when the audience figures and your salary confirm it is your personality and not just the music that attracts the listeners.

Nonetheless you should not be afraid to let your personality emerge, and make the show your own. Although the type of music is the main reason the audience tune in, a very close second to that comes the presenter. Music radio executives know that the presenter's personal style and ability to entertain and amuse can be a big draw for the audience, which is why top presenters on both BBC and ILR stations command large salaries.

ILR presenters, aiming for a younger audience, tend to sound more 'in your face'. Local BBC presenters, working to an older audience, often have a warmer, more laid-back feel. But these are not hard and fast rules. You can still be warm and relaxed even when broadcasting to younger audiences. Jo Wylie on Radio One – a youth network if ever there was one – has a much gentler feel to her presentation style than many of her colleagues. It is still possible to be yourself within the parameters of an overall station style.

Of course it really helps if you enjoy the music you are playing. However desperate you are to get into radio, never work on a station where you hate the play list – you will find it very difficult to shine there.

Weather and travel

I include these two together because the pitfalls are often the same. Weather and travel news are an integral part of any broadcasting day. Arguably, they are more important to large sections of the audience than anything else. With the unpredictability of British weather, it is not surprising we have a national obsession with it. Meanwhile, in what is supposed to be an increasingly mobile society, our roads get ever more clogged, trains grind to a halt, planes get delayed. Yet broadcasters persist in using a throwaway delivery for weather and travel, as if they were irrelevant.

Weather and traffic are such habitual features of your programme that it is hard to keep your style of delivery fresh. When you are in a nice centrally-heated, air-conditioned studio where the temperature remains constant most of the day, it is easy to forget that some people are out in that weather you are rattling through so dismissively. As you mention the temporary traffic lights on the ring road for the third time that week, it is difficult to remember that there may be some poor devil passing through the area, tuned to your station for the first time, stuck in a mile-long queue and needing that information.

Of course you've done it a million times, you could read it in your sleep. Traffic news or weather may seem boring because you deliver it every day, but it *really matters to someone*. The best way of improving your performance is always to have that someone in mind, so you avoid falling into a throwaway pattern.

Here's a typical example. It's clearly a radio report, but I've heard TV forecasters doing the same:

> And the weather – rain TONIGHT, but brightening skies towards MORNING, chilly for the time of YEAR with a TOP TEMPERATURE of 15 degrees CELSIUS. The outlook for later in the WEEK, showers with sunny PERIODS. IT'S – five o'CLOCK!

In any weather report, there will probably be only a handful of key words essential for the listener/viewer to hear. But if you look at the example above (you can also listen to it on the CD-ROM), you can see that all too often the words that the blasé or bored presenter stresses are the very opposite of those that should be made clear. This is how it might have been better signposted:

> And the WEATHER – RAIN tonight, but BRIGHTENING skies towards MORNING, CHILLY for the time of year with a top temperature of 15 DEGREES celsius. The OUTLOOK for later in the week, SHOWERS with SUNNY PERIODS. It's FIVE o'clock!

Clear vocal signposting is just as critical in travel news, because your audience need to be alerted when their particular traffic hot spot is mentioned. If you have any trouble with that concept, please join me on the motorway sometime to enjoy the delights of negotiating a stop–start tailback while someone reads the travel news so fast you can't pick out which junction to turn off at for the alternative route.

Sports broadcasting

Sports broadcasters are easy to satirize. They get so very excited when they are commentating on a live event – apart from cricket commentators, who ever since the days of the great John Arlott and Brian Johnston seem to have made a speciality out of not getting excited at all.

But there is nothing wrong with getting excited – after all to its devotees, sport *is* thrilling. A sports broadcaster needs to reflect the audience's eagerness to discover the outcome of the match. To outsiders who find the sport in question boring, the excitement seems ridiculous, but we must assume that they have long since turned off or will be using the sports bulletin on their favourite breakfast show as an opportunity to nip off and clean their teeth.

Although sport is part of mainstream broadcasting, you can safely proceed on the basis that you will be broadcasting to fellow fans. But that does not mean you should assume all your audience share the same level of knowledge about sport. I may not be able to name every player on the field for Aston Villa, but I am still interested to know how the team is doing in the Premiership. (Probably not so well, judging by past form.) Nor should you assume that all your listeners are equally interested in every sport you are going to mention. There are people who are listening avidly because they are waiting for the latest on Formula One, but they couldn't give a stuff about the golf.

So *signposting* is especially important in sports bulletins. Radio listeners in particular need it to alert them to the moment their particular sport or team is mentioned.

Unfortunately, many sports broadcasters seem blissfully unconscious of this. They rattle through the bulletin in throwaway style, following what seems to be a rhythmic, prescribed pattern of intonation that every sports broadcaster learns at their father's knee. They seem to be particularly prone to picking up bad habits from each other, so much so that I find they are genuinely shocked when I suggest that some of them might engage the brain and put thought into changing the pattern of their delivery. 'But that's how sports reporters sound!' said one. 'You're *supposed* to give it a rhythm!'

You can still sound enthusiastic and excited without gabbling. Rhythmic speech, however fast, sends the audience into a trance. By all means, reflect the thrill of sport to your listeners or viewers, but give them a bit of help too by using intelligent intonation, so they can understand why this particular piece of news or sporting history is so significant.

NON-MAINSTREAM GENRES

Working outside the mainstream is often a good way to learn the craft of broadcasting, and many broadcasters got their start on hospital radio or in-house networks.

Hospital radio

Hospital radio presenters have the unique experience of broadcasting to an entire audience who are not well. It may seem obvious; but it is important how you deal with that. People vary in their response to illness. Some are going to be feeling rotten; others may feel they are on the point of being back on their feet, ready to go out into the wider world. But the one thing they won't want from you is sickly sentiment. They don't want to be pitied; they prefer to be treated like a perfectly ordinary audience. It is your job to distract them from the fact that they are stuck inside this place, with very little to do except worry about their illness.

But don't let that make you become over-cheerful. If you think back to your own experiences of being unwell, even if it's not to the same degree, you will realize that the worst thing in the world when you feel bad is the falsely hearty friend.

It is a fine balance, and probably one of the hardest jobs in broadcasting to get exactly right. I have huge admiration for good hospital

DJs; no wonder so many go on to careers in professional broadcasting. The best ones do rather more than just go in for their shift. They take the time and trouble to get to know their audience, and the relationship they build up with them is what makes them such good broadcasters.

In-shop radio, shopping channels, and corporate video

It's perhaps a little unfair to lump these three together, but broadcasters working in these media are different in one important respect from others. Their job is to sell.

You could argue that all broadcasters are 'selling' something – the news, their network, the reality show viewer-voting lines, themselves. Mostly though the aim of the mainstream broadcaster is to entertain and inform, not to persuade the listeners or viewers to part with their money.

But selling doesn't mean you should put on an act. If your job is to make people buy, or buy into something like a corporate ethic, you need to embrace that whole-heartedly. You need to find within yourself a genuine enthusiasm for the product, just as a non-selling broadcaster needs to find a genuine enthusiasm for the story. If you feel embarrassed or cynical about what you are doing you shouldn't have taken on the job. The audience, remember, have those built-in insincerity detectors – their ears. You can be sure that your voice will give you away, however good an actor you think you are. And if they suspect even for a moment that what they're hearing is a cynical act, they won't buy.

In-shop radio has become an area of broadcasting that has expanded recently, and many big chain retailers have started to dabble in the field. Some of the most successful I have heard have been in music stores, where they work particularly well because they are staffed by music fans doing what they would naturally do anyway – enthuse about music.

To be successful on in-shop radio, you need not only genuine enthusiasm but also exceptional *clarity*. Your voice has to cut into the reverie that most shoppers wander round in. Unlike a normal broadcasting audience, they have not switched on to listen, and they are probably doing their best to ignore you.

But even though it is your job to grab their attention, you have to moderate that with knowing you must not irritate them. Too aggressive a delivery could send them back out onto the street in droves. Again, it is a case of knowing and wooing your audience. So if you work for a chain of young people's clothes shops, you can bounce around and be much more of a personality than if you were working for an upmarket department store.

People *choose* to switch onto a **shopping channel**, so at least you have the comfort of knowing that unlike the in-shop radio presenter, your audience actually want to hear you.

There are a lot of jokes at the expense of people who work on shopping channels, but they are remarkably good training for a career in the wider world of broadcasting. With very little time to prepare, you learn to handle props live in front of a camera, chatting away blithely, needing to be clear in your explanation of what this gadget does, enthusiastic enough to sell it, and concise enough not to bore people into switching off if they are not interested in that particular product. You learn to talk to time, you learn to work with co-presenters, and you learn to use your personality to draw an audience.

But what if you find yourself having to sell some gizmo that frankly, you would not give as a Christmas present to your least favourite auntie?

This is a trick that I think requires particular mental agility. An insincere hymn to its virtues is not going to be successful, unless you can really make yourself believe in that moment that this is the best product of its kind. You must try and understand why it might actually be a useful article. *You* might not want it, but there just might be someone who will not only part with hard cash for it but also think their money well spent. Try and imagine that person and why it would be so very appealing to them. The secret of the good salesperson is to know their customer, and not to despise them, even though they may not share their tastes.

Corporate video clients generally want an up-beat but traditional style. Most have rather conservative tastes in the kind of voices they go for and will either prefer a big name, or a smooth, warm, classless RP voice. Until recently, it was still surprisingly hard for women to get work doing voice-overs for corporate clients.

If you want to work in this area, you need to make a show reel or voice tape, selling the quality and range of your talents as a voice-over artist, and tout it round the studios and production companies that make corporate videos. It may well sit on a shelf there gathering dust, so follow up with phone calls. But to do well in this field, unless you are already a well-known name you need an agent.

Potentially you can make a lot of money from corporate voice-overs. But it is a very hard market to break into if you do not have the contacts. Many people who think it might be fun to give it a go end up disappointed, because most producers rely on voices they already know.

TELEVISION VOICES

Should television voices have a different style from those in radio? In a bi-media world, broadcasters cross back and forth between the two with no difficulty. Essentially it is the programme content and the audience, rather than the medium, which sometimes force a change of style on a broadcaster. Jeremy Vine began to moderate his tough *Newsnight* delivery when he moved from television to radio, because barking out the questions at interviewees would not have been appropriate in the cosier setting of a Radio Two lunchtime programme.

But there is one important difference between radio and television, and we have touched on it briefly already in Chapter 9 when we talked about writing for broadcast.

In radio, voice carries almost all of the work of communication. In TV, voice supports pictures. You should be thinking of your voice as providing a commentary, not the full story – an explanation and an enhancement for the pictures.

TV voice-over

A helpful tip that you might like to bear in mind if you are doing a TV voice-over is to think about where you position yourself in relation to your audience. We have already talked about imaginatively placing yourself in the same room or space with the listener or viewer. But you should bear in mind that you occupy different amounts of their attention, depending on the medium.

In radio, you effectively face your audience. It is as if you are sitting on the chair opposite the listener. You have one-to-one eye (and voice) contact and you are trying to hold their full attention.

In television, you should not necessarily think of the viewer as facing you (unless you are doing a PTC, or reading a bulletin in vision). When you are out of vision, doing a voice-over, the viewer's main attention is focused on the pictures on the screen, and it is as if you were leaning on the back of the sofa just behind them, tapping them on the shoulder to point out the aspects of the pictures that need explanation.

This is a useful technique to employ especially when you are doing a voice-over to a programme where the pictures largely speak for themselves. It has given rise to a particular style of voice-over that I think of as 'the whisper in the ear' – not literally a whisper, but a rather more intimate, slightly under-projected, wry style of delivery that can in some circumstances be very effective.

The 'whisper in the ear' must be used with caution. I tried it out once on a documentary and thought at the time it sounded rather fine. When I actually watched the documentary go out on air, I realized it hadn't been so much a whisper as an uninflected mutter! But you can still make use of the idea behind it – the sense that you are interjecting to draw the viewer's attention to something interesting, helping to explain what they are seeing.

But the more important the information you are trying to convey, the more up-front you should be in your voice-over style. Not a 'bellow in the ear', of course, but a firm, crisp, concise delivery to make sure what you are saying grabs the viewer's attention. Remember always that your voice should not be competing with the pictures. It should be working together with them and enhancing them.

MOVING TO NETWORK

Is there any real difference between network and local style? Moving from a local radio station or a regional television centre to a national network can seem a big step. At first, you will be stunned by what seem like limitless resources and facilities, after the budgetary constraints of local broadcasting. (Don't worry, you will soon be moaning again about not having enough money or time to make the programmes to the standards you would like.) In real terms though you may have to make very little adjustment in your style. Usually the biggest hurdle to overcome is your own sense of awe: 'What on earth am I doing here?'

When I first moved from local radio to a daily programme on a national station, I couldn't help feeling I had somehow got the job on false pretences. I was convinced that now I was on network I would have to sound more grown-up. I didn't understand freshness was exactly what the editor wanted from me, and by trying to change myself to fit what I imagined was the network approach, I actually lost the very qualities that had got me the job in the first place. It took me quite a while to find myself again.

Carolyn Brown, the Radio Four newsreader who appears on the CD-ROM accompanying this book, went through something very similar. Previously, she had been news editor on an independent local radio station. One of the reasons Radio Four gave her the job as a continuity announcer was because she had a lively voice with a warm Northern accent, and they were trying to get away from what was in those days an overwhelmingly rather formal Southern sound. But the first time I heard her on Radio Four, I almost didn't recognize her voice. Instead of being herself, she was trying to sound as she imagined a Radio Four continuity announcer should: smooth, bland, and decidedly un-Northern. In time, she relaxed and took off the metaphorical dinner jacket to become one of the network's most popular continuity and news voices.

I have since trained a number of people making a similar leap, going through exactly the same anxieties about whether they are really up to the mark (of course they are, how else did they get the job?), and squashing all the life out of their performance as a result. Often they sound bland, over-polite, and over-anxious to please, because they feel they dare not be themselves.

Stop putting yourself down. You wouldn't be there if you hadn't already demonstrated talent and potential. Don't let yourself be squashed by the over-powering feeling that network is somehow 'different' from what you have already been doing. They employed you because you had a quality they liked, something new they hoped you would bring to the programme. You don't need to put on a voice or adopt a false persona to give yourself network credibility.

SUMMARY

- To key in to a station or programme style, listen to the output, and be aware of who your audience is likely to be.
- Don't feel you have to slavishly imitate others to get the style right.
- Play to your strengths – if you don't like the job, get out.
- Never get blasé or cynical about what you are doing.
- Don't be over-awed by a new job.

16 Star quality

What additional requirements are there for the voice of a presenter? How does the role differ from being a reporter or occasional contributor to a programme? The presenter stands in a slightly different relationship to the audience, and so must bring something extra to their delivery.

For every broadcaster who has made it to the top of the profession in television or radio, there are hundreds – no, thousands – of hopefuls who would like to be in their shoes. Presenting is often seen from the outside as the top job in broadcasting. It isn't, of course – the real power lies in the hands of a few men or women who have realized that clawing your way up through the management structure gives you far more control over what actually hits the airwaves. Nonetheless, presenting is where the glamour lies. It can also, at the very top, be where the money lies. But I wouldn't advise you to go into presenting if you want to get rich. Only a very few reach that level.

All the same, whatever kind of presenter you are there is nothing like that heady, if illusory, feeling of being the one who matters. It is *your* show, and that feels very different from being one of the backroom staff or a reporter or contributor.

So what is it that separates the few who actually become presenters from the thousands of wannabes? Is it a matter of looks, talent, personality, being in the right place at the right time, who you know, or even – since this is a book about vocal performance – your voice?

Any or all of those things can be helpful. But after watching and listening to and working with a whole variety of presenters, my belief is that in the end it comes down to Ingredient X: something that is almost impossible to define, but whose presence we can all recognize when we come across it.

Presenters often have good voices. But what makes them great presenters is more importantly *distinctive* voices. We're really looking at a different kind of voice here, the kind of 'voice' people describe writers as eventually finding – the inner voice which is about who you are and what you have to say to the world. Unless you can find that, you will never become more than one of the also-rans.

WHAT MAKES *YOU* SPECIAL?

Where does that Ingredient X lie? Does it help if you have looks? Personality? Or is it, as I've heard many a cameraman or woman mutter, all in the bones?

Actually, as one who generally looks like a blob in front of a camera, I can't help feeling there might be some truth in that. Some people's faces just seem to work so much better on camera than others. They may not even be hugely good-looking in everyday life, but the camera brings out some special geometry in their features. You can envy them – but you shouldn't necessarily despair if you weren't born with that happy accident of bone structure.

The same goes for voices. You can have rich and beautiful tones that the microphone seems to adore. But if beauty is all that your voice contains, you might as well go and work in a call centre.

I have watched presenters who look fantastic on screen, and yet fail to engage the viewer. Conversely, I've seen presenters who are physically quite unremarkable, yet still draw you in so that you hang on their every word and gesture. The historian Simon Schama is a great example of this. I'm sure I am not the only middle-aged woman who has a secret crush on him. Every time he wriggles his shoulders – a mannerism I would find immensely irritating in any other presenter – I shudder with delight, waiting for whatever gripping historical nugget he's about to impart.

What makes Simon Schama work so well on screen is not just his historical erudition, but his obvious enthusiasm for his subject. Enthusiasm is catching. He makes us feel excited by subjects that might have bored us in school.

And enthusiasm works all the better if it is allied to warmth. Michael Parkinson, a veteran amongst presenters, still engages us because of his genuine feeling for the people he interviews. You get the idea that if you somehow accidentally ended up sitting next to him in the pub, he would talk to you with the same degree of interest and friendliness. He's a man who exudes confidence in front of the camera, but he also has a humbleness that instantly gets you on his side.

THE PRESENTER'S RELATIONSHIP TO THE AUDIENCE

Being a presenter is a very different thing from being a reporter or a contributor to a programme. You only have to listen to one of the zoo-format shows on radio to realize that. There is a whole gang of people chipping in to the show, but however anarchic it gets there is never any doubt who is in charge – the person whose name is on the programme, the presenter.

You can be the bubbliest weather-girl in the world, the most informed reporter, but *it isn't your show*. Sometimes the weather girl or the witty reporter gets a chance to stand in when the presenter goes on holiday; and that is the moment where they are really put to the test. Could they be a presenter? Being bubbly or clever often isn't enough.

A presenter stands in a different relationship to the audience. In family terms, the reporter or contributor might be seen as something like a brother or sister. They might know a bit more than you, or be the family joker, but they are without a shadow of a doubt on your level. There's a sense of equality between the listener/viewer and the reporter/contributor.

But the presenter is more than that. They are the head of the family, the leader of the pack. That doesn't necessarily imply that they are the mother or the father (though there are some presenters who assume exactly that role) but they are indisputably the key character. You may not always agree with them; they may sometimes charmingly admit to their own vulnerabilities; yet they will be the one who sets the tone of the occasion.

Or perhaps you could think of the presenter as the one person in a gang of friends to whom everyone listens, the one the gang actually seems to revolve around. What is it about that person? They may just be the loudest and the funniest, like Graham Norton. They may be the cleverest and most knowledgeable, like Melvyn Bragg. They may be the bounciest, like Davina McCall. They may even be the quiet and thoughtful one, who without being over-assertive makes everyone shut up and listen. There could be other people in the gang who have one or more of these qualities, but at the end of the day you know those are team-players, not the captain.

To take another analogy, the presenter is someone who can make people follow him or her, rather like a good officer in the army. We shouldn't push this idea too far, because a presenter may well be a bit of a maverick, and a questioning attitude, prodding at the establishment, pushing the limits, is essential to good presenting. But the idea of *leadership* is important. The reporter or contributor is the guy with the radio who trots over with the news from HQ, or the observer who has crawled back on her belly from the frontline. You, the listener/viewer, might think of the reporter as a comrade with a specialism. But the platoon leader – you know without question they are in charge. They have the authority.

Ah, there it is again – that familiar quality which is so important in your voice as you broadcast. Remember I said earlier that authority comes from *knowing what you're talking about*? A presenter needs authority, even more than a reporter or contributor does. Authority is what makes us listen to leaders, even when we disagree with them.

So as you take on the role of presenter, you need to rethink your relationship with the listener/viewer. You need to build in an extra level of confidence – just at the very moment when you are possibly thinking 'What on earth am I doing here?' But don't doubt yourself or your abilities. Someone gave you the job of presenting because they believed you could do it. You might feel fear but this is not the moment to show it. Instead, it's the moment to remind yourself of how far you have come in broadcasting, and how much you have already learned about your craft.

OWNERSHIP

One of the most difficult tasks is to take on a presenting role on a flagship programme that is already strongly identified with another presenter. On the day that you take over the breakfast show on your local station, or stand in for the regular presenter on a network TV show, it's easy to imagine the faceless listener or viewer at home making comparisons.

As long as you think of yourself as 'only the stand-in' you won't be able to take ownership of the programme. Tell yourself you have a right to be there. They wouldn't have given you the job if they didn't think you were capable of it. You may not be John Humphrys or Jenni Murray or Trevor McDonald or Sara Cox, but it is no good imagining you are the poor man's substitute. Be yourself, and feel that you are taking that presenter's chair in your own right. Claim the programme for your own and stop worrying whether you are as good as the regular presenter. You can be, especially if you remember you are inevitably going to be different.

Don't be too proud to ask for help

Your first job as a presenter, or the moment you take on a new presenting role such as moving to a network show, is the moment to reassess your voice. You will probably already be an experienced broadcaster, but now that your relationship to the audience has changed you may find it useful to look afresh at the assumptions you have made about what broadcasting is, to see if you can develop your voice further.

For instance, just how good is your connection with the listener or viewer? After several years in the trade, you are so used to broadcasting that you may have convinced yourself it is no longer necessary to personalize the viewer or listener in quite the way you did at the start of your career. Perhaps you feel a personal listener is a childish prop, like an imaginary friend whom you can put away now that you have 'grown up'.

I don't think there is anything 'childish' about using this technique. It is one I have returned to time and time again, to help me with a difficult broadcast. You ignore the listener/viewer at your peril, and to personalize them is as good a way as any of reminding yourself that they are there. Indeed, finding the *right* person to whom to picture yourself talking is often a way of finding your own distinctive presenting voice.

I once worked with a lovely reporter who had just got the job of his dreams, fronting a daily current affairs show on the network. But it wasn't working out as he had planned. He found himself surprisingly uneasy in the role, and he did what we all do when we feel insecure – he put on an act.

You can't pretend to be a presenter. You must, as I have stressed throughout this book, be real. He had temporarily misplaced his identity – his 'voice' – and I had to help him find it again.

'Who are you talking to?' I asked him. Of course, he had forgotten. At the start of his career, he had usually pictured himself talking to his grandmother. Apart from the fact that the good lady had long since tuned in to celestial radio, being twenty years dead, I suggested that he might find it easier to pick one of his friends who would be genuinely interested in what was being said on the programme. Whoever it was, it was important to give them a name and a face, or he was unlikely to be able to visualize them in any real way.

There was quite a bit of muttering – he clearly thought I was a bit of a madwoman. But gamely he went along with the idea. After that I didn't need to convince him. Suddenly he sounded confident, relaxed, authoritative – simply because he was picturing himself explaining the story to someone who was interested. 'I find I'm actually thinking about what I'm saying', he said, surprised. 'It all seems to make sense. And I've stopped worrying about whether I'm doing the job right, whether I actually sound like a presenter. I just *feel* I am.'

IDENTITY

Some of the wisest words I ever heard about on-air identity came from the mouth of an eighteen-year-old, just starting his career in local radio. 'It seems to me that presenting is a bit more complicated than just being yourself, warts and all', he said. 'It's about looking at your personality like it's a hank of wool, and finding the right strands to pull out to show the audience.' In other words, you need to understand not just who you are on air, but which parts of your personality and experience will make this broadcast work.

I have always liked his metaphor, that personality has strands, as if you were running a skein of multi-coloured wool through your fingers and plucking out a combination of colours to weave with. It means you can always be yourself on air – you just choose to show different aspects of yourself at different moments.

Not everyone has to like you

One of the commonest mistakes a presenter can make is to want to be loved by everyone. If you want too much to be liked you will be drawn into putting on a bland persona, for fear of offending someone. You won't be yourself.

As I have said before, there is no room for politeness in broadcasting. I don't mean that you should be rude to the audience – there certainly is a place for *courtesy*. What you should avoid though is the kind of artificial politeness that masks a fear of not being loved enough. Do you think John Humphrys has sleepless nights over whether or not the audience like him?

Some of the best broadcasters are people the audience loves to hate. They are uncompromising in being themselves. It shows supreme confidence in who you are. You don't have to be liked for people to listen to you.

The prima donna factor

It isn't always easy to be supremely confident as a presenter if you are naturally a shy and retiring person. Nobody likes a real prima donna, but sometimes you may have to resort to tricks to boost your own confidence and to remind yourself that you have a right to be doing the job.

I used to play a rather silly but effective game whenever I went into the studio. I would invariably ask for a different chair.

There was actually some logic behind this. I am rather short, and sitting on the usual studio chair I found that I felt almost as if my chin was resting on the desk top – which reminded me unhelpfully of a little girl pretending to be one of the grown-ups. I needed to feel as if I had a bit of height in front of the microphone.

So I would ask for an adjustable chair, which caused raised eyebrows at first. I was always perfectly polite about it but would insist that I needed to feel comfortable. It became part of my pre-performance ritual, to get me not only into the right physical position, but also into the right frame of mind. It reinforced for me that I was in control, and I am ashamed to confess it was very gratifying to have studio attendants leaping to do my bidding. After a while, the adjustable chair would magically appear in the studio whenever I was going to broadcast, and I stopped being quite so neurotic about my identity.

In my other incarnation as a producer and TV director, I have noticed that other presenters behave in a similar way. It's a means of asserting themselves, of bolstering their own fragile confidence, and it is always the role of the support team to make sure their whims are catered for, so they will produce the best possible performance. One presenter I used to work with always made a point of insisting there was an en suite bath whenever we booked her a room for an overnight stay. A shower wasn't good enough; it *had* to be a bath. Nobody minded. It was a foible we indulged, to make sure she was happy and in the right frame of mind for the shoot. And out on location, in pouring rain, doing take after take at the director's whim, she never complained and showed the utmost professionalism. She *deserved* that bath to soak in at the end of the day.

Of course, this can be taken too far, and nobody likes working with a presenter who makes unreasonable and arrogant demands then fails to deliver the goods. But I think there is no harm in finding your own pre-performance ritual to help you feel in control. A presenter is after all 'the talent', and however disparagingly TV crews use that phrase sometimes, we do recognize that the programme cannot work without a good presenter.

HUMILITY

After suggesting you should sometimes allow yourself to behave like a prima donna, it may sound contradictory then to stress that one of the most vital attributes for a presenter is humility.

You have been given the presenter's job so you can make a bridge between the programme and the audience. Confidence is one

263

thing. Arrogance is another. A runaway sense of self-importance interferes with your ability to communicate.

However great their leadership qualities, a presenter is still part of a team. You have to rely on that team to support you, and you must keep them on your side by being prepared to muck in sometimes. Good broadcasting is all about teamwork, and you have to share the responsibilities and the hard work.

Great broadcasters are also humble in recognizing what they share with the audience. So never forget that when it comes down to it you are really no different from those who are watching and listening to you.

If you are ever tempted *not* to be humble, let me tell you something one of my friends said to me when I was moaning that my career as a presenter seemed to have stalled. 'Presenting is a fashion business', he said, his eyes taking on the distant bruised look of One Who Speaks From Experience. 'One month you're in, the next you can be out.'

Some presenters do have incredible staying power and remain successful throughout their careers. But most at some point feel the chill winds of being rather less in demand than they would like. If you really want to be a presenter, you will have to accept that's the way it is. Personally, I don't feel it is entirely a disadvantage, because it means you will constantly have to re-invent yourself. And a spell out of fashion works wonders in reminding you that you need to be humble as well as confident in your abilities. After all, how long will the names of yesterday's presenters be remembered?

AND FINALLY...

Like far too many of my colleagues, I can never resist a good broadcasting cliché (though *you* should). I can't tell you what the particular Ingredient X is that will make you a star, but what I can guarantee is that it must be something that is distinctively you.

For that is what all this advice on the broadcasting voice boils down to. Be yourself.

Bibliography

On voice

Cicely Berry, *Your Voice and How to Use it Successfully*, Harrap, London, 1975.

Gordon Luck, *A Guide to Practical Speech Training*, Barrie & Jenkins, London, 1975.

Michael McCallion, *The Voice Book*, Faber and Faber, London, 1988.

Patsy Rodenberg, *The Actor Speaks*, Methuen Drama, London, 1997.

J. Clifford Turner, *Voice and Speech in the Theatre* (ed. Malcolm Morrison), A&C Black, London, 1993.

On the craft of broadcasting

John Simpson, *News From No Man's Land*, Macmillan, London, 2002.

Janet Trewin, *Presenting on TV and Radio*, Focal Press, Oxford, 2003.

USEFUL ADDRESSES

The Society of Teachers of the Alexander Technique (STAT)
Ist Floor, Linton House, 39-51 Highgate Road, London NW5 1RS. Tel: 0845 230 7828. www.stat.org.uk

Voice Care Network UK is a charity dedicated to helping people keep their voices healthy and to communicate effectively. They are not broadcast specialists, but can put you in touch with a range of voice teachers and speech therapists.
29 Southbank Road, Kenilworth, Warwicks., CV8 1LA. Tel: 01926 864000.
www.voicecare.org.uk

Index

Bold figures denote major sections or chapter topics

Focal Press   www.focalpress.com

Join Focal Press online
As a member you will enjoy the following benefits:

- browse our full list of books available
- view sample chapters
- order securely online

Focal eNews
Register for eNews, the regular email service from Focal Press, to receive:

advance news of our latest publications
exclusive articles written by our authors
related event information
free sample chapters
information about special offers

Go to www.focalpress.com to register and the eNews bulletin will soon be arriving on your desktop!

If you require any further information about the eNews or www.focalpress.com please contact:

USA
Tricia Geswell
Email: t.geswell@elsevier.com
Tel: +1 781 313 4739

Europe and rest of world
Lucy Lomas-Walker
Email: l.lomas@elsevier.com
Tel: +44 (0) 1865 314438

Catalogue
For information on all Focal Press titles, our full catalogue is available online at www.focalpress.com, alternatively you can contact us for a free printed version:

USA
Email: c.degon@elsevier.com
Tel: +1 781 313 4721

Europe and rest of world
Email: j.blackford@elsevier.com
Tel: +44 (0) 1865 314220

Potential authors
If you have an idea for a book, please get in touch:

USA
editors@focalpress.com

Europe and rest of world
ge.kennedy@elsevier.com

****

The CD-Rom has been made using Macromedia Flash. To ensure th
CD-Rom's playback is of the best quality possible, quit all other run
ning applications and check that your machine meets the minimun
system requirements.

Minimum System Requirements – Windows
300 Mhz processor
Windows 95, 98, 2000, ME, XP
128 MB of RAM
256-colour monitor capable of 800×600 resolution
4×speed CD-Rom drive

Minimum System Requirements – MacIntosh
233 Mhz G3 processor
System 9.0 or later
128 MB of RAM
256-colour monitor capable of 800×600 resolution
4×speed CD-Rom drive

****